W9-BLF-678

ILLUMINATE

Ignite Change Through
Speeches, Stories,
Ceremonies, and Symbols

*by Nancy Duarte
and Patti Sanchez*

Portfolio / Penguin

PORTFOLIO / PENGUIN
An imprint of Penguin Random House LLC
375 Hudson Street
New York, New York 10014
penguin.com

From Nancy

To Patti, my beloved friend, who helped me see things through others' eyes. Writing this book was an expedition into a vast unknown. We explored great ideas, cut great ideas, and made great discoveries together. There's no one I would have wanted by my side more than you. My heart leaps when I think of you, because the imprint you made on my heart changed me forever.

To Mark, my sweet husband, who lets me drink deeply from his well of strength, wisdom, and peace.

From Patti

To Nancy, my dear colleague and constant inspiration, who grabbed me by the hand and led me down the rabbit hole on an adventure that would turn my life topsy-turvy in the best possible way.

To James, my sweet companion and best friend, who taught me that mindfulness, rest, and the occasional burst of silliness can heal all things.

To Ellen, my wise mother and first mentor, who showed me that everyone has a great story inside them and all I had to do was be curious and listen well to learn it.

To all of the teachers, in business and in life, who saw some kind of spark in a shy little girl and nudged her to let that light shine.

CONTENTS

FOREWORD

Leaders See the Future

by Nancy Duarte

According to the U.S. Bureau of Labor Statistics, less than 50 percent of small businesses successfully make it past six years of operation. Yet my firm, Duarte, Inc., has thrived for twenty-five years, in large part because we've stayed ahead of the curve by inventing and reinventing our services and process.

Even though we've successfully managed several transformations at Duarte, we have to continue to change to keep driving the industry forward and offering clients the right products and services to ensure that their needs are met. Leading us from our early days as freelancers to our visual storytelling practice of today, I have developed an uncanny ability to anticipate what's ahead, as if the future is illuminated for me in a way that others can't see. The dream of a new future turns into fire in my belly and I carry that idea forward like a torch, lighting the path so others can thrive.

Each time I see the business starting to settle into a state of comfort, I begin to envision our next transformation. I study the market, listen to clients and employees, and use that information to dream about our next gutsy move. This process is how and why my award-winning firm has grown into the largest communication company in the Silicon Valley, the fifth-largest woman-owned business in the area, and partner to the top brands in the world.

Meanwhile I have watched other Silicon Valley companies come and go, seeing firsthand how staying in the same place creates stagnation. A pool of standing water eventually becomes foul rot unless you stir it up and let oxygen back in.

My team would tell you that I am great at stirring the water to avoid the rot, but I was not always great at helping them understand why all that change is good for them and not just good for the business. I've never been great at communicating empathetically. I'm passionate about my ideas, which gets me pretty far, but I would rarely factor in how others may process my messages.

As I grew into a leader, my lack of empathy was holding me back. I struggled to create the connective tissue employees needed to understand how my new ideas

Duarte, Inc.,
Transformations

1987–1990
Freelance

Mark Duarte spent the summer of 1987 schlepping furniture from the old California Microwave building in Silicon Valley to earn enough money to buy an Apple Macintosh Plus. That Macintosh inspired a dream to start a design business at home with our baby daughter in his lap while I worked at a "real job." Employees eventually bronzed that Mac as a symbol of great fortune.

1990–1997
Service Bureau

I cold-called Apple, NASA, and Tandem (now HP) to peddle Mark's illustration skills and landed large projects at all three. I quit my "real job" in sales at an electronics distributor to join Mark. Since Apple was the first company to project slides from a computer on a conference-wide scale, serving them created a niche for us. Demand for slide production grew quickly across the valley, and thanks to our responsive service and "the show must go on" creed, our business grew rapidly. Our staff of five employees no longer fit comfortably working from our house, so we moved into a "real office" above a coffee shop.

1997–2001
Design Firm

We began to attract degreed designers and recruited a creative director to transform us into an award-winning design firm. She implemented a new creative process, including critique methods and design exploration. The dot-com boom lured us into designing print and web in addition to presentations. It was a gold rush, and the business doubled.

Each S-curve is a tranformation driven by leadership.

2002-2005
Presentation Specialists

The dot-com bubble busted and 9/11 shocked the world. Jim Collins's *Good to Great* was released at just the right time. His Hedgehog Concept states that if you can be best at, be passionate about, and make money at one thing in the world, do just that one thing. In a counterintuitive financial move, we shuttered our print and web services to focus solely on presentations. It was the best decision we've ever made.

In 2013 Duarte, Inc., moved into one of the 35,000-square-foot buildings Mark moved furniture from in 1987.

Duarte, Inc.'s, (re)dream is to infuse leaders with communication skills that ignite transformation.

2006-2009
World Leader in Presentations

Al Gore's *An Inconvenient Truth* won an Academy Award and the world understood what a great presentation looks like. My first book, *slide:ology*, sold like hot-cakes, won awards, and created an unexpected demand for pre-sentation training, so we launched a second business model, Duarte Academy. Large corporations began outsourcing presentation cleanup to India, so I made a trip there to determine when Duarte, Inc., would be im-pacted by the trend. While there, I determined that extensive out-sourcing would happen within a decade, and that helping clients with content in the form of a story would make our services more valuable.

2010-2012
Storytellers

Convinced that only designing slides wasn't sustainable, our shop expanded into design thinking and storytelling services. Instead of dolling up slides, we began to rethink them altogether and adopted a cinematic storyboarding process to visually reexpress client messages. Our storytelling book, *Resonate*, spawned a TEDx talk that got more than a million views total. We built a world-class content team (led by coauthor Patti Sanchez) to infuse storytelling practices into persuasive presentations. But we scaled at unprecedented speeds and things began to crack. The frenzy to get volumes of work done with an inability to ramp the org compromised our quality and wore employees thin.

2013-2015
Breakthrough Momentum

For the first time in our history, we had to focus on an internal reinvention of our process and culture instead an external reinvention of our services. Knowing this would be a brutal and uninspiring process, we launched innovative labs so teams could engage in reimagining our business in the future—even as massive organizational change was afoot. We were taming a beast and at the same time incubating new ideas for new products and services. That polarity of energy kept the staff motivated through massive upheaval of aligning the organization and positioning it for growth.

To learn more about our venture, see page 275.

would benefit them. They would distance themselves from my future because to them it felt like it was solely my venture, not theirs. In turn, I was frustrated that they didn't jump in with the reckless abandon I wanted.

Knowing I could not transform my organization alone, I had to learn new behavior and architect models for empathy so my team would jump in. (And if many of you are completely honest, you could be more empathetic, too.)

Duarte, Inc., has been through several transformations but none was as difficult as our most recent one (described at the end of this book). Most of our ventures have been about adding new services or preparing for scale. However, our last shift dramatically changed our internal processes and reporting structure, almost bringing us to our knees because it dramatically impacted every role in the organization. While the change may have been difficult, it was the logical next step in a long line of Duarte, Inc., transformations.

We often help our clients communicate their ideas during seasons of transformation but we had never gone through this much intense pressure ourselves. This dramatic season of reinvention taught me a whole new level of empathetic storytelling skills that, when applied to our own situation, helped us cope with the brutal realities of systemic change.

When taking risks you have to persuade others to come along. Some of your more adventurous travelers will jump in, and others will create roadblocks to slow things down because they prefer things to stay the way they are; they'd rather stick with what they know than jump into something new.

Great leaders visualize the journey through the eyes of others. Patti and I have created models to help you understand where you're at in your venture, communicate empathetically, and motivate others to see your dream through to completion.

Leading transformations has been an exhilarating ride for me, from our humble beginnings schlepping furniture in 1987 to influencing how the world presents and keeping Duarte, Inc., at the forefront of that industry. Yet I have scar tissue from the bumps and bruises of mistakes I've made along the way. Sometimes I've communicated well. Other times I've failed. But no matter what, I brush myself off, am changed from the challenge, pick up the torch, and keep going.

Communicators Guide the Way
by Patti Sanchez

Though Nancy is a seer of the future, my gift is the ability to see things from another person's perspective. I'm naturally wired to notice what others are feeling, sure, but using what I observe to make ideas resonate with people is a craft that I've developed over many years.

I've made a career out of helping companies pitch their products to customers, partners, investors, and more. The formula was simple—deliver the right message to the right people at the right time. It often worked quite well: High-quality content led to high-quality leads that converted to high-quality sales. Yet every now and then, a marketing campaign failed miserably, even though the product was great, the messaging was clear, and the audience seemed a perfect fit.

Sometimes ingenious and timely products failed to win any support at all in the market. Despite all the creativity and money I could throw at a great idea, it could still flop simply because people hate change. I've seen the same thing happen with internal initiatives. Otherwise sensible, even nice, people can squash an idea with a strong business case because it threatens to disrupt their world. Smart leaders who shoot from the hip instead of planning their communications for an important meeting can end up wreaking havoc because they didn't consider how others would react to their words.

Watching the way humans respond to change of all kinds, I've learned the hard way that coming up with ideas is easy and getting others to embrace them is not. I've come to believe that knowing where to go is important, but explaining why and how to get there is even more important. Because change of any kind is frightening to most people, leaders have to narrate the journey from here to there and back again with clarity and conviction and, most of all, empathy.

While Nancy and I were writing this book, our company went through an internal restructuring. The shift disrupted nearly every role in the organization and naturally caused some angst. Even worse, it came at a time when business was booming. The majority of our employees felt as if nothing was broken, so they didn't understand why anything needed to change.

When Nancy told me her vision for the future of Duarte, Inc., I saw a different scene play out as I contemplated how our staff would react. I imagined what they would feel as we sprung the new vision on them and how it would affect their daily lives. I asked myself what we should say, show, and do to make transformation less daunting and more exciting to them.

The concepts in this book have been road tested. As we applied these models to our own business, I watched Nancy's vantage point shift as she began to see things more clearly through the eyes of our employees and our clients. Together, we found common patterns in communication to help our team—and yours—navigate the unknown and venture forth confidently into the future.

The future is a formless void,
a blank space waiting to be filled.
And then a Torchbearer envisions a new possibility.

That vision is your dream, your calling,
and it burns like a fire in your belly.
But you can't create the future alone.
You need Travelers to come along.

Yet the path through the unknown is dark and unclear.
You have to illuminate the path for travelers.
Torchbearers communicate in a way that conquers fear and inspires hope.

Some say being a torchbearer is a burden.
Some say it's a blessing.
Either way, those who light the path
are the ones who change the world.

———

CHAPTER ONE

Leaders Move Others Forward

Leaders anticipate the future. They stand at the edge of the known world, patrolling the border between "now" and "next" to spot trends. They help others see the future, too, guiding people through the unexpected and inspiring them to long for a better reality. The leader's role, your role, is to light the way for your team through empathetic communications—to be a torchbearer.

Leaders don't just anticipate the future, though; you also shape and bring it forth. Making something out of nothing is the mark of the greatest leaders. Look around you right now: The smartphone in your hand, the artisanal coffee in your cup, and the floor covering under your feet all exist because a fearless creator hatched an idea and communicated an inspiring vision.

A healthy organization should be in constant motion, always embracing and adapting to a new future. The rate of change in business today happens so quickly that you can no longer plan comfortably in advance—instead change is a state of mind. You have to practice change perpetually so that your organization is ready and capable to adapt for the future. Without this willingness and drive to change, your products or services may not be relevant in just a year or eighteen months. Torchbearers such as Steve Jobs, Howard Schultz, Ray Anderson, Anne Mulcahy, Lou Gerstner, Dr. Martin Luther King Jr., and other leaders profiled in this book achieved greatness by mastering the art of invention, reinvention, and reinvention again.

The most common symbol in business for moving from a current state to a future state is the S-curve. The shape of the curve plots the life cycle of a business as it starts, grows, and matures. Once success is achieved, stasis often sets in and the business begins to enter a state of decline. To avoid this fate and continue to thrive, your organization must continually reinvent itself by launching new products or initiatives, which take it through new S-curves. As you anticipate future needs to make sure you arrive at the right place in the future, one S-curve leads to the next, stringing together an epic tale of growth and achievement.

Venturing into the Future Is Scary

The desire to build something significant simmers inside torchbearers; how you communicate determines whether or not you achieve that goal. Leading people requires not only sensing change afoot, but imagining a brighter future and communicating it in a way that motivates others to follow you there.

Yet no one sees the future with perfect clarity. At times, it feels close and attainable. Other times it appears distant and turbulent, or as a dreamy, faint image lacking in detail. The path forward is full of twists and turns because you will adapt your plans as you listen to feedback and learn new insights along the way.

Because there is no map, the future scares most people. The ones you need to come with you on your venture, or "travelers," as we refer to them, will have to start from the bottom of a deep ravine to get to the top of a tall mountain far away, with formidable predators and treacherous passages in between—all to help realize your vision. The trek will not be a simple "point A to point B" progression for the people traveling alongside you. You'll need many others, such as employees, customers, partners, and investors, to sign on as fellow travelers on the journey. This won't be

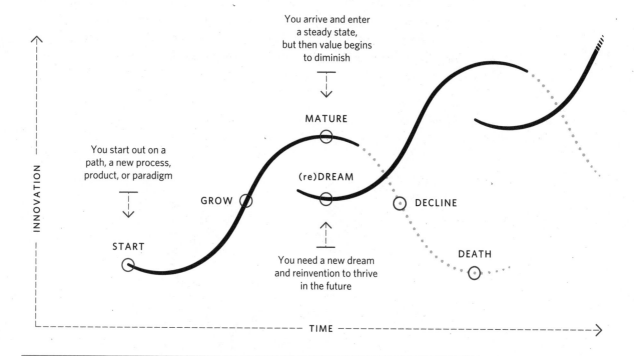

Innovation Life Cycle

You start out on a path, a new process, product, or paradigm

START

GROW

(re)DREAM

You need a new dream and reinvention to thrive in the future

You arrive and enter a steady state, but then value begins to diminish

MATURE

DECLINE

DEATH

INNOVATION

TIME

an easy decision for them, making your empathy and guidance even more important to light the way.

Uncertainty Makes Your Travelers Conflicted

From your perspective, your plan helps create a brighter future, but your travelers may not see it that way. Many have taken stock of what you're asking them to do and prefer their world the way it is; they don't want it disrupted. In general, the more they stand to gain in the future state, the more likely they'll sign on, and the more they'll lose, the harder they'll fight to preserve the status quo. Most would rather stick with the task at hand and get through their own pile of work than jump into something new, especially because they know change is hard and risky. In order to guide your travelers toward that future, you have to anticipate their reactions by imagining each step along the path as they might experience it.

Transformation Impacts Travelers

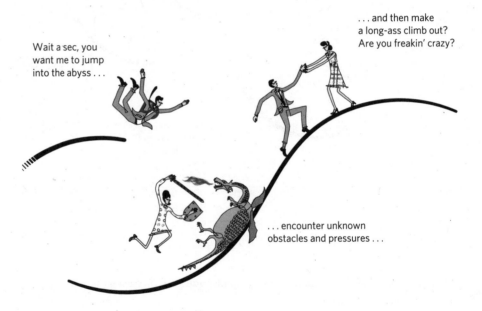

Each curve is a transformation, in which travelers will experience a range of emotions throughout the venture.

Some stages of the journey will be easy enough to navigate, and in those moments your travelers are more likely to be committed. Other stages will be uncertain, which will make them more likely to resist change. Their reluctance might come across as stubborn refusal to you, but understand it's a natural fearful reaction to the unknown. As people process and explore what you're asking of them, they will go through a range of all imaginable emotions. These feelings are valid and real, and can't be ignored.

Map the Stages of Your Venture

In order to lead people through this venture, you need to understand the stages you and your travelers will encounter. After studying successful movements in business and society, we've identified the five stages that every venture contains: Dream, Leap, Fight, Climb, and Arrive. Understanding these stages will help you create galvanizing moments that shape how your travelers experience the journey and sustain their energy so you arrive at achieving your dream.

As a torchbearer, you need to hone your ability to communicate in a way that galvanizes hearts and minds at critical junctures, such as when they first launch an idea or celebrate its completion. But the real trick is to sustain the interest and commitment of the travelers over the long haul with an ongoing stream of meaningful and timely communications.

To foster hope, you must articulate the nature of the journey, what you're undertaking together, and your vision of the destination with as much clarity and certainty as possible to inspire your team to commit. Imagine if you could fly overhead, study the topography, and anticipate the obstacles, and then use that insight to map out a clear path. Provide this bigger-picture view to help orient travelers to where they've been, where they are, and where they are going.

Anatomy of a Venture Scape

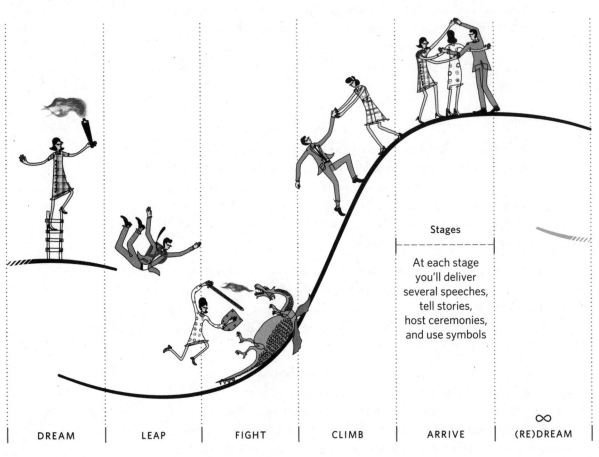

Stages

At each stage you'll deliver several speeches, tell stories, host ceremonies, and use symbols

DREAM | LEAP | FIGHT | CLIMB | ARRIVE | ∞ (RE)DREAM

Transformation Follows a Story Structure

You'll notice that, like a story, your Venture Scape has a beginning, middle, and end. Change has an identifiable pattern to it, and it follows the structure of an epic adventure, the oldest kind of story there is. Ancient epics such as *Beowulf*, *The Odyssey*, the *Mahabharata*—or even modern epics such as *The Hobbit* and *The Lord of the Rings*—are tales of transformation on a grand scale. In these stories, the protagonist is like your travelers, leaving familiar territory and traveling through unknown worlds to seek a reward. Along the way, the hero is tested, challenged, and ultimately changed, returning home weary but wiser.

People love stories about epic adventures because they show us how larger-than-life heroes grapple with great challenges and somehow emerge transformed. Stories like these also feel true because they mirror the kinds of struggles we encounter and hopefully overcome in our lives.

Stories have the power to convey transformation, and using a story structure as the framing device for your own epic venture will keep you and your travelers motivated. It also orients you to see their plight and helps you navigate the journey through their eyes. Travelers need to readily understand what you need from them as they jump into your venture to pursue the reward.

Similar to a classic epic tale, a Venture Scape covers a wide territory and spans a long period of time. Because the scope is vast and the sequence of events is often complex, epic tales have a narrator—essentially the torchbearer of that story—who explains events and interprets their meaning.

As the story's communicator, the narrator typically knows what others can't or won't understand and uses that insight to illuminate everything, including developments in the past, present, and future. He or she usually possesses an uncanny ability to see the unknown and hear the inner dialogue of characters in the story, helping the audience empathize with the hero.

As the torchbearer of this venture, you are similar to the epic narrator because you communicate the significance of the trek and illuminate events along the way for your fellow travelers. Torchbearers spring travelers into action at critical moments and heighten their excitement about the venture ahead.

Picture your venture as an epic tale about beloved travelers as they tackle obstacles in a grand journey that changes them and their world.

The Five-Stage Venture Scape Is Like a Story

Story Beginning

A relatable and likable hero jumps into an adventure.

Story Middle

The hero encounters seemingly insurmountable roadblocks that test his or her resolve.

Story End

The hero attains the object of desire and the journey transforms him or her.

Dream Stage

Your travelers face a choice to stay put or believe they play an important role in making your new DREAM come true.

Leap Stage

Travelers have to accept that things won't be the same and count the cost of the sacrifice before committing to the LEAP.

Fight Stage

When travelers are faced with opposition, their trek becomes long and difficult. It tests the depth of their commitment. No sooner do they FIGHT opposition . . .

Climb Stage

. . . than they have to muster the resolve to CLIMB out of the pit, which usually takes a long time. And then travelers must fight, climb, fight, and climb again.

Arrive Stage

When they make that last gallant push, travelers ARRIVE at their destination, seize the reward you've promised, and are celebrated for their effort. They feel bound together and buoyed by the valuable skills they've learned, just in time to undertake another venture.

You can see that the middle stages, Fight and Climb, are a struggle. If your venture were a movie, these stages would be where most of the action transpires and the protagonist's will gets tested. The tension of those middle stages pushes your venture forward because it stirs your travelers' resolve to continue when the going gets tough.

Controlling, framing, and conveying the narrative of your venture is the torchbearer's primary role. To motivate travelers, you'll need a torchbearer's communication toolkit: You will deliver speeches, tell stories, hold ceremonies, and use symbols to ease transitions and keep up spirits.

Use Galvanizing Moments to Keep Travelers on Course

Each stage in your venture is composed of a string of moments that marks progress while creating space for your travelers to breathe. In moments like these, speeches, stories, and ceremonies provide a forum for communicating and sharing ideas, but they also provide a welcome break from the grind of everyday activity. When you plan your strategy, identify these moments and think of ways to mark them. Put work on the back burner briefly to allow travelers to come together and share communal experiences.

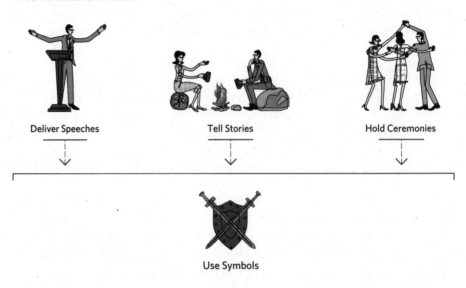

The Torchbearer's Toolkit

Deliver Speeches

Tell Stories

Hold Ceremonies

Use Symbols

When people gather for a shared purpose and brush shoulders with one another, the effect can be magical. Sociologist Émile Durkheim coined the term "collective effervescence" to describe the feeling of such experiences. They can be powerfully unifying, especially when the group is focused on pursuing a goal together.

During a moment of collective effervescence, people's individual identities subside and they feel part of something larger than themselves. Durkheim described the transformation this way: *"At the same time all [a person's] companions feel themselves transformed in the same way and express this sentiment by their cries, their gestures, and their general attitude; everything is as though he really were transported into a special world."*

That feeling of belonging to a larger whole helps instill shared values, beliefs, and norms within a group. Transcendent moments like these can also be cathartic, helping to concentrate and release emotions at points during the journey when tensions have built up. They create a charged atmosphere that refreshes your travelers and gives them fuel for the journey.

Once you've successfully come to the end of a stage in your venture, use speeches, stories, and ceremonies to create galvanizing moments again to orient them to their spot in the journey. This is a time to celebrate what they've accomplished so far so that they can transition into the next stage with confidence and determination.

During civil rights demonstrations, activists would sing freedom songs to lift their spirits. Galvanizing moments like these fill travelers with a feeling of effervescence that gives them fuel for the journey.

Galadriel gives Frodo a light.

An Elven Princess Lights Frodo's Path

In Peter Jackson's film adaptation of J. R. R. Tolkien's *The Fellowship of the Ring*, the opening sequence is narrated by an elven princess, Galadriel, played by Cate Blanchett. Beautiful and wise, she recalls the tale of a magical ring, forged long ago, that nearly destroyed the world until it came into the hands of hobbits, who would soon *"shape the fortunes of all."* Galadriel helps Frodo throughout, and later in the film lets him look into her Mirror of Seeing, which reveals the future by showing him *"things that were . . . things that are . . . and some things that have not yet come to pass."* When Frodo cowers after seeing frightful images of events that could occur if he shirks his duty, Galadriel encourages him, saying, *"This task was appointed to you, and if you do not find a way, no one will."* Haltingly, Frodo replies, *"Then I know what I must do. It's just . . . I'm afraid to do it."* Galadriel reassures him, *"Even the smallest person can change the course of the future."* Before Frodo and his fellow travelers depart for the dark land of Mordor, Galadriel presides over a gift-giving ceremony in which she gives Frodo a crystal phial filled with light, saying, *"It will shine still brighter when night is about you. May it be a light to you in dark places, when all other lights go out."*

The gift of light that Galadriel gave Frodo eases his burden of carrying the One Ring and helps him overcome obstacles on his journey to destroy the ring. In the same way, torchbearers illuminate the path for their travelers. The light you carry is expressed through speeches, stories, ceremonies, and symbols culled from your own experience as a well-seasoned traveler. Verbalizing your experiences helps your travelers navigate the path successfully, too.

CHAPTER TWO

Listen

Listen Empathetically to Light the Path

Every venture begins with a leader's vision. You may see the path ahead with clarity, but the outcome of your venture is not really up to you. Your idea is the spark, but you need others to carry the fire on the long trek ahead. Whether you're trying to get your internal team on board, asking investors to fund you, convincing customers to buy your product, or imploring the public to donate to your cause, your success depends on others' support. They are the ones who can make your dream a reality, but only if it becomes their dream, too.

In order for your venture to be successful, you need to see the journey through your travelers' eyes. Try to imagine how their world will change if they embrace your dream. When you understand how they'll be affected, you'll be able to communicate in a way that resonates with their emotions and mind-sets. You'll also gain insight from your travelers that will help you refine your venture.

Listening empathetically from the start will help you fine-tune your dream, or even reveal a better outcome than the one you'd imagined. You probably have strong convictions about the direction you want your venture to take, and you may even feel like it's the only option that makes sense, but it's possible that your dream is based on incomplete information. The picture that you see from your vantage point likely differs from what people on the ground are experiencing in their day-to-day lives. If you don't understand the obstacles they're grappling with or learn how your vision could affect their lives, you run the risk of investing everything in a plan that is destined to fail.

Listen empathetically as you go through each stage of the Venture Scape to check in on people's progress and course-correct if you need to. Share information openly about where you are and what's coming next, and invite your travelers to be equally transparent about how the journey is unfolding from their perspective. Ask them to tell you whether your dream is achievable or not, if the path is smooth or if obstacles need to be removed, and whether they're energized and able to keep going or whether it's time for you to ease up and give them a rest before taking the next hill.

In addition to its power as a two-way communication vehicle, empathetic listening helps people cope with the chaos of change. In moments of seismic upheaval, people need a safe atmosphere to let off steam, vent frustrations, and attack new ideas to test their validity. By deeply and thoughtfully considering the perspectives of other people, you can identify your next step while softening the blows of change and building support for your vision.

Empathy Creates Solidarity

Empathy is a fundamental requirement of healthy human relationships, and it's learned very early on. When a toddler sees her mother laugh, she instinctively starts to giggle in unison so they share the fun together. When she hears her little brother cry, she may sob in solidarity. Empathizing brings people closer and makes them feel more connected. That connection makes people more willing to help and cooperate with one another.

The same principle holds true in our professional relationships. A 2007 study found that leaders who show empathy toward others are viewed as higher performers, and for good reason: People who care about others demonstrate higher motivation, productivity, and creativity. "Emotional intelligence," which includes empathy as a core skill, has been proven to increase business success in numerous studies by Daniel Goleman, author of *Emotional Intelligence*. When employees feel that their leaders care about them, they feel more optimistic about the future and are more committed to the organization.

Empathy also increases trust and alignment in thinking, which can speed adoption of new ideas. High-performing teams are built on empathetic relationships that encourage people to share information freely with one another. And when people feel listened to and acknowledged by others, they're more receptive to hearing those people's perspectives and changing their own views.

Empathy exercises are used to increase business success in many fields. Retailers use secret shoppers to pose as customers and record their observations. Product developers brainstorm scenarios to imagine customers interacting with a product. Negotiators use role-playing to imagine opposing points of view. You can listen empathetically in a variety of ways, and your job as the torchbearer is to create conditions that give everyone a voice in the venture.

Torchbearers Start by Listening

Executives who are new to an organization often embark on listening tours with employees and customers to get a firsthand account of problem areas and opportunities, let people vent, and help them move on. Before rolling out a new strategy when she took over as CEO of Xerox, Anne Mulcahy spent three months talking with employees. She said, *"What I found out was that the more obvious problems were masking more fundamental problems."* To dig deeper into employees' concerns and settle their nerves, she held a dozen live television broadcasts, sent out over forty letters, spoke at more than eighty town meetings, hosted hundreds of roundtables, and logged about two hundred thousand miles visiting sites in more than a dozen countries. Mulcahy later reflected, *"The response was overwhelming. Defections slowed to a trickle. Hope rekindled. Energy returned."*

In addition to healing cultural rifts, empathetic listening can inform innovation. When planning to launch their revolutionary personal computer in 1984, the Macintosh team came across a brand-new type of market research pioneered by the social scientist Arnold Mitchell and his team at SRI International. SRI's groundbreaking Values, Attitudes, and Lifestyles (VALS) study used psychological principles to describe American mind-sets and to group people into categories based on what motivated them to buy. When the Macintosh team saw the VALS study, they knew the "achievers" segment, made up of knowledge workers, should be their target. Knowledge workers—who spent the majority of their day reviewing information and making decisions—often didn't have the time or inclination to learn programming. To reach this group, the Macintosh team created messaging that appealed to knowledge workers by speaking to their frustrations directly, even making it seem as if the computer itself empathized with them.

The Macintosh was very different from the traditional computers at the time. In the early days of information technology, computers were huge, complex machines that could be operated only by technicians who knew sophisticated programming languages. Businesspeople, who knew nothing about programming, often had to wait days or weeks to get a simple report. Managers felt that information was being held hostage by these massive mainframe systems and the companies that made them, such as IBM. During the first live demo, the Macintosh computer was programmed to speak directly to these frustrated customers, saying to the crowd, *"I'd like to share with you a maxim I thought of the first time I met an IBM mainframe: NEVER TRUST A COMPUTER YOU CAN'T LIFT."* The crowd erupted in applause. The Apple team echoed this theme of distrust with the famous ad directed by filmmaker Ridley Scott, broadcast during the Super Bowl. In the ad, Apple positioned their rival as an oppressor who kept knowledge workers in shackles, invoking the frightening Big Brother figure from George Orwell's novel *1984*. Though Apple's board of advisers nearly killed the bold ad, it resonated deeply with viewers and sparked excitement about Apple's crusade to liberate people from the shackles of bureaucracy with simple yet powerful technology.

Imagine Yourself in Your Travelers' Place

Most leaders have an innate talent for connecting with other people—it's key to forming relationships and gaining trust. Yet leaders often assume that the value of their ideas is self-evident, so they're surprised when they encounter resistance.

If you're being completely honest with yourself, though, even you have resisted change at some point in your life. Rather than bury that difficult time, use your hard-won experience to help others move through a time of transformation gracefully. Look back on times when you've been asked to embrace something you didn't want to. Make note of your experiences. What were you thinking, feeling, and doing when the change occurred? What did you struggle with, and what helped you endure?

Now continue the exercise by imagining that you are the travelers on your current venture. Step inside their minds to explore how they see things, to understand what they're feeling, and to anticipate what they might do (or resist doing) at each step of your venture.

Think	Feel	Do
Imagine their thoughts about moving from the present to the future. What beliefs do they hold about the past? How will their perspectives affect their responses to your call to action? Think through the mind-sets that might challenge them.	Imagine all the emotions that your dream might evoke in your travelers. How do they feel about the change and what you're asking of them? How will the challenges affect their moods and motivation? When might they feel most excited and inspired?	Imagine their potential reactions by walking through the actions your vision will require of them. What might they do in support of your dream, or to protest it? How will the process affect their routines, and will those changes be readily adopted or resisted?
I think this idea is…	**This idea makes me feel…**	**This changes my routine by…**
I imagine it will be like…	**It motivates me because…**	**It requires new actions, such as…**
I believe it will be easy or hard because…	**It demotivates me because…**	**It makes me want to do (or not do)…**

Analyze Gains and Losses

Your travelers will rarely all feel the same way about the venture you propose. Each person will weigh the pros and cons of the new endeavor on a virtual scale in his or her mind and make his or her own decision. They'll assess whether the sacrifice is worth the reward and decide what they have to gain or lose. You can get out ahead of that process and tip the scales in your favor by weighing the costs as they might.

Think about all the people you wish would sign on in support, beyond the obvious allies, such as employees, customers, and partners. Include those who will indirectly enable or hinder success, such as funders, advisers, and influencers, as well as adversaries, such as competitors and those whom your dream threatens the most.

Next, assess what each of them stands to gain or lose if your dream succeeds. Consider how your venture stands to benefit your travelers. These include things like opportunities to challenge themselves or learn new skills, more authority or advancement in their job, or the happiness and satisfaction that come with an improved situation. Each of these benefits is a reward for those who embrace your idea.

Also think about the ways that your venture may hurt them; these are the sacrifices you are asking them to make to bring your idea to fruition. Perhaps they'll be giving up the safety and predictability of the world they know, losing some of the independence that they had before the new challenge, or temporarily taking on a larger workload. List some of the possible rewards and sacrifices to determine what your travelers stand to gain and lose in your new world. The list is limitless; below are just a few:

Reward		Sacrifice	
Opportunity	Learning	Safety	Anonymity
Challenge	Fame	Ease	Blissful ignorance
Advancement	Happiness	Kinship	Restlessness
Authority	Belonging	Predictability	Craving
Responsibility	Satisfaction	Uniformity	Independence
Flexibility	Abundance	Equality	Ambition
Variety	Growth	Freedom	Comfort
Independence	Empowerment	Protection	Stability

Finally, reflect on your own experiences with major change. Mine moments from your past to help you communicate that you know exactly what your travelers are going through. Think about what helped you navigate change, and offer up those lessons as well.

Leaders who want to drive significant change must listen to their travelers, make them feel a part of the process, and communicate empathetically if they want their venture to succeed. Read on to learn how a leader at IBM listened well, and how a leader at Market Basket did not.

——

IBM

Embarking on a major organizational change is likely to ruffle many feathers and stir up a lot of fear. To prepare for a big shift, torchbearers do a lot of asking and listening before they start telling and acting. When you start by listening empathetically, you'll uncover the root causes of problems and build a coalition of support to help you solve them.

A Behemoth Is Born

Formed in 1911 from the merger of three office equipment companies, IBM was destined to be big. Thomas Watson Sr., who took the helm in 1914, believed that large companies like his had a role to play on the global stage, an ambition that showed in the slogan "World peace through world trade," which was carved into IBM's building in New York. In the 1920s, the company even published a book of songs meant to fill employees with pride, including a ditty that went like this: *"International is our name, it well befits our line. Serving in all nations we're known in every clime. Just watch us grow from year to year until the end of time."*

Through the decades, that ambition drove the company to innovate in many areas, from tabulators and calculators to mainframe computers, storage systems, and application software. Each innovation spawned new lines of business and complicated the organizational structure, which over time turned the once-nimble company into a sprawling and slow-moving bureaucracy. Because of that bloat, IBM lost touch with its customers' needs and struggled to keep up with rapid technology shifts in the 1980s and 1990s.

During that time, companies such as Apple introduced smaller, easier-to-use personal computers. Soon the move toward flexible "client/server" environments that PCs enabled ate away at IBM's premium-priced mainframe business. Meanwhile, process inefficiencies and uncontrolled spending eroded IBM's once-healthy profit margins. By 1993, the company had racked up $8 billion in losses, and the threat of bankruptcy loomed.

IBM's board of directors began searching for a candidate to replace then-CEO John Akers, who had been with the company for thirty-three years. Convinced that an infusion of fresh blood was the best way to turn the company around, the board hired Louis Gerstner Jr.—the first CEO to come from outside IBM's ranks.

Understanding the Emotional Landscape

Gerstner had been following IBM's troubles in the press and had already met with board members and key executives to get the lay of the land prior to his first official day of work. Even though he had ideas about what needed to be done in his first ninety days, he knew he had much more to learn. So he set out on a listening tour, meeting with employees far from the company's main office in upstate New York to hear the unvarnished truth.

In his first month on the job, Gerstner traveled to offices on every continent to meet with executives and worker bees alike, asking for briefings on the state of the business. *"It was clear that at all levels of the organization there was fear, uncertainty, and an extraordinary preoccupation with internal processes,"* he later wrote.

The emotional temperature was quite different outside IBM. Gerstner had to speak at the company's annual shareholder meeting, even though he didn't yet have a complete plan for turning the company around. Hostile stockholders railed at IBM for letting the stock tumble, obliterating the funds of older retirees who depended on stock for their income. Some turned to personal attacks on Gerstner, questioning why he was getting a $9 million compensation package his first year when the company was bleeding so badly. Gerstner stayed calm, acknowledging the company's bad decisions. Yet he reassured them, *"We can bring IBM back. It's going to take boldness, brilliance, vision and teamwork. And, it's just going to take an awful lot of plain old hard work."*

Customers were equally angry, as he discovered weeks later during a summit meeting of chief information officers. They felt that IBM had taken advantage of them with exorbitant pricing and convoluted processes that made the company difficult to work with. To prove that he was open to their feedback, Gerstner abandoned the presentation he had planned to deliver and instead held an informal Q&A session.

He told them, *"One of the most important things I can say to you is there is now a customer running IBM."* Then he told stories about experiences that he had as a user of IBM technology at his previous companies, RJR Nabisco and American Express, which showed how deeply he understood their pain. One frustrated customer, clearly losing patience, asked when Gerstner was going to start doing something to fix the situation. *"Now. We're going to put a blowtorch to these things,"* Gerstner said.

"Bear Hugs" Reshape the Culture

Armed with early insights from employees and customers, Gerstner moved into problem-solving mode. The company needed to come up with a plan to resolve the issues that emerged from his listening tour, but he also wanted to involve his leadership team in developing the solutions. He called a meeting of the fifty top leaders in the company so he could debrief them on the issues he had uncovered and give them their marching orders.

Then he gave them an assignment he called "Operation Bear Hug." He gave each executive and their direct reports three months to meet with their top customers to demonstrate concern for their satisfaction, ask about issues they were grappling with, and uncover ways that IBM could help. Managers then had to recap the conversations in memos. At the same time, Gerstner called customers on his own.

He "bear-hugged" employees, too, touring the company's various sites and hosting gatherings to share updates, test ideas, and tackle concerns. He held ninety-minute unscripted Q&A sessions with the staff, talking to twenty thousand workers directly. *"I listened, and I tried very hard not to draw conclusions,"* Gerstner said.

All of the listening that Gerstner did informed his strategy-making process, helping his executive team build plans to make IBM relevant, competitive, and profitable again. It led to an even larger and longer-lasting shift in IBM's culture, moving it from an inwardly focused bureaucracy to a market-driven innovator.

Market Basket employees protest the ouster of their beloved CEO.

Market Basket

The most successful organizational transitions happen when the strategic decisions are made after empathetically understanding the impact on those most affected. When replacing a leader, for example, look at the values of the culture to make sure the new leader is a good match. If there is a vast gap in values, travelers will reject the leader and start a venture of their own.

When Tables Turn and Travelers Demand Change

In an era of corporate greed, increasing inequality between haves and have-nots, and demonstrations on Wall Street by the 99 percent, it's hard to believe that the employees of Market Basket actually launched a grassroots venture to win back a beloved CEO. Can you imagine being ousted as CEO by your board—which is led by your cousins, who own 50.5 percent of the company—and then being reinstated because employees refused to work for the new leadership and customers boycotted your products? That's just what happened to Market Basket's president, Arthur T. Demoulas.

Two cousins, Arthur T. and Arthur S. Demoulas, inherited a small grocery store from their grandfather, and Arthur T. led the growth of the company into a seventy-one-store chain. Tensions over control of the company had raged for decades, with, according to *Time*, *"battles for power including tactics that seem like they would only be found in fiction—fake identities, secretly taped meetings, and more."*

Employees had long perceived Arthur T. as their advocate, fighting his cousins to assure Market Basket workers good wages, bonuses, and a generous retirement plan (some employees retired with more than a million dollars in their accounts). He was known for emphasizing people over profits, and he developed a strong bond with the staff. Employees and customers often shared stories of his generosity and thoughtfulness. He made personal calls to check on ill workers, regularly asked how their kids and spouses were doing, and attended employees' funerals. Market Basket workers often described the company as a family and likened Arthur T.'s ouster to the loss of a father.

A Test of Values

In 2008, following the financial meltdown, the company's profit-sharing plan lost $46 million of employee retirement funds, and Arthur T. insisted the firm cover the losses out of its own portion of profits. Cousin Arthur S. objected, shifted board sentiment, and fired his cousin Arthur T.

Installed as the new leader, Arthur S. did not have a history of putting employees first the way his cousin did. Arthur S. hadn't anticipated or listened to what the Market Basket employees wanted from a leader, and employees swiftly leapt into action. They were determined to continue to work for a company led by someone who put them first. Outrage over the removal of their beloved CEO motivated them to fight the change of leadership and insist on the reinstatement of Arthur T.

Fight Hard and Fast

To enlist customer support, employees stuffed customer grocery bags with flyers that read, *"We are Market Basket and we need your help."* Customers began to boycott the store. Shortly after, more than two thousand employees rallied outside the headquarters, calling for Arthur T. to be reinstated, showing up despite receiving warnings that they may be fired if they missed work to attend protests. Market Basket made good on that threat and started firing people, including Tom Trainor, who'd worked for the chain for more than forty years. The outrage built and employees rallied again, with five thousand people gathering to protest and listen to Trainor speak:

> "Yesterday I was fired. Today I'm fired up. I am Market Basket. And I always will be Market Basket. We started something on Friday and that job is not finished yet. At Market Basket we always finish; we always stay until the job is done. We know you're afraid; we all are. This is history in the making. Never before has a company galvanized together from top senior management down to part-time/ front-line workers for one goal. That goal is to bring ATD back!"

Trainor repeated the phrase "Bring ATD back," referring to Arthur T. Demoulas, several times throughout the speech and the eager audience chanted it back in unison. He reminded the employees that they had warned Arthur S. that employees would shut down the company if he fired Arthur T. Shortly after, almost seven hundred employees walked off their jobs and they began picketing stores and posting Arthur T.'s pictures throughout store aisles. An employee-run blog, *We Are Market Basket*, was created.

Customers also got involved in the fray. Some taped receipts from competitors on store windows. When employees approached customers with a petition, more than forty-five thousand signed it. Customers felt that the workers were doing the right thing and stood with them, wearing T-shirts printed with *"I'm the customer, you can't fire me, I quit!"* Customers hung signs on the store doors stating, *"Please come back Arthur T., I had to shop at Shaw's this week."*

The "We Are Market Basket" Facebook page garnered almost ninety thousand likes. When donations started pouring in to help support the employees who had walked out, the board instructed store directors to stop taking donations. The protests brought the company to a virtual standstill for six weeks.

The *We Are Market Basket* blog featured a moving statement to remind the activists of their significance:

> "We are in the midst of what will most likely be the biggest and most important cause any of us will ever be a part of. The eyes of the nation are on us as we march forward with unwavering resolve to get ATD back in charge and put Market Basket back on track. Our fight has been joined by tens of thousands. Associates, vendors, media, politicians and most importantly, our customers."

The Generous Leader Returns

With Market Basket operations at a standstill, Arthur T. raised funds from a private equity firm and bought out the opposing family members' shares for $1.5 billion. Once he was reinstated as CEO, Arthur T. celebrated with a speech held at the company headquarters:

> "You're all so very, very special and all I can say is it's great to be back together again. . . . Words cannot express how much I miss you and words cannot express how much I love you. [The audience applauds, cheers, and shouts, "We love you, we love you."]

> "You have demonstrated that in this organization here at Market Basket, everyone is special. You have demonstrated that everyone here has a purpose; you have demonstrated that everyone has meaning and that no one person is better or more important than another.

> "You proved, all of you, that your grassroots effort to save your company and harness thousands and thousands of people was not about a family conflict or Greek tragedy [the audience laughs and shouts, "We love you!"] but more about fairness, justice, and a solid moral compass that unites the human soul. [extended applause and cheers]"

When the news of Arthur T.'s return was announced, employees, vendors, and customers rejoiced. Some embraced, wept, and danced in the aisles at the news. Employees and vendors then worked hard to rapidly restock shelves. A palpable buzz of excitement could be felt in the stores. Those who had led the venture recognized that the journey they'd been on would shape their collective consciousness in a new way and that the values Arthur T. stood for would become an intrinsic part of the organization moving forward. After they reached their ultimate goal, employees on the *We Are Market Basket* blog stated:

> *"Many causes in this world start small and grow into something big only to dissipate entirely when resolution comes about. We Are Market Basket has become more than just a cause; it has become the embodiment of a culture made up of associates, customers, vendors and concerned citizens all over America. Now that we have successfully helped to save the Company and CEO we love, the challenge becomes a new one: how do we cultivate the 'We Are Market Basket' way?*

> *"Now that the fanfare has faded we can concentrate on business while at the same time being acutely aware of the fact that while our company has not changed, the image of it has been altered forever. It is now a beacon of hope for employees everywhere that their voices matter in the cold, shareholder driven business world. It has a social conscience which places the welcomed responsibility on our shoulders to be good, charitable members within the communities we serve."*

It was a stunning reversal that proved the power of the people's resolve to have a leader who shares their values. As David Lewin, a professor of management at UCLA, told the press about the effort, *"To have an internal uprising of just about everyone, without a union, is very unusual in American industry. And it's even more unusual for workers to say, 'We want this guy to come back'—and to have him actually come back."*

———

CHAPTER THREE

The Torchbearer's Toolkit

Once you've envisioned your dream and imagined it as reality, you've got to motivate others to help you realize the dream. Whether they sign on or not is determined by how well you communicate. You need to first empathetically understand your travelers and then use the right communication tools at the right stage of the Venture Scape to express your vision, communicate progress, and inspire them to keep going.

Understand Your Travelers' Inner Journey

Travelers from a beloved story—like the hobbit Frodo Baggins—experience a physical adventure. Frodo physically moves through landscapes; fights Ringwraiths, orcs, and a spider; and climbs mountains to vanquish an enemy and return with new skills. But the protagonist in a story also goes on an inner journey, a journey into the depths of the soul that challenges fears, frailties, and insecurities. Frodo has to find inner strength to complete the task.

Your travelers take an inner journey during your trek, too. In each stage of your venture, they'll be asked to do things that will stretch their abilities far beyond their comfort zone. At some point, they'll hit a wall that will dent their self-confidence and they'll doubt whether they can finish the job. These times will test your travelers' resolve, and they will be faced with making a decision to keep going and stay committed or refuse to continue and become resistant.

Keep in mind, the terms *committed* and *resistant* capture the polarity of possible choices. The vast group falls somewhere in between, waiting to see how others respond. So, even though committing and resisting are portrayed here as black-and-white choices, most travelers are operating in various (at least fifty-one) shades of gray skepticism.

Appeal to the Mind-sets of Your Travelers

Your travelers may even switch sides along the journey. Those who are committed initially may turn resistant if they sense too much uncertainty or if setbacks scare them, causing them to choose security over adventure if the reward isn't worth the risk. Inspired by your empathetic communication, those who are initially hesitant will pick up the torch and help you lead the way forward.

Your travelers may wrestle with internal dialogue as they vacillate between committing and resisting. In *The Lord of the Rings*, Sméagol was originally a hobbit, who was corrupted by the One Ring and became known as Gollum. In the screenplay, the character has internal conversations between Sméagol, the committed traveler, and Gollum, the resistant one.

FRODO

You will lead us to the Black Gate.

CUT TO: GOLLUM scrambles quickly through the rocky crags,
looking back to make sure the HOBBITS are behind him.
ANGLE ON: FRODO and SAM struggle to keep his pace.

SMÉAGOL

To the Gate, to the Gate!
To the Gate, the master says. Yes!

CLOSE ON: GOLLUM sports an EVIL FACE.

GOLLUM

No! We won't go back. Not there.
Not to him. They can't make us.
(coughing)
Gollum! Gollum!

He scrambles on further and stops atop a rock.
His FACE turns suddenly SOFT.

SMÉAGOL

(pleading)
But we swore to serve
the master of the precious.

GOLLUM

No. Ashes and dust and thirst there
is, and pits, pits, pits.

Your travelers will experience similar internal counterarguments. Each person will weigh the pros and cons of the new endeavor in his or her mind, assessing whether the sacrifice is worth the reward. Travelers want to see a positive outcome but have to wrestle with doubt before signing on to help make the dream a reality. They may also resist because they see flaws in your vision or strategy that you don't see. So use your empathetic listening skills to uncover their concerns because those doubts may be harbingers of difficulty you could encounter later.

Communicate with Emotional Polarity

Because your travelers will face the choice to commit or resist at each stage of your venture, you need to address both with communication that alternates between positive and negative poles. Use motivating communication to help your travelers commit, and warning communication to ease them away from resistance and back toward commitment.

Committed	Resistant
Motivating	**Warning**
Use motivating communication when your travelers are energized and feeling adventurous about pursuing your dream. Even though they're committed, keep them uplifted with extra encouragement to stay engaged.	Use warning communication when travelers seem stuck or are heading in the wrong direction. They may resist based on personal biases or even justifiable concerns. Warning them about the possible negative outcomes of staying put or straying from the course can push them away from resistance.

Both motivating and warning communications can spur your travelers into action at each stage. Think about what's at stake for them and then empathetically listen to see if your travelers are ready to commit or if obstacles stand in their way. Your communication tools—speeches, stories, ceremonies, and symbols—can help your travelers cross a threshold of decision. By illuminating the rewards of committing and the costs of resisting, you can help them keep moving forward.

Move People Through Speeches, Stories, Ceremonies, and Symbols

You can communicate your vision to your travelers in many ways. But the spoken word has the ability to grip hearts in a way no other medium can. The oral tradition has thrived because it expresses information and emotion powerfully. When you use the spoken word in speeches, stories, and ceremonies, reinforcing it with meaningful symbols, empathetic communication makes each moment feel significant and builds energy that makes your venture feel attainable.

While your outbox might be crammed with memos explaining your strategy and the status of key initiatives, only when you pull people together in a room are you able to create a unique opportunity for human connection. Speeches, stories, ceremonies, and symbols become your unique torchbearer toolkit to help communicate your dream in a compelling and desirable way, helping your travelers long for and help achieve it.

THE TORCHBEARER'S TOOLKIT

Deliver Speeches

When you deliver a speech, you have the opportunity to explain your ideas and directly address resistance to change. By contrasting the current situation (*what is*) with the improved reality travelers will enjoy if they embrace your dream (*what could be*), you'll be able to make the future more alluring than the present. Speeches motivate forward movement because the gap between *what is* and *what could be* creates tension that your travelers will want to resolve. Your goal is to distance them from the current reality and impart a vision of the future (*new bliss*) that your travelers long to see come true.

Tell Stories

Whereas speeches structurally move back and forth between the present and the future, a story follows a single protagonist's transformation. Observing a protagonist try, fail, and then overcome stirs potent feelings that resonate on a deep, psychological level. We remember stories because they connect our hearts and minds to an idea. The three-act structure also makes stories easier to recall and share with other people so the ideas contained in them are more likely to spread.

Hold Ceremonies

Ceremonies fulfill a need to express emotion collectively, resulting in communal catharsis. Ceremonial acts help travelers envision new behavior or purge old mindsets so they can move forward unencumbered. Pausing to gather and express collective emotions gives travelers a much-needed reprieve. Use ceremonies to mark important transitions to provide your troops the opportunity for community and commitment.

Use Symbols

Symbols are ordinary artifacts that take on meaning because they were part of a speech, story, or ceremony. They express ideas and emotions in concentrated form. Because of their resonance, symbols become the visual language of a social group. They express people's thoughts, feelings, and values in a shorthand and sometimes highly charged way. There are visual, auditory, spatial, and physical means to create emotionally charged artifacts that remind your travelers of key moments along the venture.

SPEECHES

Persuade with Speeches

Speeches often contain stories, ceremonies, or symbols that amplify ideas and heighten emotion. Speeches differ from stories because stories typically unfold in a chronological sequence, whereas speeches aren't bound by the constraints of time and place. A speech gives you the freedom to unveil insights in the order that conveys information in the most persuasive and engaging manner possible.

For important persuasive information, deliver a speech. Whether a formal address to many travelers or informal remarks to a small gathering, an effective speech builds tension and then releases it. Great speeches have the potential to hold an audience's interest just like good stories do, but they do something unique: Speeches call your audience to action, imploring them to adopt your idea and run with it.

In order for your travelers to embrace your vision for the future, they will need to undergo their own transformations. Before your travelers hear your speech, they may believe or behave one way, but after they hear your speech, they should behave or believe differently. To help your travelers understand what is needed to achieve your vision, articulate where you need them to move from and where you need them to move to. Then make everything in your speech support that transformation.

Christine Lagarde, managing director of the IMF, speaks at Davos.

Persuasive speeches establish a gap between *what is* and *what could be*, and then resolve it by introducing a *new bliss*. Just as a great story creates and resolves tension, the gap between *what is* and *what could be* creates tension that jolts audiences out of complacency. When this gap is effectively communicated, an imbalance is created that will make your travelers crave resolution, which can be achieved only by taking action to close the gap. You are asking them to leave the comfort zone of their current reality and venture to a new place that is closer to the future you envision.

End the speech with a *new bliss*, describing what you think the future should look like so that your travelers long to get there. Motivate them by describing the possible future with wonderment and awe to show them that the reward will be worth their efforts. Then conclude the speech by explaining not only why your idea is possible but that it is the better choice to make.

Three-Act Persuasive Speech Structure

Christine Lagarde, managing director of the International Monetary Fund (IMF), delivered a speech in 2013 in Davos, Switzerland. The theme was "Resilient Dynamism," which must be a goal for all countries if they are to survive another significant economic downturn.

Beginning: What Is	Middle: What Could Be	End: New Bliss
Paint a realistic picture of the current world and what's at stake if your travelers stay there and do nothing.	Introduce a new potential future into the present reality. Contrast the gap between what is and what could be so they can see the transformation needed.	The imbalance is resolved and the speech ends with everyone understanding the reward they'll gain by creating a better future.

Beginning: What Is

"I know we are all still deeply concerned with the state of the global economy. Where do we stand? Well, thanks to policy actions taken over the past year, we have seen some respite and some stabilization in financial conditions.

"But it is not all good news. The recovery is still weak, and uncertainty is still high. As the IMF announced just a few hours ago in our World Economic Outlook, we expect global growth of only three and a half percent this year, not much higher than last year. The short-term pressures might have alleviated, but the longer-term pressures are still with us."

Middle: What Could Be

"So how can we successfully navigate our way into this future world? There are no easy answers. So where to begin? I think it starts with the new generation on the march—in a world that is flatter, more closely knit, more interconnected than ever before in history.

"This new generation thinks differently. It is a generation weaned on immediacy, democracy, and global reach of social media. . . .

"Perhaps we can lay the groundwork for future success by embracing some of the emerging values of this new generation."

End: New Bliss

"I believe we are standing in the antechamber of a new global economy, marked by rapidly shifting circumstances and new modes of thinking.

"Yes, this new economy will be geographically different, driven more by the dynamic emerging markets and developing countries. But it will also be generationally different, shaped by different values and principles.

"What we need today is a 'new moment in history' that embraces the values of a new era—more openness and cooperation between nations, more inclusion and solidarity among peoples, and stronger accountability of those responsible for the global economy."

Speeches Motivate Action

The gap between *what is* and *what could be* allows your travelers to move from the familiar to the unfamiliar. Though people are generally more comfortable with what they know, conveying the opposite creates conflict that they feel compelled to resolve. Audiences enjoy experiencing a dilemma and its resolution; it keeps them interested as you speak.

When your speech is over, your travelers should have a heightened sense of *what could be* and clearly see that staying with *what is* will bring stasis and decline if they choose to resist rather than commit to your idea. The *new bliss* helps them see how they and their world will be transformed for good, making them want to dive in.

STORIES

Engage with Stories

The fact that the five-stage Venture Scape follows a traditional story plot makes storytelling a particularly effective communication tool during your venture. People love stories because they are fascinated with transformation. When we observe someone else mastering his or her own transformation, it gives us hope that we can, too. If told effectively, stories also create a common bond between you and your travelers that will open them up to hearing your unique perspective more readily.

Stories can be told from a number of perspectives, including "I," "we," and "they" vantage points, with each one creating a different emotional effect. "I" stories relay the personal experiences of you as the torchbearer, inviting the audience to enter your inner world and feel closely connected to you. "We" stories convey the shared experiences of a group, which emphasizes common experiences and uniting principles that bind everyone together. "They" stories share what happened to others, usually in another place or time, which allows a diverse set of experiences to be represented and understood because you can pull from any point in history.

Regardless of the vantage point, stories of all kinds follow a deceptively simple three-act structure: A likable protagonist is introduced and then he or she faces hardship and is changed during the process. You root for the hero to muster courage, vanquish enemies, and eventually snag the prize.

Three-Act Story Structure

Beginning

A relatable and likable hero jumps into an adventure.

The hero (protagonist) is a central figure of action who drives a story forward. He's likable and you want to root for him. As he treks through his ordinary world, an inciting incident occurs and he needs to choose whether to jump in or not—which would require the hero to enter the unknown.

_____

Four simple, amiable hobbits from a rural region known as the Shire . . .

Middle

The hero encounters seemingly insurmountable roadblocks that test his or her resolve.

After he commits to the adventure, the hero realizes that this new, special world is harder to navigate than he thought. He encounters roadblocks, trials, and adversaries and possibly risks losing something valuable. Through the challenges he faces, he becomes emotionally vested in the outcome of his adventure and at his darkest moment must resolve to recommit to the end.

_____

. . . are thrust into an epic conflict over the fate of the most powerful object in the world, the One Ring. Frodo encounters nearly unbearable burdens while his friendship with Sam is heartbreakingly tested. Pippin has to serve a crazy leader and Merry joins the army to fight against Sauron's forces.

End

The hero attains the object of desire and the journey transforms him or her.

As the hero struggles through the final ordeal, he returns to his ordinary world having mastered new tools, destroyed an enemy, picked up wisdom, and bonded with other travelers. He is honored as a wiser and stronger hero and the world is changed by his journey, too.

_____

The four hobbits set right the balance of good and evil and return home to find the Shire under oppressive occupation. With their newly found confidence and experience, they root out the corrosive influence and take leadership roles in their community. (NOTE: This sequence is not in Peter Jackson's movie, but it's how Tolkien demonstrates that the hobbits were transformed by their journey.)

Stories Transmit Potent Information

Ever since humans first sat around the campfire, stories have been used to create emotional connections. In many societies, they have been passed along nearly unchanged for generations. Today, stories are becoming more pervasive in business because they make ideas, data, and plans relatable, recallable, and repeatable by associating information with powerful feelings.

According to psychiatrist Bruce Perry, presenting information in a variety of forms, including metaphors and stories, instead of merely reciting facts increases attention levels and reduces boredom. When stories are crafted using techniques from literature and film, they keep us engaged by constantly building and releasing dramatic tension.

Stories also help us make sense of our world by giving us mental models, or schemata, for visualizing and describing it. Myths in early societies explained the origin of the world and outlined its boundaries—sky above, earth below, water near or far—along with identifying landmarks such as mountains, trees, rivers, and seas to help navigate around it. In the same way, people today use storytelling as an orienting device to understand where they are, where they came from, and where they're going.

By narrating your venture as you would narrate a story, you help your fellow travelers transition from their current world into the future world that you envision for them. You can bring that world to life in even more full-bodied form through ceremonies.

CEREMONIES

Immerse with Ceremonies

Like stories, ceremonies depict the process of transformation. For thousands of years, almost all cultures have used rite of passage ceremonies to mark changes that humans undergo at critical moments in our lives.

When anthropologist Arnold van Gennep first introduced the term "rites of passage," he wrote, *"All societies use rites to demarcate transitions"* in life. He saw them as rites of regeneration, in which the old self must ritually die before a new self can emerge. Modern rite of passage ceremonies include the bar mitzvah, debutante ball, graduation, baptism, wedding, coronation, and inauguration.

Since both authors of this book had the privilege of marrying Mexicans, we chose the quinceañera rite of passage to illustrate how transformation is represented ceremonially. Fifteen-year-old Hispanic girls go through this coming-of-age ceremony to symbolize their passage from girlhood into womanhood. Following a three-act structure just like a story does, the girl metaphorically changes form, arriving at the ceremony as a child and emerging at the end as a woman.

Three-Act Rites of Passage Structure

Beginning: Separation	Middle: Transition	End: Reincorporation
The individual withdraws or detaches from current status or social group. She experiences metaphorical death as she leaves her old life behind.	The individual symbolically changes her appearance or behavior to signify transformation.	The individual returns and commits to a new role and to living by a new set of principles.
• Wears normal clothes	• Changes into white dress	• Honors her purity
• Wears a headpiece	• Exchanges headpiece for tiara	• Is a princess before God
• Has no scepter	• Is given a scepter	• Takes on more adult roles
• Wears no jewelry	• Puts on earrings	• Is reminded to listen to God
• Wears flat shoes	• Exchanges flats for heels	• Dresses as a woman
• Carries her last doll	• Gives doll to a young girl	• Leaves behind childish things

The Rite to Pass

Ceremonies are deeply rooted in nearly all known cultures. Gathering to ceremonially acknowledge transformation strengthens the deepest values of a collective group. When coworkers share drinks after a layoff or an organization marks a successful venture with a balloon drop, they are performing ceremonies. Today, many organizations are larger than some historical civilizations, yet they overlook this important communication device. If life is like a series of passages from one state to a new state, and if most cultures observe these thresholds, shouldn't leaders today acknowledge them, too?

Some ceremonies communicate the anticipation of a new beginning and others demarcate an ending, but they all help people understand where they are in the transformation. Ceremonies help your travelers cope by honoring sacrifices and pain, providing renewed energy to face challenges, and expressing joy and gratitude about good fortune or achievements. At points of triumph or in moments of disappointment, it's important to use ceremony to keep travelers motivated. Victories should be celebrated, but even dark passages—whether slight missteps or utter disasters—must also be acknowledged so people can move on. A ceremony that marks a transformation is more meaningful than a simple party because it expresses group sentiment as you experience change. For example, you can mark a moment of bravery during the Fight stage by hosting a rally where travelers can jeer at their enemy, which emboldens them to face their fears.

One of the most important roles of ceremony is to affirm solidarity. Ceremonies demonstrate sentiments such as "we are serious," "this is over," and "I'm committed." Some ceremonies may even be so meaningful that they can never be duplicated, instead becoming cherished experiences that deeply bond a group. French sociologist Émile Durkheim proposed that ceremonial rituals not only maintain social order but also develop group cohesion and strong interpersonal relations.

A study by the Royal Melbourne Institute of Technology found that ceremonies also enhance communication by "eliciting arousal, directing attention, enhancing memory, and improving associations." Basically, ceremonies help people understand and process new messages and ways of thinking, making the moment more likely to be remembered.

SYMBOLS

Empower with Symbols

A symbol could be anything—an image, object, word, or place—that comes to represent something else. Most symbols take on meaning by being part of a significant moment that gives rise to a speech, story, or ceremony, and often all three.

Using moments to turn artifacts into meaningful symbols seems part of human nature; anthropologist Victor Turner identified the symbol as the smallest unit of ritual in cultures. We long to preserve and evoke the emotions of past experiences, and symbols have given us that ability from our very beginnings as human beings.

Symbols come in a wide variety of types because anything can become symbolic. Some are intentionally created, such as coins, flags, company logos, and mascots. Others take on their symbolic meaning through the course of events, such as the dollar bill from your first sale or the trophy your team won at the company picnic. Symbols sear the meaning of these events into our minds.

Visual	Auditory	Spatial	Physical
What you see	**What you hear**	**Where you are**	**What you do**
Symbols we see through images or objects that make meaning tangible.	Symbols we hear through words and sounds or group expression.	Symbolic spaces— whether sacred or historic—create another layer of meaning when people gather there.	Our gestures and outfits communicate what we feel and whom we align with.
Your venture may have an image displayed on banners, your story may reference a token hidden under audience members' seats, or fireworks may shoot off just at the right time during your speech.	A declaration may be shouted, a bell may be rung, or rousing music may be played at the end of a speech. Travelers may read a new mission statement together, which feels liturgical, or sing wistfully in unity.	A story could be told at a venue where actual events unfolded, or a speech can be delivered at a historic location that makes it take on a sacred nature. A ceremony communicates meaning by creating a serene or spectacular setting.	Sad travelers may hug and happy ones may dance in the aisles at the end of a speech. Travelers may wear a button to show their solidarity with others during a ceremony.

COMMUNICATION TOOLKIT

Bring It All Together

Now that you know the five stages of the venture—Dream, Leap, Fight, Climb, Arrive—the polarity of emotion possible at each stage, and the components of your communication toolkit, you can pull them all together to create transformative moments along the way.

First, determine the stage you're in by reading across the top of the chart inside. Next, select the most effective speeches, stories, ceremonies, and symbols for that moment in time. As you can see on the vertical axis of the chart inside, there are two types of speeches, stories, and ceremonies that you can choose from at each stage— motivating or warning—depending on the emotional polarity that your travelers are feeling. Look at the content of your speeches, stories, and ceremonies to identify potential symbols and then listen to the emotional connotations they seem to hold for your travelers.

Listen to the Message in Symbols

The most effective symbols emerge from an organization's or group's shared experience, such as when employees create a T-shirt to wear in solidarity with those who are working long hours to get a product out. Torchbearers should keep a close eye out for artifacts that could become symbols and use them to amplify ideas in speeches, stories, and ceremonies.

Symbols can have a powerful effect on business. In the blink of an eye, something ordinary can become imbued with meaning and charged with emotion. Symbols should not be imposed on an organization, though—doing so rarely feels authentic or meaningful. Instead, amplifying existing symbols is a good way to tap into culturally understood meanings and messages. By observing what your travelers do when they gather and listening to the stories they tell, you can uncover the symbols that are meaningful to them. When you integrate those symbols with your communication you show appreciation for the sentiments they express by amplifying them and rallying everyone around them. But be aware that symbols have enormous power to both rally and rile sentiment, so use them with respect.

WE ARE LASER-FOCUSED

Starbucks's Howard Schultz delivers a speech to store managers in front of a commitment wall they signed in New Orleans.

———

Starbucks

*Some of the most enduring companies have transformed themselves
again and again to stay relevant in the future, and Starbucks is no exception.
It has undertaken several ventures since its founding as a small local
coffee shop in 1971 to become the global brand that it is today. But
one of the toughest transitions occurred in the early 2000s, requiring
its leader to undertake an epic venture to return the brand to greatness.*

Starbucks Purges Growth's Bitter Aftertaste

When Starbucks was thriving, Howard Schultz resigned from his daily oversight
as chief executive officer and assumed the role of chairman in 2000. Eight years
later, in the midst of a global economic crisis and a rapid decline in profits, he
returned to the ceo* role in early 2008. Schultz felt that the soul of the brand was at
risk because the company had allowed the pursuit of growth to cover up operational
mistakes and distract from its core mission. In a voice mail he left for employees

———

*Starbucks uses lower case for all employee titles.

(whom the company calls "partners") upon his return, he said, *"Going forward, we will be refocusing our entire organization on the Starbucks Experience by going back to our heritage and what made us so successful in the first place: putting the customer back at the center of everything we do."* Starbucks needed to innovate rapidly and reclaim its customer-centric values. The following events show the impact as Schultz rolled out his dream across the organization; his experiences are chronicled in his book *Onward: How Starbucks Fought for Its Life Without Losing Its Soul* and the Starbucks website.

Create a Customer-Centric Dream

Empathetic listening ▶

One of the first things Schultz did upon returning as ceo was to convene his top twenty executives alongside a diverse group of partners from throughout the company. Before they began the tough work of charting the future, they spent time just seeing. The team went to an off-site location in Seattle to get out of their familiar spaces and routines so they could open their minds about what the company had become, honestly examine how it had lost its way, and embark on fresh thinking about turning it around.

Dream ceremony: ▶
Immerse Deeply

Dream symbol: Auditory ▶

The meeting began on a sensory note, with music and visual images, to transport the leaders into a creative mind-set. When they walked into the meeting room, iPods loaded with Beatles music and posters of the Beatles were laid on the table. Each person was given a Sharpie and six index cards. Their assignment was to reflect on "What does it mean to reinvent an icon?" Though it was humbling to compare Starbucks to the Beatles, it helped their minds make observations about Starbucks from a different context. Leaders shared answers such as *"The band took risks," "They took us on a journey at a time when the world needed cultural leaders,"* and *"They kept reinventing themselves, but at the same time, stayed true to their music."*

At the end of the first day of brainstorming, the team split up into smaller groups and went into the city to immerse themselves in some of Seattle's most compelling homegrown retailers, such as Pike Place Market, Beecher's Handmade Cheese, and Theo Chocolate. Their assignment was to observe and report back what they saw, heard, tasted, smelled, and felt. At Beecher's Handmade Cheese, near Pike Place Market, Schultz was struck by how easily he chatted with the woman behind the counter. He asked her, *"How did you get to be such an expert on cheese?"* and he was floored to learn that she'd known nothing about the subject only six months earlier. That made him consider Starbucks's thousands of baristas. How could he breed passion in them so they did a better job sharing coffee knowledge?

Signs of Change

To begin to reignite the baristas' passion and knowledge about coffee, in February 2008 Schultz closed 7,100 stores for three and a half hours, at a cost of approximately $6 million in profit. The company used the time to retrain baristas to make the perfect espresso. Upon closing, a sign posted on the door of every store explained, *"We're taking time to perfect our art of espresso. Great espresso requires practice. That's why we're dedicating ourselves to honing our craft."*

Signs are posted at stores so customers understand Starbucks's commitment to coffee.

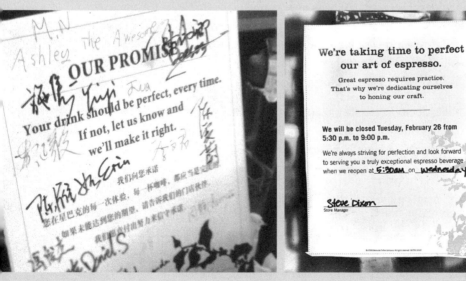

Leap ceremony: ▶
Pledge Commitment

The day after, baristas replaced that sign with a new one, autographed by the baristas, that read, *"Your drink should be perfect, every time. If not, let us know and we'll make it right."* The coffee quality scores went up and stayed there. Schultz reflected on the decision by saying: *"We had to restore the passion and the commitment that everyone at Starbucks needed to have for our customers. Doing so meant taking a step back before we could take many steps forward."*

Recommit to the Dream

After the core team of executives had convened, Schultz gathered his next tier of leaders: two hundred senior managers from around the world. He recalled, *"I could not discern a cynic from an optimist. Who believed in Starbucks—or, for that matter, who believed in me?"* He decided that all he could do was speak from his heart, saying,

Dream story: ▶
Heed the Call

"Ladies and gentlemen, let's be honest with one another. We are not doing this as well as we once did, and the mediocrity that we have been embracing cannot stand any longer." This moment required honesty about the situation as well as sincere optimism. They spent three days together talking about transformation and fine-tuning their mission statement together. The session was among the first steps the company would take to revisit and rewrite its mission. The original stated, *"To establish Starbucks as the premier purveyor of the finest coffees in the world while maintaining our uncompromising principles as we grow."* And they eventually changed it to *"To inspire and nurture the human spirit—one person, one cup, and one neighborhood at a time."*

Schultz understood that he should not simply demand that they follow him. He had to make the case for change, and then ask for, and earn, people's fellowship. He did so by delivering a speech with a powerful and authentic personal story.

> *"A week before I came back as ceo, both my children asked me, 'Dad, why are you going back? You don't need this.' I told them that if I think about the two things I love in my life, it is our family and this company. There is not anything I would not do for my family . . . and there is nothing I would not do for this company. I will hold myself to the highest level of accountability. I will walk through and climb over every wall to make sure that we get to the place that we deserve*

Leap story: Seek the Reward ▶

Leap speech: Pursuit ▶

. . . but no one in this room, including myself, can do this alone. There has never been a time in the history of the company that we needed each other more than we need each other now."

Just as he'd done with the smaller group of leaders a few weeks earlier, Schultz had the two hundred leaders visit Seattle's most inspiring retail shops. Their instruction was to consider each retail experience not as a merchant or an operator, but from the point of view of a customer. This underscored just how critical it was that the company refocus to place the customer at the center of every business decision.

◀ Empathetic listening

At the close of the event, Schultz took the stage and said, *"Over the last few weeks . . . we began to look at a piece of paper that has been in place now for 25 years, and that is the mission statement of Starbucks."* He felt that Starbucks had strayed from its original mission during its meteoric growth, and as they reexamined the mission in light of the new transformation, they updated it. He continued, *"[We] updated it in a way that would capture the passion we have for the future and the respect we have for the past. But give the people . . . a new way to look at the company."*

◀ Climb story:
Lose the Way

◀ Fight ceremony:
Rally Spirits

Schultz picked up a paper and began to read the overarching theme that framed the document. He read the first line aloud: *"To inspire and nurture the human spirit—one person, one cup, and one neighborhood at a time."* Then, without a cue, a vice president stood up from her chair and read the next line of the mission statement, then a UK vice president read the next. One by one, leaders read aloud the mission statement. The moment was emotional and subdued; several people cried.

◀ Leap ceremony:
Pledge Commitment

After the new mission statement was introduced, doors opened so everyone could exit the meeting room. As they did, they entered a larger room, where, to their surprise, museum-like displays depicting the mission statement's themes had been constructed as a visceral experience. Excerpts from customer letters and e-mails covered one wall. On another, one thousand coffee cups were handwritten with various experiences customers had had at Starbucks, such as *"I came up with an idea for dinner"* or *"I played with a wandering child."* Each display was designed to bring the company's values to life, and to remind the company's leaders why they needed to keep the customer first. Then something happened that stunned Schultz.

Individuals turned back in to the meeting room and began approaching him to sign their copy of the new mission statement. A line began to form. Schultz shook hands with and thanked the leaders who signed more than 150 mission statements in an emotional display of their commitment.

Leap ceremony: ▶
Pledge Commitment

Pike Place Roast is released as a symbol of transformation.

Hark Back to Move Forward

Among the steps the company took to reestablish Starbucks as the definitive leader in coffee was expanding its coffee offerings. New products included a brewed coffee with a flavor profile that Starbucks deemed more "approachable" than its darker roasts and traditional blends. They launched the new blend with flair and began grinding beans in the store again, a ritual they'd abandoned in order to serve customers more quickly. The new brew gave Starbucks partners something exciting to rally around, and freshly ground beans filled stores with a rich aroma, ushering back some of the theater that had been missing from the Starbucks experience. They named this milder blend Pike Place Roast, after the first Starbucks store, located in Seattle's historic Pike Place Market. It was a sign to partners (employees) and customers that the company was going back to its roots—a nod to the past while embracing the future, as Schultz explained it, adding, *"Pike Place Roast had the potential to be a powerful catalyst for a symbol of our transformation and prove the company was actively reclaiming its coffee authority."*

Losing One Battle and Closing 600 Stores

With Starbucks stock value continuing to fall, the board challenged Schultz to close stores and cut expenses. Six hundred stores were selected to be shuttered. Shockingly, 70 percent of all stores slated for closure had been opened during the last three years of the company's aggressive growth period—another sign that Starbucks had lost sight of some of the fundamentals. In a memo to partners on July 1, 2008, Schultz announced the hard, yet necessary, decision to close stores:

> *"By far, this is the most angst-ridden decision we have made in my more than 25 years with Starbucks, but we realize that part of transforming a company is our ability to look forward, while pursuing innovation and reflecting, in many cases, with 20/20 hindsight, on the decisions that we made in the past, both good and bad. However, I strongly believe that our best days are ahead of us."*

◄ Climb speech: Crossroads

Schultz made it clear that the decision was difficult and painful, and that the people who worked in those impacted stores would be treated with dignity. He explained the benefits they would get and that their managers would strive to be honest and transparent with the process. He explained why this painful decision was a step in the right direction:

> *"We believe that building an enduring, great company requires the thoughtfulness and, at times, the courage to make some very tough, difficult decisions. This is one of those times. . . . And I promise you that I understand the magnitude of closing so many stores and the emotional impact it will have on our partners. I assure you that we have taken all of this into consideration in doing what is necessary to strengthen our company for today and the future."*

Mourn the Loss of a Thousand People

Store closings and layoffs had slashed costs but they still weren't deep enough to assure a victory. On July 29, 2008, Starbucks announced that it was going to eliminate one thousand non-store positions and asked 550 partners throughout the organization to leave. The very next day, Schultz addressed a gathering of one thousand Starbucks partners at the company's headquarters. He knew the layoffs were devastating for those who had to leave as well as those who remained at the company and were in the audience that day.

> *"I apologize if anyone in this room feels that we have fractured the culture and values of the company with what has happened over the last few weeks, and specifically yesterday."*

Climb speech: Crossroads ▶

He empathized with them by explaining how upsetting it was for him and acknowledging the pain and grief they felt because of the decision:

> *"This is a defining moment like no other for Starbucks Coffee Company, and moments like this are quite difficult and emotional so let me specifically address yesterday. I never anticipated, nor was I emotionally prepared for, the decisions that led to asking passionate, talented, deserving partners to leave our company. . . . I know people are angry and grieving and I know people are mad."*

He explained that the decision had to be made for the long-term sustainability of the company, and that together the company had to move forward.

Immerse Everyone in a New World

Only a few months later, thousands of store managers would gather for a conference to recommit to transforming the company. Store managers are the on-the-ground leaders who nurture the customer relationship, and Schultz wanted to communicate to them directly, expressing what was at stake and what he was asking of them and of all Starbucks partners. Transforming the customer experience would happen only if the managers understood they held the power to make Starbucks successful.

Store managers invest thousands of hours rebuilding the Ninth Ward in New Orleans.

So Schultz and his team hosted a large gathering in New Orleans of 10,000 partners (8,000 store managers and 2,000 regional and district leaders) at the considerable expense of $30 million. Keep in mind, this convened a month after the global economy took a beating, in September 2008. Some leaders and board members advised him to cancel the event because they thought it was too large an expense, but Schultz felt there was no question it was the right thing to do.

New Orleans was chosen because the city played a historic role in the coffee business as the first U.S. port to receive shipments of coffee. But more important, the city had endured a great struggle to recover its glory after Hurricane Katrina. A full three years after the storm, the city was still suffering, with some neighborhoods still in tatters. Schultz was determined that the veritable army he'd brought to town would not just focus on rebuilding Starbucks but would also help rebuild the New Orleans community. Each day of the conference, about two thousand managers wearing T-shirts bearing the slogans "Onward" and "Believe in the Power of 10,000" joined local nonprofit groups for five hours to paint homes, install fences, plant trees, and build playgrounds.

◀ Climb symbol: spatial

◀ Climb story:
   Endure the Struggle

At the opening session of the conference, Schultz spoke from his heart, with no script. He wanted to strike a balance between harsh realism and belief in the future. Standing onstage in front of a huge screen that read "Onward," he said:

> *"We are here to celebrate our heritage and traditions and also to have an honest and direct conversation about what we are responsible to do as leaders. . . . We are not a perfect company. We make mistakes every day . . . but we have lots of issues that we are trying to balance."*

He went on to highlight challenges, including the weak economy and increasing competition. Then, expressing empathy for the store managers, he asked a series of rhetorical questions about the business from their viewpoint:

> *"What does it mean when approximately 50 customers a day are not coming into our store versus last year? What does it mean when at eight o'clock in the morning the line is out the door and a customer peels off and leaves? What does it mean when you see a customer you recognize with a cup of coffee that is not ours?"*

He then laid out the challenge and offered his pledge to help the store managers return Starbucks to greatness:

Climb story: ▶
Lose the Way

Managers listen to heartfelt customer messages.

Managers rake warm coffee beans to emotionally reconnect to what they do.

> *"These are serious questions, and what they mean, I have always believed strongly, is that we have to take accountability and responsibility for the things that we observe. The things that we experience. And the things that we learn. . . .*
>
> *"I will do everything humanly possible to represent you the way that I ask you to represent the company. Passionately. Honestly. With great sincerity and humility and doing everything I can to exceed your expectations to make sure our future is as great as our past."*

And Schultz didn't rely on words alone. As part of the conference, a series of interactive, multisensory storytelling galleries were created for strolling through at the venue to bring partners through a journey of rediscovery. *"At one towering display,"* Schultz recalled, *"I could pick up a coffee cup, hold it up to my ear like an old-fashioned children's game of 'telephone,' and listen to actual recordings of customers who had called our support center with praise or critiques of their store experiences."*

In another gallery, photo montages featured candid shots of customers in Starbucks stores. In another, nearly a thousand coffee trees were placed alongside a drying patio, like those found on coffee farms, where partners could rake beans strewn

◀ Climb ceremony: Renew Commitment

◀ Empathetic listening

Store managers sign a wall and pledge to run their stores differently when they get back.

across the floor as if they were drying in the sun. They could also take a virtual tour of a coffee roasting plant or walk through dramatic scenes of coffee's journey from soil to cup.

Leap ceremony: ▶
Pledge Commitment

Schultz also asked the managers to <u>sign a Commitment Wall</u> pledging to operate their stores as if they were their own businesses.

Leap speech: Pursuit ▶

In his closing remarks, Schultz spoke from the heart in an <u>inspiring call to action</u>:

> *"The power of this company is you. We need to recognize as leaders that unlike any other time in our history, this is a seminal moment. This is a test. A crucible. A challenge for how we are going to respond. And my primary message is to share with you the pride that I have in being your partner."*

He understood that he had to empathize with where partners were on the journey by speaking transparently, even demonstrating his own vulnerability. Yet he needed to clearly convey what was at stake and that he was asking for personal accountability from them.

Becoming Profitable Again

Through the effort of Schultz and his team, Starbucks climbed back to profit. In his fiscal third-quarter-earnings call in the fall of 2009, Schultz told Wall Street, *"Over the past 16 months, Starbucks has faced both the headwind of the global economy, just as all businesses have, and our own unique set of challenges. Today I am pleased to report results for the third quarter that point to positive momentum from the comprehensive set of actions we've taken to transform the business."*

◀ **Arrive speech:** Victory

The store managers had taken the empathetic lessons from the New Orleans conference to heart. As Schultz explained on the call, *"Our partners have embraced the challenge of putting themselves in the shoes of our customers and are driving meaningful operational improvements."*

He also gave plenty of evidence that Starbucks had become a customer-centric organization again, by recounting progress made since early 2008: *"We have improved staffing models, provided increased rigor around store standards and reinforced our passion for delivering the best customer experience, all of this has significantly improved store economics."*

And he quantified the spike in customer satisfaction: *". . . partner friendliness, up 7 percentage points; taste of beverage, up 7 points; speed of service, up 11 points; and most importantly, overall customer satisfaction, up 9 points."*

"One of the real lessons I share from this experience," Schultz later recounted in 2011, *"is that people need the unvarnished truth. . . . I think the openness allowed people to be part of the solution rather than being outside of it. I honestly believe without that seminal event [in New Orleans] we would have not been able to transform the company and do it so quickly."*

Starbucks Venture Scape Summary

Starbucks had been driving rapid expansion globally but in the process the company had lost some of its magic with customers. In an eighteen-month period, ceo Howard Schultz and his leadership team undertook a venture to reframe the company's mission, shift employee mind-sets, and reinvigorate the customer experience to bring Starbucks back to its roots.

01
Schultz returns as chief executive officer of Starbucks after realizing the company's rapid global growth was destructive to the health of the brand.

02
Schultz gathers twenty top executives and a diverse group of partners in an immersive visioning process.

03
Executives rewrite the company mission and commit to transform Starbucks.

04
Starbucks closes 7,100 stores for three and a half hours to retrain baristas on how to make espresso-based beverages. Baristas commit to customers to make better drinks and recommit to the brand.

05
Two hundred top leaders gather at the Global Leadership Summit. They commit to the transformation.

06
Leaders ask Schultz to sign their copy of the new mission statement.

07
Starbucks launches Pike Place Roast coffee, symbolizing its commitment to return to its roots.

DREAM

LEAP

08

Starbucks announces the closing of six hundred stores.

09

Starbucks cuts one thousand support positions and 550 people are asked to leave.

10

In spite of the global economic crash in September 2008, the company hosts a leadership summit in New Orleans for ten thousand store, regional, and district managers.

11

Starbucks lays off seven hundred more employees.

12

On July 21, in the Fiscal 2009 third-quarter-earnings call, Schultz claims to have achieved positive momentum.

13

Starbucks reignites its commitment to global responsibility and promises to focus its efforts on ethical sourcing, environmental stewardship, and community involvement.

∞

FIGHT   CLIMB   ARRIVE   (re)DREAM

CHAPTER FOUR

DREAM

Dream

Moment of Inspiration

When you kick off a vision, initiative, or product, it sets in motion a new season of transformation. In the initial stage of your venture, your travelers need to understand your vision and find inspiration in the journey ahead.

Torchbearer leaders dream about how to move from the present to the future. In this first stage of your venture, you take the future you've been modeling in your mind and start to imagine how to create that potential future now. It could be an internal process that will transform how your team functions today, a new product or service that will improve your customers' lives, or a different way of thinking or acting that could make the world a better place somehow.

Once you can picture your dream as a reality, you can communicate it to others, which is the vital first step in your venture. The more clearly you can envision it, the more urgency you probably feel to run toward it. Yet while you may see utopia in your mind's eye, it may still be a hazy, faraway place to your travelers. You'll need to paint a vivid portrait of the future you desire so that others can see it clearly, too. Even then, you'll have to convince people that it's better than the status quo.

This stage requires both determining the direction in which you need to go and declaring a compelling vision that instills longing to get there. Getting your travelers to pull up their tents and trek into the unknown is no easy task. For many, the largest stumbling block to progress is letting go of the world they know. To help people move forward, show them how their attachment to the current state holds them back, and lay out how the proposed future can and will be better for them.

Start by empathizing with your travelers to show that you understand the benefits and disadvantages that their world today provides them. Then help them visualize the end state by describing your dream in alluring detail and what they stand to gain in it. Finally, communicate the whole path from present to future, clearly articulating the journey from where you've been to where you are now, and where you're headed in the long run.

Understand What Your Travelers Are Feeling

When you're planning how to communicate the dream to your travelers, you'll need to assess how they're currently feeling. Using the empathetic listening skills described earlier in this book, you should have already initially identified what they could gain or lose if your dream is realized. Those who will gain a lot are likely to commit more readily, while those who have more to lose will probably resist more. Use motivating communication to help energize the committed ones and warning communication to coax the resistant to come along.

If They're **Committed**, You'll Hear Them Say . . .	Use **Motivating** Communication to Keep Them Going.
"I'm on board." **"I see a new possibility."** **"There's a better way."**	Generate hope and excitement by showing people that what they have to look forward to is far more attractive than the current state. Reveal the visionary picture of the future. Instead of being afraid to tread into the unknown, your travelers will boldly go because they're motivated to pursue the vision you've portrayed. Connect the choices that they are—or aren't—making today to the possibility of tomorrow. Reinforce how your vision will fulfill their potential.

If They're **Resistant**, You'll Hear Them Say . . .	Use **Warning** Communication to Get Them Unstuck.
"I just don't see how this could work." **"The whole idea is wrongheaded."** **"Everybody thinks this makes no sense."**	If travelers are cemented to their present state and seem immoveable, show them how their refusal to move on could play out negatively in the future. But also reveal how, by making changes now, they can avoid those negative outcomes. Help them understand why continuing on the current path will hinder their and everyone's ability to thrive. Bring closure to outdated attitudes and processes and inspire them to imagine a better way.

Dream Communication Toolkit

Armed with insights about your travelers and what inspires them, you're ready to share your dream. Using speeches, stories, ceremonies, and symbols you can express your vision and help your travelers experience it firsthand through words, images, and actions that bring it to life.

DREAM SPEECHES

The spoken word is a powerful persuasive communication tool, so delivering speeches throughout your venture is important to keep your travelers aligned. In the Dream stage, speeches explain the end state you see in your mind's eye and contrast it with the current state. If your dream builds on the positive aspects of the present state to create an even brighter future, use a motivating Vision speech. But if your team members struggle to understand your dream and resist, jolt them out of their attachment to the status quo with a Revolution speech.

Motivate with "Vision" Speeches

Vision speeches are aspirational and often poetic. They fire the imagination and open minds to new possibilities by creating images of the future that embed in people's memories. They emphasize that business as usual is going away because a major positive change is around the corner.

For example, in 1993, Nelson Mandela was awarded the Nobel Peace Prize for his work in ending apartheid in South Africa. In his speech, Mandela spoke of a country remaking itself: *"We live with the hope that as she battles to remake herself, South Africa will be like a microcosm of the new world that is striving to be born. . . . Let a new age dawn!"*

Similarly, when speaking about your vision, show what your idea offers that the current state doesn't. By communicating the promise of an improved future and contrasting it with a present situation that's less desirable, you'll make the dream more attractive than today's reality.

///

Ray Anderson, CEO of the carpet manufacturing company Interface, declared a bold vision for sustainability. To convey his dream to employees he first exposed the current ecological crisis facing the planet. Then he contrasted that dire situation with an inspiring picture of how Interface could do its part to avert further disaster and leave a positive legacy for future generations.

What Is: *"Many believe that we are exceeding the capacity of the earth now and will continue to do so at an increasing, accelerating rate until catastrophe strikes, unless somebody or somebodies do something to arrest and reverse the tide."*

What Could Be: *"Who can take the lead? Industry [is] the most powerful, pervasive institution in the world, and the one doing the most damage. People coming together and acting in concert as in businesses like ours can make a big difference."*

New Bliss: *"What if Interface became the first industrial company in the world to achieve sustainability? Once we're sustainable we'll become restorative by helping others become sustainable, putting back more than we ourselves take. Imagine the favorable reaction of the marketplace, not to mention the example that we would set."*

When Lou Gerstner Jr. took the helm of IBM in 1993, he famously told reporters, *"The last thing IBM needs right now is a vision"*—a statement that got him a lot of flak. He meant that he needed to stem the bleeding first by cutting spending and slashing bureaucracy so that the struggling behemoth could stay alive a little longer while he figured out a new direction for IBM. While he stabilized the company, which took more than a year, Gerstner also listened to customers and studied market trends. He soon realized that networked computers—connected by a new thing called the Internet—would change everything about how business got done. In 1995 at the technology trade show COMDEX, he delivered a speech that foreshadowed IBM's next evolution as a provider of Internet solutions, ushering in the "e-business" era.

> **What Is:** *"We are at the threshold of the next major phase of computing. It draws upon many of the technologies we've already discussed, but one in particular— high-speed, high-bandwidth networking—which is why we refer to it as network-centric computing."*

> **What Could Be:** *"As stewards of our industry, we will step up to the challenges of social responsibility. We will improve the world, and the way we work, the way we communicate, live and learn as people."*

> **New Bliss:** *"We have grown, we have innovated, and we have prospered at a rate unsurpassed by any other. It's been an amazing, breathtaking ride. It can continue—and accelerate—if we remember that our future rests on how well we respond to the total needs of society and of our customers all around the world."*

Warn with "Revolution" Speeches

Revolution speeches incite travelers to rise up against the status quo and demand a better future. Something, or someone, is keeping you and your travelers from starting this epic journey, so you must turn things upside down before you can all move ahead.

When the American colonies were still under British rule, a band of colonists decided enough was enough and gathered to plot a path to independence. A Virginian named Patrick Henry moved his peers to act with these words, which became a rallying cry for the revolution: *"I know not what course others may take; but as for me, give me liberty or give me death!"*

Without a doubt, revolution speeches are confrontational. They describe in stark detail the injustices or losses that will occur if the current condition isn't overturned. But they also move people to seek justice by painting a picture of life back in balance when wrongs are made right.

///

When Graham Weston, cofounder of the cloud services company Rackspace, based in San Antonio, discovered that talented tech-savvy people were choosing to settle elsewhere, he warned community leaders that San Antonio was at risk of becoming irrelevant. In a speech to the city council in 2012, he outlined the opportunity available to the region if San Antonio reinvented itself as a technology center, but he warned that the city would lose the battle for talent if its leaders didn't take action soon.

> **What Is:** *"Tomorrow's reality is cloud-computing, on a massive scale—and we're not ready for it. . . . We're gonna need a lot of skilled workers but we're not going to be able to find them."*

> **What Could Be:** *"San Antonio is well-placed to become an educational and business hub for cloud-computing with a thriving industry. . . . An entrepreneurial culture and cloud education would create a highly trained workforce with a clear path to good jobs, attractive, affordable real estate, and an attractive lifestyle."*

> **New Bliss:** *"The future will be in cloud technologies and San Antonio is the best place to start preparing our workforce and our industry for tomorrow's needs."*

The computer security industry is justifiably risk averse and after many years that avoidance of change led to apathy. In his 2014 keynote at a security industry conference, Nawaf Bitar, of Juniper Networks, aimed to stir security decision makers to feel outrage and take bolder action against nefarious hackers or suffer the consequences.

> **What Is:** *"Our privacy is being invaded. Our intellectual property is being stolen. But you know what? I don't think we give a damn. You in this room have the prowess and capital to demand better, yet we stand by. We are complicit."*

> **What Could Be:** *"Our information is one of our most important possessions, and we should treat it as such. . . . If an enemy shot down one of our passenger airliners, we would go to war. If a nation-state compromised our air traffic control system and two of those passenger airliners collided, wouldn't we not also go to war?"*

> **New Bliss:** *"It's time for a new type of defense: a type of active defense that disrupts the economics of hacking and challenges convention. . . . It's time for all of us to turn the tables on the attackers, or we can do nothing. We can continue to turn the other cheek and we can passively wait for the next world war to begin."*

DREAM STORIES

When declaring your vision during the Dream stage, a persuasive speech helps your travelers see the possible future that you're seeing. A story underscores that vision by making the future seem more tangible, especially if you are proposing an innovation or concept that's radically different from anything travelers have ever known. That's where stories come in: They make abstract ideas relatable on a visceral, personal level and transport your travelers into the scene.

Motivate with "Heed the Call" Stories

Filled with vivid descriptions, Heed the Call stories set the scene of the epiphany you had that helped you imagine a new possibility and how that utopia will benefit your travelers. How will today's wrongs be made right? What will the benefits be? Who will enjoy them? These stories will rally your team to feel more impassioned about your vision and move everyone to the next stage of leaping.

///

In the previously mentioned speech Graham Weston wanted to inspire city leaders to believe that San Antonio was capable of becoming the cloud-computing hub of the U.S. To show what was possible when people banded together to build a new capability, Weston used an anecdote from American history. He set the scene this way:

> "In 1939, at the beginning of WWII, the U.S. Air Corps had 1,200 planes and the U.S. Army was ranked 17th largest in the world. Among American industries, aerospace ranked 41st—the industry could barely make 2,000 planes a year. And then the future caught up with us: the German blitzkrieg on Holland, Belgium, and France. President Roosevelt appeared before Congress and called for 50,000 planes every year. The United States aggressively ramped up aircraft production—factories ran 24 hours a day, six or seven days a week. . . . The country rose to the challenge and created a huge industry where one barely existed before, hired and trained millions of skilled workers, and wildly succeeded. We're facing a similar challenge today in San Antonio."

The cofounders of Airbnb, Joe Gebbia and Brian Chesky, frequently tell the origin story of their company and how their opportunistic response to a hotel shortage gave way to a brand-new business model. As Gebbia told it at the PSFK conference in 2011,

> "Brian and I both quit our jobs to become entrepreneurs . . . [but just then] our rent went up and suddenly we found ourselves unable to afford our apartment. . . . That same weekend a design conference was coming to San Francisco that was so big all the hotels had sold out in the city. . . . We started to think creatively: What if we were able to blow up an air mattress, put it in our living room, and rent it out to designers who need a place to stay for the conference? We could go so far as to cook them breakfast, and by the end of the night we had this concept called Airbed and Breakfast. . . . Within twenty-four hours . . . we had people who started

writing us from all over the world who wanted to stay in our living room. We made a thousand dollars and they saved our apartment."

Warn with "Neglect the Call" Stories

No matter how compelling your vision is, some of your travelers won't be charmed by it. They may be so attached to the way things are that they're blind to the need for change. Use Neglect the Call stories to help them understand the costs of avoiding change in a tangible way. Neglect the Call stories take a trip through a disappointing past and dystopian future. What inefficient, unprofitable, soulless, unrewarding reality could come to fruition if your dream isn't embraced?

///

When CEO Indra Nooyi talks about PepsiCo's quest to conserve water in all the countries where her company operates, she drives home the point by describing what it was like for her to live in a water-scarce area of the world. When Nooyi was growing up in India, her mother would get up before four a.m. to collect water from the trickle that the corporation in town would release from the central reservoir. Each family member was given a small amount of water to use throughout the day for everything from bathing to doing laundry, left to figure out how to make it last. Meanwhile, the same corporation would use large amounts of water to operate its business. Years later, Nooyi used this very personal example to illustrate her approach to balancing the needs of shareholders and other stakeholders:

> *"When you're running a company or part of a company, you have to focus on the shareholder. There's no question about it. But there's more to a company than just the shareholder. There's a multiplicity of stakeholders and you've got to worry about all of them because when you're worried just about today and just the shareholder, you don't want to add cost to society that somebody else has to clean up."*

Civil rights lawyer Gary Haugen, CEO and founder of International Justice Mission, dreams of a day when poor people all over the world no longer have to suffer. To help audiences understand the human cost of poverty, Haugen shares stories about individuals he has met in his travels around the world that foster empathy for its victims:

> "[Venus] described what it was like when the coals on the cooking fire finally just went completely cold. When that last drop of cooking oil finally ran out. When the last of the food, despite her best efforts, ran out. She had to watch her youngest son, Peter, suffer from malnutrition, as his legs just slowly bowed into uselessness. As his eyes grew cloudy and dim. And then as Peter finally grew cold."

DREAM CEREMONIES

Spoken words, whether through speeches or stories, help you describe your dream, but ceremonies will enable your travelers to experience it as if it already exists. Engage their senses through interactive experiences that allow them to see, hear, touch, smell, or taste the future to heighten their desire for it. Alternatively, ceremonies can ease the transition into the future by giving travelers a chance to say good-bye and shed their attachment to the past or present in order to make way for what comes next.

Motivate with "Immerse Deeply" Ceremonies

Immersion ceremonies create an atmosphere that helps your travelers imagine your potential future. These moments suspend disbelief, even if just for a moment, and open everyone's mind to new realities. Creatively transport travelers during kickoff strategy sessions, brainstorms, and vision meetings to imbue these moments of invention with a richer sense of possibility.

A sleek Ford Mustang concept car from 1962

///

The Mustang was Ford's most successful car of the 1960s. The original, built in 1962, was a concept car meant to symbolize the vehicle of the future and never went into production. Ford ceremonially put it on tour, taking it to the Grand Prix, to car shows, and to college campuses around the country. They introduced a young market to how stylish a high-performing car could be. When the actual Mustang debuted, even though it didn't look anything like the concept car, demand was so strong that dealers received more than twenty-two thousand orders its first day on sale.

When Jack Ma, founder and executive chairman of Alibaba Group, announced his bold vision to create an e-commerce site to compete with eBay in China, his team thought he was insane. So Jack said, *"I want you all to stand on your heads."* One executive team member said, *"I have never done that in my life, and I am too old for that."* Jack Ma said, *"No excuse, I'm the oldest among this group. We'll stand upside down on our heads."* Everyone in the room managed to stand upside down. Afterward Ma said, *"When you stand upside down, you'll see the world from a new perspective."* Then he told the executive who had never stood on his head before, *"You see, you can do things that you have never done before."*

Warn with "Mourn Endings" Ceremonies

Mourning ceremonies help those who might cling to old beliefs and behaviors to prepare themselves to change and make room for the new. These ceremonies help travelers symbolically close the door to the past; it becomes harder to reopen that door when there's finality to its closure.

///

When Nike discontinued one of its most beloved soccer shoes, it designed a limited-edition "Lights Out" shoe. The original shoe, the CTR360 Maestri, was multicolored, but the Lights Out edition was completely black. Each pair was also given a unique serial number. Nike design director Denis Dekovic said, *"We know this boot has a lot of fans so we wanted to say goodbye with something special."* Even die-hard professionals could appreciate this farewell, despite having to move on to a new shoe.

Members of the training department of a Fortune 100 company gathered every Friday for status updates and doughnuts as they migrated to a new global learning management platform. On the day the new platform launched, the manager had pallbearers carry a box of doughnuts to this final meeting to signify that the old system was gone. Interestingly, when the team continued to meet every Friday to kick off a new project, serving doughnuts felt like sacrilege, so they opted for healthier choices.

DREAM SYMBOLS

Motivating symbols created during the Dream stage represent hope for a brighter future. Warning symbols bring closure to something that needed to end so your travelers can embrace a new dream. Either may emerge from the moment when you saw the need for change or from the event where you declared the dream itself.

Motivating Symbols

- **Visual:** The Mount Sustainability graphic (page 98) that Ray Anderson of Interface sketched over and over to explain his vision for sustainability is now deeply embedded in Interface's heritage.

- **Auditory:** To process their transformation from another context, Starbucks executives listened to Beatles songs to reflect on what it's like to be an icon.

- **Spatial:** The CEO of Airbnb includes a photo of the apartment where he founded the company in his presentations.

- **Physical:** Jack Ma of Alibaba had his leaders stand on their heads to symbolize taking on a new vantage point of their role in the world.

Warning Symbols

- **Visual:** The building at Facebook's headquarters used to be the home of Sun Microsystems. Instead of replacing the sign, CEO Mark Zuckerberg chose to turn it around and put the Facebook logo on the back to remind employees what happens when you take your eye off the ball.

- **Auditory:** Rackspace's Graham Weston repeated a rhetorical question to the citizens of San Antonio: *"When your kids return from college, are they going to want to return to San Antonio or live in Austin?"*

- **Spatial:** Whole Foods raised awareness of honeybee die-offs by temporarily removing pollinator-produced foods from the salad bars in their stores. Later the company took every pollinator-related food off store shelves to shed light on the problem.

- **Physical:** Market Basket employees walked off their jobs and marched in protest when their beloved CEO was fired and replaced with a board member known for not being generous toward employees.

SUMMARY

To create moments of inspiration for your travelers at the start of your venture, use these tools of speeches, stories, ceremonies, and symbols to kick off the dream with fanfare. Just as the new year is greeted with revelry, a ship's maiden voyage is christened with champagne, and a representative rings a bell when a company goes public on the stock exchange, you should clearly demarcate the moment your dream launches to generate enthusiasm.

Yet, look at that list. New Year's rings in the new and out the old. The ship christening celebrates both the completion of the build and its launch into the ocean. The stock exchange bell signifies the end of a privately held company and the launch of a public one. They combine beginnings and endings both. Kicking off your beginning well catapults your travelers forward with memories they can use for fuel along the way. Bring closure to what your travelers cling to that slows them down and mark this new beginning as an inspirational moment in time. Usher the venture in with wonderment and awe.

Interface founder Ray C. Anderson motivated his colleagues to dream big.

Interface

Torchbearers know that to stay ahead of the curve, they have to anticipate market trends and respond ahead of time with new products and services. But sometimes the future arrives seemingly out of the blue and threatens to turn your world upside down unless you seize the opportunity to transform.

Interface Reimagines the Nature of Business

Adaptable furnishings and modular carpet tiles are common fixtures in the offices of fast-growing companies. But carpet tiles were still a futuristic concept when Ray C. Anderson founded Interface forty years ago. While attending a textile trade show in England in the late 1960s, he saw a demo for a new kind of floor covering—carpet tiles—that blew his mind. Convinced that they were the next big thing, Anderson founded the modular carpet company Interface in 1973.

His decision turned out to be exactly the right move at exactly the right time. The rise of knowledge-worker jobs in the U.S. led to offices getting built across the country, and those offices were being designed with technology in mind. Workspaces would need to be outfitted with a floor covering that could be easily lifted when wires needed repairing or relocating as businesses changed. Through word-of-mouth recommendations by architects and interior designers, customer demand for Interface's beautiful and functional products exploded. The company grew exponentially for two decades, becoming the world's largest supplier of carpet tiles.

A Simple Question Provokes Change

In the 1990s, ecological concerns rose higher in the public consciousness and industrial companies came under scrutiny. In 1994 Interface's own customers began asking, *"What are you doing for the environment?"* And Anderson didn't have an answer—yet. So he pulled together a small task force of seventeen people from Interface's business units to research the company's impact on the environment and come up with a plan to fix any problems they found.

Arrive story: ▶
Learn the Lesson

Looking for some direction, the task force asked Anderson to kick off their first meeting with a speech that would illuminate his environmental vision for the company. *"To be quite frank, I did not have a vision,"* Anderson later admitted. *"For 21 of our 22 years of existence, I never gave one thought to what we were taking from the earth* [sic] *or doing to the earth, except to be sure we were in compliance."* He fretted about what he would say for weeks. Then in an odd coincidence—or what Anderson called a moment of "pure serendipity"—an Interface saleswoman sent him a book called *The Ecology of Commerce*, written by Paul Hawken, founder of Smith & Hawken garden supply. Anderson devoured the book and was devastated by what he read.

Dream story: ▶
Heed the Call

He realized that his petrochemical-intensive carpet business was exactly the "plunderer of the Earth" that Hawken railed against. Anderson said this epiphany hit him like a "spear in the chest," shaking him to his core and causing him to question his purpose. This moment transformed him. He would no longer be merely the CEO of a carpet company—he would become a forerunner in the sustainability movement for manufacturing and industrial companies.

A Vision Is Unveiled

Anderson delivered his vision to the Interface task force in a speech that challenged them to think big about how to solve this problem. To show them what was at stake, he immersed them in the reality of environmental degradation using shocking statistics from Hawken's book about the damage being done to the earth by humans. Then he declared his ambitious goal for Interface to *"become the first industrial company in the world to achieve sustainability."*

◀ **Dream speech:** Vision

◀ **Dream ceremony:** Immerse Deeply

Anderson felt urgency to turn the tide on environmental damage and wanted his task force to feel equally impassioned. So he stretched the boundaries of the dream further, saying, *"Once we're sustainable, we become restorative by helping others become sustainable."*

He closed by asking them to take up the cause and lead the way forward:

◀ **Leap speech:** Pursuit

> *"Let us commit with this kickoff to not just sitting here and talking to each other but doing something. Specifically to doing what? I don't know—you must tell me, when you're ready. I know you'll figure it out."*

In perhaps the most important speech of his life so far, he felt he'd made a clear and compelling case for change. But when he got done speaking, the room was silent. *"It surprised me and stunned them,"* Anderson said. He had been so fired up about his vision that he hadn't considered how the dramatic data and audacious goals he shared would impact his team emotionally. He'd spent three weeks reading, contemplating, and formulating ideas and working through his own feelings of remorse over not having acted sooner. Their journey, however, was just beginning.

Dealing with Doubt About the Dream

The task force felt like a bomb had just been dropped on them. The scale of the world's environmental problems was overwhelming, and they couldn't help but feel guilty about their role in the earth's degradation. How could just one company possibly turn the tide? One employee noted that the *"vision seemed to violate the basic laws of thermodynamics."*

Changing seemed impossible. Sensing their resistance, Anderson appealed to their pride, telling his staff, *"Any business can do it, and no one will have an excuse not to do it. . . . Who should lead this effort if not us?"* Interface was the world leader in its industry; becoming a sustainable company was not a choice but an obligation.

The task force raced into action and after two days of intense brainstorming they expressed their commitment to a specific goal: Interface would achieve sustainability by the year 2000—just six years from that day. They soon realized that this challenge was too big for just their committee to handle, so they began recruiting others throughout the company to join the effort.

Leap ceremony: ▶
Pledge Commitment

Selling In the Vision

Knowing that the goal of achieving total sustainability—or zero impact on the environment—would be as daunting to all his employees as it was to the task force, Anderson searched for a simple way to describe the vision and make it still seem attainable. It was like climbing a mountain "taller than Everest," he thought. Anderson called it *"Mount Sustainability"* and visualized it using a hand-drawn triangle being climbed by a stick figure. The graphic was so basic that he could reproduce it anywhere—on a notepad in a one-on-one meeting, or as a slide in a formal presentation.

Dream symbol: Visual ▶

Having a symbol to summarize the vision was crucial because Anderson would have to explain it many, many times to get it to stick. During the next two years, he gave hundreds of speeches that won converts one by one.

"I was presenting my vision to our European contingency and many in the audience were skeptical," he said.

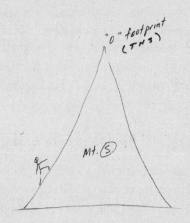

Ray Anderson drew his sustainability vision as a mountain, which became a symbol of Interface's venture.

"After the speech was over and the group dispersed, I found one of my European managers sitting alone in the auditorium with a copy of my transcript in his hand. He was clearly emotional. He looked up at me and said, 'I've heard this before but I just want you to know that I get it now.'"

◀ Leap story:
Seek the Reward

Not everyone joined as easily. Some didn't believe Interface had a sustainability problem in the first place or that it was their problem to solve, while others thought Anderson had just plain lost his marbles. In 1995, one investor who thought Anderson had *"gone round the bend"* dumped many shares of stock. Undaunted, Anderson used resistance as a learning opportunity. He read opposing viewpoints and engaged in conversation with his critics. He even empathized with detractors, saying, *"Honest people of good will and with good intentions can disagree. They can interpret the same data differently and even reach opposite conclusions."*

◀ Empathetic listening

While he understood these opposing viewpoints, Anderson never lost his clarity of purpose. He would boil the debate down to a moral dilemma in his conversations with doubters, saying, *"We are each and every one a part of the web of life. The continuum of humanity, sure, but in a larger sense the web of life itself. And we have a choice to make during our brief, brief visit to this beautiful blue and green living planet: to hurt it or to help it. It's your call."* With that question, he turned a theoretical debate into a practical, personal matter that put the responsibility squarely in the laps of the people he was trying to persuade.

◀ Leap speech:
Renunciation

Traction Builds Momentum

Anderson's persistence paid off. Over a three-year period, Interface implemented more than four hundred initiatives to reduce the company's environmental footprint. Many of the ideas they executed originally came from employees via a competition called QUEST, which incentivizes workers from accounting to the factory floor to the loading dock to submit conservation ideas.

◀ Empathetic listening

As each idea was implemented, Interface measured the resulting savings and reported back to the staff, keeping everyone motivated to continue climbing. Anderson recognized the best ideas with awards and published stories of employees' accomplishments in company newsletters.

By 1997, these combined improvements had saved the company $49.7 million. These savings freed up funds for Interface's next sustainability venture: transforming the way it designed, distributed, and decommissioned its products. This initiative would be an even more difficult undertaking that would affect every aspect of the way it did business and require its suppliers to change, too.

To start, Interface needed to involve each of its senior leaders in collectively imagining how to make the transformation happen. So that spring, Anderson planned a gathering for his leaders during a weeklong off-site at the Grand Wailea hotel, in Maui, Hawaii. This was a significant time at the company because the following year would mark Interface's twenty-fifth year in business. He wanted to commemorate the occasion by refocusing everyone's energy for the road ahead. Anderson hoped the meeting would unite people around a new dream that would propel them farther, faster, toward the summit of Mount Sustainability.

Sparking Bigger Thinking

To put everyone in the right frame of mind, Ray Anderson asked Paul Hawken, author of the book that had changed Anderson's life and business, to set the tone with an opening keynote, called "The Global Village." While planning the presentation, Hawken gathered data about the environment and how growth of the human population was impacting it. In looking at the data, he realized that the attendees were a perfect microcosm of the world's population at that time: Each of the eleven hundred people could in effect represent five million people on earth. He decided to use them as a living infographic, involving them in his presentation to show the impact each person could have.

When Interface's leaders entered the meeting room on the first day of the off-site, a Polaroid photo was taken of each person. Each also received a piece of paper with a set of numbers on it, but they weren't told what for just yet. Once everyone was

the global village

Ecologist and author Paul Hawken gives a speech to dramatize the negative impact that humans are having on the world.

seated, Paul Hawken began his presentation by discussing ecological concepts in general. Then he started to reveal the effects that humans were causing. *"Would all who have the number one please stand? You are the people of Earth. Please be seated."*

Hawken called another number and twenty-six people stood, representing 135 million babies who would be born that year. As he continued to call their numbers, Interface's leaders saw firsthand just how many people would soon be consuming food, water, and energy. They fell silent, heavy with the burden of responsibility: How could our earth possibly feed and care for so many people with such a finite amount of resources?

After Hawken's presentation, Anderson addressed the room. First, he celebrated how far the company had come since 1973, including giving awards to overall top performers in the company. He said, *"Today, twenty-four years later, we draw the curtain on the past. I'm proud, very proud of our successes. But our work together is not finished."*

◀ **Dream ceremony:**
Mourn Endings

◀ **Arrive ceremony:**
Honor Heroes

Then he segued into his vision for the next evolution of Interface:

> *"I personally am projecting ahead to another day . . . a day from which I will be looking back again at the company I will be leaving behind. The company I want to leave behind [is] the prototypical company of the twenty-first century, with its interconnected, hooked-up people, capital, processes, customers, suppliers, community, place, and product. And you will see that it will sell, that it will be a winning strategy for Interface and for all of our partners in the climb."*

Anderson closed by asking each leader in the room to do his or her part to bring that brighter reality to pass, using a touching image from his childhood coupled with a philosophical appeal:

> *"When I was a child, we learned a song in Sunday School. The words went like this: 'Brighten the corner where you are. Brighten the corner where you are. Someone far from harbor you may lead across the bar. Brighten the corner where you are.' . . . So brighten the corner where you are. What if you did it and you did it, and you did it? What if everybody did it?"*

Leaders Sign Up for a New Challenge

To signify their commitment to transform Interface into that prototypical company, leaders signed a "personal legacy wall." Next to the Polaroid photos taken of them that morning, they wrote statements pledging to make a difference. How would they

Interface leaders write promises to help the planet on a personal legacy wall.

(re)Dream speech: ▶ Vision

Dream symbol: ▶ Auditory

Dream story: ▶ Heed the Call

Climb ceremony: ▶ Renew Commitment

Tribal leaders from the island of Maui, Hawaii, express gratitude for Interface's generosity.

personally play a part in transforming their industry and the world? Their commitments were gathered and published in a newsletter to inspire everyone across the company to make their own pledges.

At the end of the event, everyone attended an emotional closing ceremony. Members of Maui's tribal communities had been invited to hear Interface leaders talk about the promises they had made to better the planet. During the off-site, Interface leaders had decided to create a charitable foundation, funded in part by employees, that would award grants for environmental projects on the island. To express their gratitude, tribal leaders and a choir of local children sang traditional Hawaiian songs while Interface's leaders looked on in tears. The musician John Denver capped the moment by performing an original song called "Blue Water World," which he composed just for that event. He sang, *"We are a promise for the future, and we cannot be denied. To somehow make a difference, to find a better way, we give ourselves completely to each bright and shining day."*

◀ Leap ceremony:
Pledge Commitment

◀ Leap symbol: Auditory

◀ Leap symbol: Auditory

Employees show their solidarity by forming the shape of the Interface logo while a helicopter catches the scene from above.

Leap symbol: Spatial ▶

In a final expression of their unity, attendees gathered on the lawn outside the hotel. As a helicopter hovered overhead snapping photos, they formed the shape of a giant circle bisected by a straight line—the Interface logo. It was a living symbol of their shared intention to make Interface a better company.

The Lasting Legacy of Leadership

The year 1997 was a major turning point for Interface. All of the leaders who attended the off-site returned to work as evangelists for the cause, more deeply invested in transforming their own processes and teaching their own teams how to become truly restorative by giving back more than they took. As a result, sustainable thinking became even more deeply embedded in the company's culture. The changes that Interface made also rippled throughout the carpet industry. After attending the company's 1997 off-site, executives from Aquafil, an Interface partner that supplies carpet fiber, were inspired to invent the world's first completely recycled nylon fiber—a feat no one had believed was possible.

Sadly, Anderson passed away in 2011, before all of the company's sustainability goals were realized. Three months after his death, Interface's leaders embarked on a global listening tour to understand how employees interpreted the vision and identify what might need to be done to rededicate everyone's energy to the cause in the wake of their founder's passing.

◄ Empathetic listening

What they uncovered astounded them: Employees around the globe had taken sustainability to heart in their homes as well as their jobs. They were volunteering to plant trees, clean up streams, and start recycling initiatives in their communities. Employees even found creative ways to reuse waste materials on their own, turning discarded shipping containers into BBQ pits and unusable carpet into dog beds. By envisioning and pursuing the dream of sustainability, Interface had not only transformed its organization but also transformed its employees' lives.

Current CEO Dan Hendrix summed it up in a speech to company leaders in 2014, twenty years after Anderson's environmental epiphany:

◄ Arrive speech: Victory

> *"Had we not begun that metaphorical climb up Mount Sustainability, we'd likely still be a brown company in a dirty industry, maybe making a green product here or there and never really rising above our competitors, who would likely be doing the same thing. . . . We would never attract the kind of talent we attract today who want to come to work for a company with a strong moral compass. . . . That transformation defined us in the marketplace, set us apart from our competition, insulated us from market swings, and created a space for us that very few companies enjoy."*

Interface Venture Scape Summary

Environmental concerns launched the carpet provider Interface on a multiyear venture to reimagine the way it designed, manufactured, and distributed its products. Inspired by the radical vision of founder Ray C. Anderson, employees, suppliers, and customers transformed the company and its industry and set a new standard for corporate responsibility.

01

In 1994 customers begin asking Interface to explain its environmental vision, but the company doesn't have one. A dejected Ray Anderson assembles a task force.

02

The task force gathers for an off-site to explore sustainability strategies in 1994; they ask Ray to kick off the meeting by declaring his vision. He doesn't have one. Then he reads *The Ecology of Commerce* and has an epiphany.

03

Ray Anderson kicks off the task force meeting by communicating his vision: to *"become the first industrial company in the world to achieve sustainability."*

04

The task force is stunned and overwhelmed by the ambitious goal and needs to regroup.

05

Anderson tells them, *"Any business can do it, and no one will have an excuse not to do it . . . Who should lead this effort if not us?"*

06

The task force jumps in and signs up for a specific goal: Interface will achieve sustainability by the year 2000—just six years from that date. Their goal is even more ambitious than Anderson imagined. They will need everyone in the company to help.

07

(1994–1995) Anderson gives talks to anyone who asks and creates a simple visual metaphor to explain his dream: Mount Sustainability.

DREAM

LEAP

08

Anderson encounters resistance from employees and even investors who doubt it can be done. In 1995, one investor who thinks Anderson has *"gone round the bend"* jumps ship and dumps shares of stock.

09

Anderson reads opposing views and meets with skeptics of all kinds to understand their arguments. But he stays focused on his vision and boils it down to a moral dilemma few can argue with: *"We have a choice to make during our brief, brief visit to this beautiful blue and green living planet: to hurt it or to help it. It's your call."*

10

(1995–1997) Interface implements more than four hundred initiatives toward sustainability, including the QUEST program, which incentivizes employees to come up with and implement ideas.

11

QUEST awards are given to employees with the best ideas, and their stories are shared in company newsletters.

12

(1997) Approaching twenty-five years in business and three years into its sustainability journey, Interface plans an off-site in Maui for its leaders.

13

Anderson gives a speech that acknowledges their accomplishments and then frames the goal: to become an exemplary company of the twenty-first century. At the end, employees gather on the lawn in the shape of the Interface logo to memorialize the moment.

14

The company has saved $49.7M through conservation efforts and must now use those funds for the next phase of its sustainability journey. A renaissance of innovation is spurred as the company designs and delivers recycled products in partnership with its suppliers and participates in restorative commerce programs with NGOs.

∞

FIGHT   CLIMB   ARRIVE   (re)DREAM

LEAP

—

Leap

Moment of Decision

*The second stage in the venture requires your travelers to commit
to change. You need them to agree to take on new responsibilities
or change behaviors so together you can see your dream through to
the end.*

You know you're in the Leap stage when it's time to take action. You've communicated
your dream and your travelers are starting to say, "I get it." You're poised to move
forward but now you need them to sign on in support and start taking action, even
if the path ahead is still a bit unclear.

As a torchbearer who's keeping an eye toward the future, you've become accustomed
to swimming in murky waters. Plunging into the unknown doesn't faze you because
historically you've successfully overcome all kinds of obstacles—scarce resources,
stubborn roadblocks, even your own insecurities—to bring your big ideas to reality.

Some of your fellow travelers are adventurous, too, and ready to dive right in without
trepidation. But others will hesitate just long enough to let doubt creep in. If you
don't encourage them, their apprehension will develop into varying degrees of fear—
from apathy to panic—that will leave them immobilized and unwilling to act.

So how can you get these hesitant travelers to cross over in this critical stage? Combat their fears head-on. Take stock of the risks honestly and then communicate your strategy for how you'll overcome those risks and difficulties. Doing so will build their confidence, start to establish that they can trust you, and chip away at their hesitation. To encourage your travelers to actually make the leap, remind them of the reward that awaits on the other side. Reiterate the benefits of committing to your vision and why their sacrifice will achieve the outcomes they desire.

The word *sacrifice* may conjure images of blood and fire, but its origin has more positive connotations: You trade one thing for another that's far more valuable to you. Your travelers do not have to sacrifice their lives, but you may be asking them to give a significant chunk of their time, attention, effort, comfort, or resources to commit to and help actualize your vision. If the reward isn't worth the struggle in their eyes, then they will resist leaping in to support you.

Understand What Your Travelers Are Feeling

In the Leap stage, you'll be able to tell if people are committed because action will start to happen, or at least action-oriented words will be used. You can boost the confidence of the bought-in travelers with motivating communication. In contrast, the resistant ones will not have moved from where they were before you declared your dream. Think back to the listening you did at the beginning of your venture to remind yourself of what they might fear and to help address it directly.

If They're **Committed,** You'll Hear Them Say . . .	Use **Motivating** Communication to Keep Them Going.
"It's not a sure thing, but I'll bet on it!" **"We need to move fast to be first."** **"Let's do this!"**	Appeal to travelers' sense of adventure by highlighting the opportunity to explore uncharted territory, discover new ideas, develop new skills, and make big bets for bigger payoffs. Show them that the reward outweighs the effort required or you'll struggle to be able to move them to contribute anything beyond the minimum.

If They're **Resistant,** You'll Hear Them Say . . .	Use **Warning** Communication to Get Them Unstuck.
"That's not my responsibility." **"Either way is fine; it doesn't matter to me."** **"I'll wait and see how things go."**	If you sense hesitation or see outright resistance, address it directly. This is no time for spin—be honest. Fight inertia by tackling the FUD (fear, uncertainty, and doubt) that easily saps your travelers' courage. But also appeal to their desire to survive by bluntly counting the real costs of staying put and portraying the consequences of staying the course.

Leap Communication Toolkit

Understanding what will hurl your travelers forward or hold them back will help you sway them to follow you into the future. Use speeches, stories, ceremonies, and symbols to craft a moment that will move them to leap from the banks of indecision into the fast-moving stream of action.

LEAP SPEECHES

Because speeches allow you to tackle resistance head-on, they're a critical communication tool in the Leap stage. You can unpack the reasons that it makes sense for your travelers to move forward right now and even mirror the conflicting voices in their heads with the structure and content of your talk. To motivate people to take action, highlight the rewards they'll gain with a Pursuit speech. Or use a Renunciation speech to warn them about the disadvantages of staying stuck in their current ways.

Motivate with "Pursuit" Speeches

Pursuit speeches move people to decide to leave what they know and embrace the new. They often explicitly state that a choice must be made to go one way or another. In 1962, President John F. Kennedy Jr. gave a speech that made the case for spending large amounts of money, time, and energy on manned spaceflight to the moon. He made clear the choice to pursue this ambitious and potentially dangerous voyage: *"We choose to go to the moon in this decade . . . because that goal will serve to organize and measure the best of our energies and skills, because that challenge is one that we are willing to accept, one we are unwilling to postpone, and one which we intend to win."*

Begin by reminding your travelers what's at stake—the dream you want them to desire. Then explain the action required and why your travelers should go after the prize wholeheartedly. By counting the costs of the current realities and showing how the reward will be worth it, you'll persuade people to take the next step.

///

When Steve Jobs announced in 2005 that the Macintosh would no longer be using the PowerPC processor and was shifting to the Intel x86 platform, some pro-Mac/anti-PC loyalists saw the move as a betrayal. At Apple's Worldwide Developers Conference (WWDC) that year, Jobs addressed developers' fears that the transition would be difficult but that it was a continuation of successful changes Apple had navigated in the past. Then he reiterated why developers should support the platform shift by promising that it would keep them on the forefront of the market.

What Is: *"The Mac in its history has had two major transitions so far. The first one, 68K to PowerPC, happened about ten years ago. The second major transition has been even bigger: the transition from OS 9 to OS X that we just finished a few years ago."*

What Could Be: *"We want to constantly be making the best computers for you and the rest of our users and so it's time for a third transition. We are going to begin the transition from the PowerPC to Intel processors. Now, why are we going to do this? Because we want to make the best computers for our customers looking forward."*

New Bliss: *"We're going to continue to be bold and begin the third transition today to make the best machines we know how to make in the future. We've already made a big investment in this and we're fairly far along. It's time for you to get ready, too. When we meet again here next year we will have Macs with Intel processors entering the market and we will be very excited to keep pushing the frontiers."*

Civil rights lawyer Gary Haugen was appointed as the lead investigator of the 1994 genocide in Rwanda. His experiences there led him to the discovery that everyday violence, coupled with a lack of law enforcement, was undermining the world's fight against global poverty. After Haugen founded the International Justice Mission he began speaking out to raise awareness about the issue. In his eighteen-minute TED talk, he crystallized his message into an impassioned plea for action.

What Is: *"In the developing world, basic law enforcement systems are so broken that recently the UN issued a report that found that 'most poor people live outside the protection of the law.' You can give all manner of goods and services to the poor, but if you don't restrain the hands of the violent bullies from taking it all away, you're going to be very disappointed in the long-term impact of your efforts."*

What Could Be: *"It doesn't have to be this way. Broken law enforcement can be fixed. Violence can be stopped. Almost all criminal justice systems can be transformed by fierce effort and commitment."*

Gary Haugen advocates for an end to the violence that plagues people living in poverty.

New Bliss: *"When our grandchildren ask us, 'Where were you when two billion of the world's poorest were drowning in a lawless chaos of everyday violence?' I hope we can say that we had compassion, that we raised our voice, and as a generation, we were moved to make the violence stop."*

Warn with "Renunciation" Speeches

Renunciation speeches ask your travelers to change mind-sets that hold them back and to embrace a new way of thinking or acting. The changes may not happen overnight, but you need your travelers to understand that clinging to past behaviors will prevent them from reaping the reward your dream promises to deliver.

In the Gospel of Matthew in the New Testament, Jesus delivered his Sermon on the Mount, entreating people to operate under the rules of God's eternal kingdom instead of acting according to the ways of the world, for which they would be rewarded with deep and lasting joy and peace. *"You have heard that it was said, 'Love your neighbor and hate your enemy.' But I tell you, love your enemies and pray for those who persecute you, that you may be children of your Father in heaven."* In a similar though perhaps less dramatic way, you have to show why everyone must let go of old ways and begin anew to create a better future.

///

Former vice president Al Gore faced a monumental task of convincing the world that climate change is a problem. Over the course of several years he perfected a persuasive presentation that outlined a highly analytical, data-driven argument that humans are causing harm to the environment. Gore also used a strong emotional appeal to solve the problem of climate change because our very lives are at stake.

> **What Is:** *"We have solved a global environmental crisis before: the hole in the stratospheric ozone layer. This was said to be an impossible problem to solve because it's a global environmental challenge requiring cooperation from every nation in the world. But we took it on, and the United States took the lead in phasing out the chemicals that caused that problem."*

> **What Could Be:** *"Now we have to use our political processes in our democracy and then decide to act together to solve those problems. But we have to have a different perspective on this one. It is different than any problem we have ever faced before."*

> **New Bliss:** *"It's our only home. And that is what is at stake: our ability to live on planet Earth, to have a future as a civilization. I believe this is a moral issue. It is your time to seize this issue. It is our time to rise again to secure our future."*

Mashery makes tools that help companies integrate their websites with mobile applications, which is increasingly important as usage of mobile devices grows exponentially. Yet many big businesses resisted the change because they had already invested millions of dollars building websites and other applications that were meant to be accessed via traditional technology such as PCs. Totally redesigning that infrastructure was just too costly and time consuming, so businesses instead created bare-bones mobile sites with little connectivity to core applications that customers want to use. When speaking to business leaders, Mashery CEO Oren Michels explained that websites not designed originally for mobile devices create a bad customer experience, and he challenged them to rethink their web strategies to integrate mobile applications.

> **What Is:** *"Most websites offer an entrance point into your business. But then they leave it up to the visitor to slog their way through in hopes of finding their destination. People don't want to visit your site, take a leisurely browse around the tabs, and hope to find what they need. That's a terrible experience."*

> **What Could Be:** *"Whether people are using an iPad, an Android smartphone, or any other device, [mobile] apps create a direct connection between people and where they want to go."*

> **New Bliss:** *"That brings an opportunity to [serve] a huge amount of customers and businesses. The businesses that succeed will be those who integrate [mobile apps] into their strategy."*

LEAP STORIES

While your speeches explain the argument in favor of leaping into the venture, stories will show your travelers what action looks like in real terms and remind them why it matters in the first place. Telling a story about someone who was faced with the choice to leap or not to leap is particularly effective. Whether your protagonist is their peer, a competitor, or even you, personalizing the moment of decision through stories adds emotional urgency that will motivate or warn travelers.

Motivate with "Seek the Reward" Stories

Seek the Reward stories are about a person who committed to take action, setting the wheels of change in motion. Tell your travelers about a sacrifice that someone, either you or someone else, had to make to gain something of value. When did she or you realize the scale of sacrifice required to make the dream a reality? What moved her to say yes and why? Show exactly what the outcome will look like so your audience will know when they've arrived, and illustrate how it will fulfill their wants and needs.

///

To get a large group of developers motivated to build applications for the latest Macintosh platform, Steve Jobs told them a story about one software developer who had already made the choice to transfer his code to the new platform:

> *"This is a developer I've known for a long time. I gave him a call and I said, 'We've got something really secret we're working on and I can't tell you what it is, but I want you to put all your source code on a hard disc and fly out here and let's see what we can do.' And it was nip and tuck. I think you're going to be very pleasantly surprised."*

By using a developer's story about the reasons he decided to develop applications for the new operating system, Jobs reinforced the idea that all developers could benefit from the change and should make the leap, too.

The founder of the Chinese e-commerce marketplace Alibaba, Jack Ma, is a big champion for small businesses because his platform was built for them. When he spoke at a convention for small and medium-sized enterprises in 2009, he inspired them with a story about how small, agile companies are the engines of economic growth.

> *"Every economy needs an incentive package to have more small and medium-sized companies so they have hope. Every big company comes from small businesses. Without incentives to have more babies [small businesses], we are going to die. In the twentieth century, bigger was better. But in the twenty-first century, I believe*

small is beautiful. It's not about how fast your machines are or how much equipment you have; it's about how quickly you can change yourself to meet the market. In this last financial crisis, we saw a lot of big companies die, ones we would never [have] thought would, like AIG . . . the big car companies. But [if you] look at all the small and medium enterprises, we still feel pain but we are happy in our heart because we are still surviving."

Warn with "Ignore the Reward" Stories

Ignore the Reward stories warn your travelers about the risks of remaining attached to old ways. When did you realize that outdated mind-sets were holding you back? What should you have let go of and why? Emphasize what is at risk, raising the stakes by clarifying the high cost of doing nothing. Create a vivid impression of what will be lost and who will feel it most acutely.

///

Forty years before he became a famous spokesperson for the environmental movement, Al Gore was just a freshman student at Harvard University. One day, he heard a lecture by a visiting scientist named Roger Revelle, who pioneered the study of carbon dioxide levels.

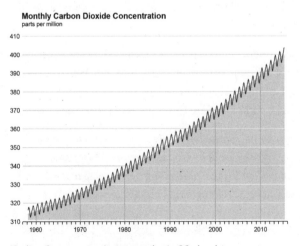

Monthly Carbon Dioxide Concentration
parts per million

Keeling Curve measuring atmospheric CO$_2$ levels

"He showed our class the result of these measurements after only a few years. It was startling to me. . . . He drew the connections between the larger changes in our civilization and this pattern that was now visible in the atmosphere of the entire planet. He

projected into the future where this was headed unless we made some adjustments, and it was as clear as day. . . . He started measuring carbon dioxide in 1958. By the middle sixties when he showed my class this image, it was already clear that it was going up. I respected him and learned from him so much I followed this. When I went to the Congress in the middle 1970s I helped organize the first hearings on global warming."

When he saw Revelle's chart that showed carbon dioxide rising to dangerously high levels, Gore was shocked to realize how bad the world's environmental problems were and made it his mission to shake others out of their complacency.

When articulating his vision for how applications should work in a mobile world, Oren Michels used the analogy of a rapid transit system to illustrate the ideal way to build application infrastructure.

Slide shown by Oren Michels, CEO of Mashery

"When subways are integrated into a city and the lives of its residents, they can make it easy to get just about anywhere. The Bay Area Rapid Transit system, known as BART, was designed to bring people into the city . . . but there aren't many stops in San Francisco [so it] can't fulfill its basic missions: getting people where they want to go. This is exactly how most businesses treat their online customers. Whenever I travel to a city with a great subway system—New York, London, D.C.—I wonder what the BART planners would do differently if they had a chance to develop their strategy today. Businesses actually have this chance—and too many of them are putting their heads in the sand and not doing anything about it. This is where things are headed. So all I can ask is: what are they waiting for?"

LEAP CEREMONIES

Committing to leap is both an intellectual and a physical decision. Not only must your travelers agree in principle, but they must match that agreement with their actions. Ceremonies that encourage them to perform an action in support of the dream and be celebrated for their commitment offer positive reinforcement for saying yes. Despite being stirred by your words, some travelers may still freeze up in their moment of decision, and perhaps for good reason. Some idea or obstacle may be blocking their path and they need your help to ceremonially remove it before they can move forward.

Motivate with "Pledge Commitment" Ceremonies

A commitment ceremony publicly declares that your travelers have jumped in and are officially signed up for the trek. They've agreed that the benefit of moving forward outweighs the cost of staying put. Commitment may be as simple as raising their hands or it may be more formal, such as signing a contract or declaring their promise to act publicly, before their peers.

One of the most important moments in Silicon Valley history happened when eight employees and two bankers decided to start Fairchild Semiconductor, which became the first successful semiconductor company. To solidify the decision, one of the bankers pulled out ten newly minted one-dollar bills and laid them carefully on

Replica of a dollar bill signed by the Fairchild Semiconductor founders

the table. *"Each of us should sign every bill,"* he said. These dollar bills, covered with signatures, were their contracts with each other. The men who signed the bills are now remembered as the founders of Silicon Valley.

When Southwest Airlines acquired Morris Air, the company leaders decided to host a mock wedding ceremony. An Elvis impersonator performed the ceremony at Graceland Wedding Chapel, in Las Vegas. Corporate mascots dressed as airplanes played the part of the wedding couple, with flight attendants from both companies serving as the wedding party. Southwest and Morris employees showered the couple with bags of peanuts. A Southwest spokeswoman told the press that it was a *"consummation . . . in an unusual way that only Morris and Southwest could achieve."* The ceremony was captured on video and shown to employees to ease the transition into one larger company.

Warn with "Dismantle Blockages" Ceremonies

In a dismantling ceremony, you symbolically remove limits or destroy barriers that block the path of your travelers and are causing them to feel hopeless or fearful. Dismantling can also help people break their attachments to an unhealthy past—whether outdated systems that have been a source of frustration or objects of affection that will no longer be relevant in the future.

Tearing down blockages, or helping your travelers tear them down, shows that you're serious about supporting them. It also shows that you've taken time to understand their sacrifice and experience how tough this transition may be for them. If the obstacle is large, a dramatic act may be required. But sometimes something as simple as granting your travelers authority for the task at hand will embolden them to jump in.

OEMS: ALL OUR PATENT ARE BELONG TO YOU

Tesla's Patent Wall, before and after it was dismantled

Elon Musk founded Tesla Motors with the goal to convert the fossil fuel–dependent auto industry to electric cars. In its first few years of operation, Tesla filed 250 patents related to its electric car technology, which were all displayed on a massive wall at the company's headquarters. Once Musk realized that other manufacturers were using the patents as an excuse to avoid committing to electric cars, he released all his patents for any carmaker to use, making it easier for them to incorporate Tesla technologies into their cars and spur wider adoption of electric vehicles. As a ceremonial gesture, Tesla dismantled the wall of patents and replaced them with a large poster of a tyrant from the Japanese video game *Zero Wing* as a reminder that Tesla doesn't want to control the market.

When Meg Whitman arrived at HP, a chasm separated management and employees, largely due to the behavior of the two short-tenured CEOs who preceded her. This divide was strikingly symbolized by a large fence, outfitted in barbed wire, surrounding the executive parking lot. One of the first things Whitman did was to remove the fence. She also moved all of the executives out of walled offices and into cubicles. The executives also now enter the same door as the rest of the employees, instead of one marked "executives only." Whitman said later, *"This was symbolic of the kind of culture that we wanted to build."*

LEAP SYMBOLS

A Leap symbol's meaning comes from the moment when you knew things had to be different and you decided that your contribution would make a difference. Maybe you were awakened to a problem and decided to change it or you removed obstacles to help people move forward. Just as exchanging a wedding ring symbolizes commitment, Leap artifacts commemorate the act of deciding to jump in—or the consequences of not taking action.

Motivating Symbols

- **Visual:** As a rite of passage initiation for new employees, Google gives them a rainbow propeller hat with the word *Noogler* embroidered on it, short for "New Google." They wear the hat to the company TGIF meeting so people can identify new employees.

- **Auditory:** In President John F. Kennedy's inauguration speech, the words *"Ask not what your country can do for you, ask what you can do for your country"* were a call to American citizens to do what is right for the greater good.

- **Spatial:** Dr. Martin Luther King Jr. delivered his "I have a dream" speech from the feet of Abraham Lincoln at the Lincoln Memorial in Washington, D.C., a historic location that underscored the former president's pledge to provide freedom for all Americans. One attendee said, *"You could feel the sense of collective will and effort in the air."*

- **Physical:** Southwest Airlines marked the acquisition of AirTran by piling executives into an Atlanta-bound AirTran plane emblazoned with "Southwest ♥ AirTran." As the plane approached the hangar, a water-cannon salute sprayed the planes, more than a

Southwest and AirTran planes "kiss" to symbolize the companies' merger.

thousand guests cheered, a local high school band played, and confetti dropped on guests as executives signed the agreement. Guests took photos in front of two planes that were parked nose-to-nose to symbolize a kiss.

Warning Symbols

- **Visual:** The carbon-levels slide Al Gore saw in college shook him to the core, and changing the direction of the chart became his life's work to prevent a terrible fate for the planet.

- **Auditory:** Members of the UK House of Commons often show disdain for ideas they disagree with by clapping, shouting, and creating distracting noises. Prime Minister David Cameron has enlisted supporters to shout words such as *weak* and *nightmare* when his opponents present their proposals to the Commons.

- **Spatial:** The large poster Tesla put on the wall to replace their patents was lifted from pop culture's first digital meme. In *Zero Wing*, the evil CATS character tries to gain complete control of all military bases. The poster serves as a reminder that Tesla had to give up control for electric cars to be adopted.

- **Physical:** A decade after Coke discontinued Surge soda, loyal fans created T-shirts that read "The Surge Movement" and organized "Surge-in days," asking fans to call Coke's hotline en masse to petition for the soda's return.

SUMMARY

This moment of decision is a critical time in your journey because you're asking travelers to take a leap of faith. To them, your dream is still ethereal—an early-stage promise that's tantalizing yet delicate, so fresh and untested that it could evaporate into thin air at any minute. But in this moment, your travelers have already begun to will the dream into existence simply by believing in themselves and in you. Their choice to move forward gave your fragile dream a scaffolding of steel that will serve it well in the next stage. And by committing yourself to helping them succeed, you have cemented their desire to journey forward with you.

Rackspace's Graham Weston
creates a vibrant, innovative
environment for employees.

—

Rackspace

Even the most well-meaning dreams can meet a wall of resistance that sets you back weeks or months. Getting everyone to move forward might even require rethinking your vision, again and again.

Rackspace Finds a New Place to Innovate

San Antonio, the second-largest city in Texas, is better known for its tourist attractions than for its digital technology. Yet on its northeast side, just off I-35, a global leader in cloud computing is rising. It's called Rackspace, and from its headquarters in south Texas—and its data centers on four continents—the company generates $1.8 billion in annual revenue. Since the early years after its founding in 1998, Rackspace has grown rapidly by nurturing an innovative culture dedicated to providing what it calls "fanatical support"—with expert cloud engineers available 24-7 to service its three hundred thousand business customers. It regularly wins coveted Stevie trophies and other awards for customer care. Rackspace extends similar nurturing to its six thousand employees, which led *Fortune* magazine to rank it as one of the top one hundred places to work in the U.S., for six of the past eight years.

One look at Rackspace's global headquarters shows that this is no ordinary company. Escalators instead of elevators carry workers between floors, plus a two-story slide serves as an express lane to the in-house coffee shop for the impatient and the merely playful. Sunny atriums filled with nooks, tables, and even ski-slope-style gondolas (salvaged from a local park) invite employees to sit and share ideas, while neon signs point the way to the food court. It feels less like a corporate headquarters than like a shopping mall . . . probably because that's what it used to be.

Back in 2007, Rackspace was located in a typical office building, but not for long. Demand for cloud services was booming and the company went on a hiring spree, adding as many as eight hundred employees per year. Soon the building it occupied became too small, prompting the search for a new place that Rackers (as employees are known) could call home.

Interior of the former Windsor Park Mall before it was renovated by Rackspace

Envisioning a Better Home

The cofounder and chairman of Rackspace, Graham Weston, looked at properties all over San Antonio. He wanted to keep the company in his beloved hometown, if at all possible. And he wanted to put all of the headquarters workers in a single building to avoid the silo effect he had observed at companies that spread workers across a campus where each department had its own building. A notorious penny pincher, Weston preferred to rehabilitate an existing building rather than construct one from scratch. But he found few affordable spaces large enough to support his ever-expanding business. Then he thought of the perfect place—the Windsor Park Mall.

◀ Dream story:
Heed the Call

The sprawling Windsor Park shopping center was so large, with more than 1.2 million square feet under one roof, that Rackers referred to it as "the Castle"—a joking reference to the British royal family's palatial residence just west of London. The mall had opened more than thirty years before, when large indoor malls were in vogue, but now it sat nearly empty, a victim of economic decline in the surrounding community. Weston calculated that the cost of buying and renovating the

Interior of the former Windsor Park Mall after it was renovated by Rackspace

downtrodden mall would be far less than building a brand-new structure, and it would offer Rackspace an opportunity to rejuvenate a part of San Antonio that was down on its luck.

Weston had deep ties to San Antonio. He was born there and had seen the city expand in the 1960s and 1970s. He then watched as other places—Houston, Dallas, and especially Austin—marched far ahead to become centers of industry and technology. Those cities, along with progressively minded metropolises across the nation, chose to invest in redevelopment projects, transportation infrastructure, and appealing housing to lure businesses and the young professionals who worked for them. Renovating the mall was central to Weston's dream of revitalizing San Antonio and competing with Austin as a mecca for innovative, creative technologists whom companies like his needed to attract and retain.

When Weston imagined the mall as Rackspace's new home, he thought, *"This is going to be awesome!"* But, he recalled, *"Everybody else pretty much thought I was crazy."* Confident that the mall could be turned into a glorious home for Rackers, Weston had to communicate his vision for the new campus in a way that would inspire his people to feel pride and excitement about moving there. He hired a renowned architect to render potential designs for the building and help Rackers visualize the future of the place.

Dream symbol: Visual ▶

Architectural sketches of the future home of "Rackers"

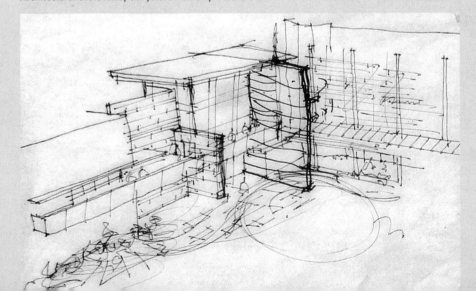

Resistance to the Vision

To build support for the project, Weston hired a consultant to work with employees, Rackspace board members, and the city councils of San Antonio and Windcrest (a community adjacent to the mall, which would annex the land as part of a complex redevelopment incentive package). Weston and the consultant mapped out the different audiences they would have to win over and how they would do so. They quickly realized that they would need to present multiple options for Rackspace's new headquarters, including the option of moving out of San Antonio altogether. They held focus groups to expose Rackers to the pros and cons of various headquarters locations and to hear their feedback. In the first focus group, the consultant presented the alternatives one by one, and things progressed smoothly. But when he got to Weston's favorite option, moving into the Castle, employees erupted into angry protest, shouting and booing him off the stage, saying, *"We can't move there—we'll be attacked!"*

◀ Empathetic listening

◀ Fight ceremony: Rally Spirits
◀ Leap symbol: Auditory

For Rackers, as for many in San Antonio, the mall had become synonymous with decay and danger. A few years earlier, during the Christmas shopping rush, a teenager had been shot and killed inside the mall. It fell into ruin as the story of that crime and others nearby circulated as evidence that the area wasn't safe. The dilapidated mall still held meaning for many longtime San Antonians, including Weston, who long ago rented his high school prom tuxedo there, and later purchased an oven there with his wife for their first home. Many other Rackers had grown up in San Antonio, too, but their reaction was far less positive. An influential member of the executive team who had grown up in the neighborhood near the mall and attended the high school right next door told Weston, *"I never want to go back."*

◀ Leap story:
Ignore the Reward

Weston would remember that comment a few years later, during an episode that helped fuel his quest to help redevelop San Antonio. Rackspace was hiring for a key executive position, and had found a highly qualified candidate who Weston felt would be a great fit. Over several conversations Weston wooed and courted the exec, but at the last moment the candidate said, *"You couldn't pay me enough to want to live in San Antonio."* The candidate joined Rackspace, but in its Austin office. By that

◀ Leap story:
Ignore the Reward

time, Rackspace had lured hundreds of highly sought senior managers and technologists from San Francisco, New York City, and other major cities around the world. It usually had the best luck hiring married candidates with children, who found San Antonio a great place to raise a family. What was more difficult was hiring young, single engineers who wanted attractive options for living in an urban core, with vibrant nightlife and public transit options. This challenge launched Weston on a quest to figure out how he and other civic and business leaders could turn the city into a place where smart, creative, accomplished young professionals wanted to live.

Reimagining the End State

Now wrestling with his vision for Rackspace's new headquarters, Weston regrouped with the architect to consider how best to deal with employees' concerns. They could build a commercial cluster surrounding the mall that would put restaurants, dry cleaners, and other service businesses just steps away from Rackers, essentially insulating them from the perceived dangers of the neighborhood. *"The architect told me we should put a wall around the building,"* Weston said. *"I asked him what it would cost and he said, 'Seven million dollars.' I said, 'Well, what if we invested that money in the community instead?'"* This was an expensive proposition, especially when the economy was starting to nosedive in late 2007 and early 2008. Yet Weston saw investing in the community as an opportunity to demonstrate the kind of change that he wanted to see in San Antonio and show the community that technology companies could use their prosperity to create a better home for everyone. He also had a hunch that the mission of transforming the community could inspire Rackers, who are exceptionally active in community groups and volunteer work.

Soon a *new dream was born*: the Rackspace Foundation, funded by contributions from both the company and its employees. *"It made Rackers the heroes,"* said Weston. *"I told them, 'Who other than you would believe that this part of town deserved something better and decide to invest in its future?'"* Today the foundation donates much of the money it takes in, up to $1 million a year, to improve neighborhoods around the mall. Grants are given to seven nearby schools and to community programs that uplift youth and transform their lives through robotics and chess classes and other

Fight symbol: Spatial ▶

(re)Dream ▶

Leap speech: Pursuit ▶

Leap ceremony: ▶
Pledge Commitment

educational activities. Funds were also funneled into the building of parks and recreation facilities where residents could relax and play.

Meanwhile, work on the new Rackspace headquarters had begun. A colony of bats had to be shooed out of one part of the mall. In another section, where police departments had conducted training, blank shell casings had to be swept up. The consultant and architect began taking small groups of employees on tours of the mall to demystify the threats they imagined and help them see how the space would be transformed when Rackspace was in it.

◄ Dream ceremony:
Immerse Deeply

As parts of the building were finished in 2008, the moment of arrival came when small groups of employees moved in. Rather than working in a dangerous and decrepit environment, they found a joyful, inspiring space that was far better than they had ever imagined. The space even honored the mall's prior days with positive symbols from its past. Meeting rooms were named after businesses that once operated there, from Gingiss to LensCrafters and RadioShack. The work of local artists is featured on the walls, and even includes a freshly painted graffiti mural along one wall that echoes the spray-painted messages and tags that had previously covered the empty mall's exterior.

◄ Arrive symbol: Spatial

The Dream Comes True

As the company has grown, doubling its workforce roughly every five years, newly refurbished phases of the mall have opened to Rackers, and each phase has been greeted with delight. The latest phase includes meeting rooms named after classic toys such as Hula Hoop, G.I. Joe, Easy Bake Oven, and Rubik's Cube. As each new area debuts, Rackers celebrate with balloons, breakfast tacos, and brief talks by company leaders. A steady stream of local and national dignitaries, school groups, and customers flows through for tours of the Castle. It has become a potent tool for recruiting employees and customers alike. The Rackspace sales team reports that when prospective customers visit the Castle, their close rate is north of 98 percent.

◄ Arrive ceremony:
Honor Heroes

◄ Arrive story:
Savor the Win

A financial analyst who closely follows the company and regularly visits the Castle, along with the headquarters of Rackspace's rivals, recently observed that many of those other companies are *"full of unhappy people."* But anyone who visits Rackspace headquarters, he said, can see that the engineers and other employees *"really enjoy helping customers"* and *"love their workplace."* At a basic level, he added, *"customers want to do business with people who are happy."*

This dilapidated Mervyn's store once anchored the Windsor Park Mall.

Once a symbol of decay, the former Windsor Park Mall is now hailed as one of the best corporate structures in the nation, and one of the most successful urban infill projects. It has been honored with awards and even a difficult-to-attain LEED certification for environmentally sound design and use of recycled building materials. What could have been a liability was transformed into an asset that helps Rackspace win customers and employees through its audaciously hopeful image. Said Weston, *"It formed the story of our culture and it shows others who we are and what we aspire to be."*

The former Mervyn's store was remade into the new Rackspace headquarters.

Rackspace Venture Scape Summary

After a period of rapid expansion, Rackspace outgrew its San Antonio headquarters. Cofounder and chairman Graham Weston had the idea to transform a defunct mall into the company's new home, but employees resisted jumping in. By listening to the concerns of Rackers, Weston engaged employees in the venture and reimagined the company's role in the community.

01

In 2007, Rackspace grows so rapidly that it runs out of space in its corporate headquarters in San Antonio. CEO Graham Weston begins the search for a new home for Rackers and realizes that the old "Windsor Castle" mall is the perfect spot.

02

Weston hires an architect to visualize his dream of converting the mall into a glorious new HQ building for Rackspace.

03

Weston also hires a communication consultant to present his concepts for the building to employees, board members, and community leaders.

04

Together, Weston and the consultant map out the audiences they need to convert and begin scheduling focus groups with employees.

05

When the consultant presents the option to move into the mall, employees erupt in anger because the building has become a symbol of danger and decay. They say, *"We can't move there—we'll be attacked!"*

DREAM   LEAP

06

Employees protest the idea of moving into the mall.

07

Stories have been told about murders that happened in the mall, which to employees is a warning to stay away from that area. Another employee grew up nearby and remembers stories from his childhood, saying, *"I never want to go back."*

08

The consultant and architect take employees on a tour of the site to overcome their fears about what it would be like to work there.

09

Weston and the architect regroup to figure out how to overcome employees' resistance. The architect suggests building a wall around the mall for $6 to $7 million, but Weston counters that they should invest that money in the community instead by creating the Rackspace Foundation.

10

Weston motivates employees to support the move by saying, *"Who other than you would believe that this part of town deserved something better and decide to invest in its future?"*

11

Work on the mall remodel begins.

12

As employees begin to move in, group by group, they tell others who haven't yet moved in how cool it is.

13

Now complete, the new Rackspace HQ incorporates symbols from the mall's past, including a graffiti mural recalling the tagging that previously covered the exterior of the abandoned mall.

14

Once a symbol of decay, the former Windsor Castle is now hailed as one of the best corporate environments in the nation.

∞

FIGHT   CLIMB   ARRIVE   (RE)DREAM

FIGHT

Fight

Moment of Bravery

When a big fight looms, your travelers need to be emboldened by their strength in numbers. In this third stage, you must summon people's courage by portraying the enemy as beatable and build travelers up for the fight ahead.

At this point many travelers have jumped into the fray, but it might not be smooth sailing yet. As your vision begins to gain traction, it will incite those who love the status quo to rise up and rage against your dream. Your opposition could be deriving from external alternatives to your idea, internal political battles, or resistance from an impassioned individual who feels that his or her future is at risk. In more dire situations, your opponents may be nefarious outside forces, such as competitors trying to steal market share, activist investors threatening a hostile takeover, or nation-states challenging the very ideals you fight to uphold.

To dampen the damage your opponents create, you'll need to help your travelers see the ways that the enemy is threatening their happiness. Stir your travelers' competitive spirit by exposing the enemy's transgressions and unite them around a common goal of protecting the dream they all wish to see fulfilled. You may need them to fight *against* an enemy, such as a competitive foe or bureaucracy that's run amok. Or you may need them to fight *for* something, such as a big hairy goal.

Either way, fire travelers up by stressing what's at risk and appealing to their sense of justice. Harness their love of a challenge and then reveal your plan for winning the battle, perhaps even reminding them of times when they have overcome seemingly unbeatable odds in the past. After a huge push to hit a major milestone or fight a difficult battle, stop to make some noise about the wins they've achieved. Celebrate successful skirmishes to keep spirits buoyed and then paint the path toward the future.

Understand What Your Travelers Are Feeling

In the Fight stage, some of your travelers will gladly take up arms either because they're competitive in nature or because they've seen the damage your opponents have done and just can't let it slide. Nudge those gung-ho gladiators into battle with motivating communication. Still other travelers will hold back, perhaps because they doubt they have the iron will to win or because they don't think your dream is worth fighting for in the first place. With them, warning communication will point out the pitfalls of standing down.

If They're **Committed,** You'll Hear Them Say . . .	Use **Motivating** Communication to Keep Them Going.
"We need to right this wrong."	Define the traits and transgressions of your adversaries, drawing a stark contrast between them and you. Who exactly are your adversaries and what vulnerabilities can you exploit? Detail a plan of attack. What talents, assets, experiences, or resources will give your troops an edge? Have you vanquished a similar foe in the past? Visualize what victory will look like. Portray your travelers triumphing to focus your allies on the success of the mission and bolster their courage.
"We can't let them win."	
"We're better than that."	

If They're **Resistant,** You'll Hear Them Say . . .	Use **Warning** Communication to Get Them Unstuck.
"They're messing things up."	Generally, some of the fear people feel is valid and some is overblown. No matter what you've asked travelers to face, they'll feel it's tougher for them to master than it is for you because you're not in the trenches. Whatever the obstacle, you must paint a clear picture of the enemy and your plan of attack, or you don't stand a chance of succeeding. Warn about the risk of succumbing to the opposition, using the threat of failure to keep egos in check.
"Let's just stop this in its tracks."	
"Hell no, we won't go."	

Fight Communication Toolkit

In this stage, you've got to remind your travelers what they're fighting for and why they've got what it takes to win. Through speeches, stories, ceremonies, and symbols you can build their resolve to stand up for the ideals that your dream represents and give them the strength to stay true to it themselves.

FIGHT SPEECHES

The boundaries of conflict are often drawn with words. When people make verbal declarations of their values, they're effectively defining the boundaries of the territory they feel compelled to defend. Fight speeches motivate your travelers to protect your dream, while warning speeches remind them to keep battling despite impossible odds.

Motivate with "Battle" Speeches

In *Braveheart*, a movie about the Scottish wars for independence, William Wallace gives a speech in the moments before battle to motivate his fellow Scots, saying, *"Fight and you may die. Run and you'll live—at least a while. And dying in your beds many years from now, would you be willing to trade all the days from this day to that for one chance, just one chance to come back here and tell our enemies that they may take our lives, but they'll never take our freedom!"*

Rousing speeches have long been used to ignite the fighting spirit. You, too, can stir people's courage by describing the damage the enemy has done and warning of potential continued harm. Expose the opponent's weaknesses and articulate how to win.

///

In 1999, Alibaba was founded in Jack Ma's apartment in Hangzhou, China, where he pulled together a group of seventeen friends and students to leverage the Internet to build a global marketplace. He described to them how their inventive technology and tireless work ethic would help them win against larger, more well-established companies in Silicon Valley.

What Is: *"Since we were working on China Pages, I've always said our competitors are not domestic websites, but overseas websites. Our competitors are not in China, but in America's Silicon Valley."*

What Could Be: *"We need to learn the hardworking spirit of Silicon Valley. If we go to work at eight a.m. and go home at five p.m., this is not a high-tech company and Alibaba will never be successful."*

New Bliss: *"If we are a good team and know what we want to do, one of us can defeat ten of them. We can beat government agencies and big famous companies because of our innovative spirit."*

Ma's prophetic words came true within a decade when Silicon Valley–based eBay shut down its Chinese operation because Alibaba's success was unstoppable.

In 2013, Google launched a technology-enabled hotline to fight a shadowy enemy— criminals involved in human trafficking. During the launch, the director of Google Giving, Jacquelline Fuller, described the state of the problem and Google's solution by comparing traffickers to deadly viruses.

Jacquelline Fuller, director of Google Giving, funds technology to stop human trafficking.

What Is: *"[Human] traffickers are very savvy about how they're using communications and how they're moving porously across borders."*

What Could Be: *"In the same way people fight the HIV epidemic, we had to figure out how to identify who's vulnerable, analyze the pathways of transmission, and figure out how the bad guys are mutating so we can get one step ahead of them."*

New Bliss: *"Our global impact partnerships will help us move beyond identifying who's vulnerable and beyond rescue into prevention."*

By donating money and technology to nonprofits, Google established itself as an ally in the fight to stop human trafficking.

Warn with "Underdog" Speeches

The British Armed Forces were in trouble in their fight against Hitler when on June 4, 1940, Winston Churchill appealed to his allies to summon the will to overcome their enemy: *"We shall fight on the beaches, we shall fight on the landing grounds, we shall fight in the fields and in the streets. . . . We shall prove ourselves once again able to defend our Island home, to ride out the storm of war, and to outlive the menace of tyranny."* The speech deepened British citizens' resolve for the war effort and Churchill's persuasive skill ultimately helped coax America to join the commonwealth as an ally.

These David-versus-Goliath moments are when you're up against a wall and the outlook isn't good. It's time to admit to your troops that you're losing the battle and may suffer defeat, but you should still paint a picture of what victory could look like if travelers don't give up. Acknowledge their suffering first and then ask them to muster every ounce of strength to pull from behind to win.

When addressing investors in 2013, Elon Musk, of Tesla Motors, explained that auto dealers were lobbying against his direct-sales model despite the fact that consumers clearly said they wanted it, jeopardizing Tesla's potential success. So in order to sell direct to consumers, Musk put pressure on the federal government by posting a petition on the White House website, getting more than 130,000 signatures from consumers.

What Is: *"Auto dealers keep saying we should grant them a franchise. But if you look at the opinion polls as to whether people want direct sales, the answer is overwhelmingly yes."*

What Could Be: *"If democracy was working properly and the legislators were implementing the will of the people something else would be happening and there would not be legislation trying to artificially restrict direct sales."*

New Bliss: *"I think customers are going to lead a revolt on this front. Because if I was in the customer's position I would not be happy about [dealers] spending money to pervert democracy."* At the time of this writing, Tesla has won the right to sell direct to consumers in twenty-one states but is battling staunch resistance from dealers elsewhere—a fight Musk clearly relishes.

One year after Lou Gerstner Jr. stepped in to turn IBM around he gathered the company's top leaders, 420 of them, from around the world for a management off-site. Organizational politics were so bad that his managers were focused more on fighting internal battles than combating threats from outside. To jolt them out of their complacency, Gerstner began by showing two charts: one that tallied the market share IBM had lost to competitors and another that listed IBM at the bottom of industry-wide customer satisfaction rankings. He riled them up by reading quotes from CEOs of competing companies, such as Microsoft's Bill Gates and Oracle's Larry Ellison, who mocked IBM. Then he called the managers to rise up against their enemies and commit to winning again.

What Is: *"We're getting our butts kicked in the marketplace. People are taking our business away. . . . What do you think happened to all those points of market share? These guys ripped them away from us and . . . I don't like it."*

What Could Be: *"We've got to generate some collective anger here about what our competitors say about us, about what they're doing to us in the marketplace. . . . We've got to get out and start winning in the marketplace."*

New Bliss: *"This is going to be a group of change agents—people who are imbued with the feeling of empowerment and opportunity and all our colleagues. Those of you who are uncomfortable with it, you should think about doing something else. Those of you who are excited about it, I welcome you to the team, because I sure can't do it alone."*

FIGHT STORIES

Stories add urgency to speeches in the Fight stage by highlighting what's at risk and how your opponents are making inroads against your dream. Show the enemy's transgressions with tangible anecdotes about the damage they're doing. Motivating stories give travelers who need it an extra push to rise up against your foe, while warning stories keep them from getting complacent in the face of conflict.

Motivate with "Overcome the Enemy" Stories

Overcome the Enemy stories are all about triumphing against the odds. In storytelling, this is the moment when the hero faces a great foe and still comes out on top. For instance, in Peter Jackson's *The Lord of the Rings*, Aragorn's ragtag army of an elf, a dwarf, a wizard, and six thousand men arrives at the Black Gate only to find massive armies of fearsome monsters defending Mordor. They are horribly outnumbered, yet hold their own. When have you or others overcome seemingly insurmountable obstacles? What helped you and them win?

Qualcomm manufactures computer chips for mobile devices, and through the tenacity of its founder and CEO, the company helped forge the digital world we know now. Back in the late 1980s, CEO Irwin Jacobs saw his industry begin to adopt a cell phone technology that he felt was headed in the wrong direction. Telecom carriers, device manufacturers, and analysts all thought the analog standard was the future of telecom but Jacobs knew better. Despite strong resistance, he fought to convince the industry that digital technology, based on Qualcomm's chips, was the way to go. Yet his technology was particularly challenging to show. Jacobs tasked his engineers with getting a working prototype ready and scheduled a demo in November 1989, inviting three hundred industry executives to the event. The day of the demo, Qualcomm engineers set up equipment for transmitting satellite signals to cell phone towers, which would relay calls to a phone in a van—revolutionary at the time. The plan was for Jacobs to explain how the technology worked and take

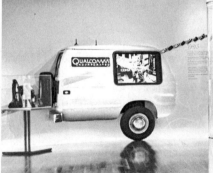

A section of the original van used in Qualcomm's demo now lives in the company's museum.

audience members for rides in the van as calls were made and received. But partway through his talk, Jacobs saw one of his engineers frantically gesturing for him to keep talking because the demo wasn't working. Jacobs spoke for forty-five extra minutes until he got the sign that he could release the crowd. Groups took trips in the van while calls were made, and the demo was considered a huge success. Jacobs later recalled, *"If that demo had failed, we probably would have been dead."* Instead, the technology he demonstrated became the industry standard that runs the cell phones we all use. The van, which is now displayed in the company's museum, became a symbol of the innovative drive and tenacity that are central to the Qualcomm culture.

When Nawaf Bitar of Juniper Networks was trying to convince his colleagues in the security industry to find new ways to fight hackers and cyberterrorists, he told the story of an injustice that taught a writer how to fight oppression:

> *"Had Henry David Thoreau been alive today, he may well have been a hacker, channeling his bold ideas to the keyboard instead of the pen. Thoreau had refused to pay his taxes in opposition to slavery. One day he ran into the tax man and he was promptly thrown in jail. He would have stayed there had his aunt not paid his taxes on his behalf and against his wishes. The taxation incident had a profound effect on him. He wrote the essay 'Resistance to Civil Government.' It was this essay that sparked the nonviolent protest movement inspiring the likes of Dr. King and Gandhi."*

Warn with "Come from Behind" Stories

Victory isn't guaranteed for your venture; sometimes the opposition is so fierce that you experience significant setbacks. In your toughest moment, when the outcome of your venture is in jeopardy, everyone's on the edge of their seats—will the hero make it or not? But like the boxer Rocky Balboa, who was knocked down for the count by his opponent Apollo Creed, you somehow struggle up from the mat to fight one more round . . . and win.

Now is the time when your travelers need to hear a story that makes them believe they have what it takes to come back. When did you or someone else fail at first but then rally to fight on? What blows did you suffer and how did you find the will to recover and win the battle?

///.

To help leaders understand how social media can—and must—be harnessed for good, Stanford's General Atlantic Professor of Marketing, Jennifer Aaker, told the story of two Indian entrepreneurs who were both diagnosed with leukemia at close to the same time.

Jennifer Aaker tells a story about cancer victims.

"For many patients, the only cure is a bone marrow transplant from a human donor. Marrow infusions require a near-perfect genetic match (ten out of ten). The highest probability lies in the same ethnic pool. Of the 7.5 million registrants in the U.S., twenty percent are minorities, but only one percent are South Asian. Sameer and Vinay did not find matches that they desperately needed in the registry. We all knew that we needed to do something. In eleven weeks, friends of Sameer and Vinay hosted 470 bone marrow drives and registered 24,611 South Asians [using social media]. Both Sameer and Vinay found a match, though tragically both ultimately died. The drives they inspired, though, allowed 266 other people to find matches within a year."

Cisco Systems executive Rowan Trollope is not only a savvy technologist; he's also an avid sportsman, and one of his favorite sports is motorcycle racing. To help his travelers understand why they needed to rethink the way they work in a volatile world, he told the story of a race he once lost.

"During one race week, I spent a couple days on the motorcycle pit crew. Our whole team was new at this, so we practiced on one motorcycle for, like, a whole day. And we were really proud of ourselves. We got our time down to fifty-four seconds! But we didn't win the race. When I wandered over to one of the factory teams to

see how they did it I realized it only took them nine seconds. They spent all year practicing this one thing and had gotten very good at it. When it was my turn to fix the wheels on a bike I did it all with one drill, but the professional guys used four—two for each wheel. They were the epitome of efficiency; no energy wasted. As I watched them, I could see how a perfectly efficient, perfectly coordinated team really works. But what happens to one of those pit crews when fifteen different kinds of motorcycles pull into their pit stop? All that training they do, all the tools they use . . . it's all focused on performing one set of operations on one particular motorcycle. Efficient tools and processes aren't cutting it anymore."

Trollope went on to explain that today the organizations that succeed will be not "efficient" but "agile," and if travelers wanted to win, they needed to be agile, too.

FIGHT CEREMONIES

To amplify courage in the face of conflict during the Fight stage, turn to ceremonies. The interactive, immersive qualities of events like these give your travelers a feeling of power that comes only through practice. Whether it's a motivating rally or a fear-quenching preparedness drill, people will leave the room feeling ready to take on the world.

Motivate with "Rally Spirits" Ceremonies

Historically, when preparing for battle, tribal cultures engaged in war dances to get amped and scare evil away by chanting and shouting. Acrobatic displays of strength or mock combat also served to stir up the ferocity of warriors as they showed off their skills. Today at professional ball games you may see players sway, cheer, dance, or clank helmets. Likewise, summon courage in your travelers by showing your unified strength and sounding a battle cry when the fight stage begins, and continue to host rallies at junctures along the way when spirits are flagging. These rousing moments embolden the spirit and make travelers feel like anything is possible.

The Macintosh team started as a small, rebellious group, but as it grew, it became bureaucratic. Steve Jobs changed the dynamic of the group by moving it into a new space and hoisted a flag embroidered with a pirate symbol over their new building to let people know that they were a small band of rebels again.

Pirate flag hoisted by the Macintosh team.

In the early 2000s, J. C. Penney made some significant strategic missteps, including pricing and store layout changes that confused customers, resulting in financial losses and huge layoffs. Former CEO Mike Ullman was brought back in August 2013 to lead the company out of this tumultuous period and he immediately empowered a small group of employees who called themselves "Warriors" to help him rebuild the company. They were known to end work e-mails with the battle-cry hashtags #FunFightWin and #WarriorSpirit. In one of their first acts, the Warriors brought back a longtime tradition at J. C. Penney that had taken a hiatus—the pep rally—bringing in cheerleaders from the local university and a high school marching band to rouse employees' spirits. Red banners emblazed with the rallying cry "Fun. Fight. Win." flanked walls around the building and employees waved pom-poms to fuel everyone's competitive spirit.

J. C. Penney employees cheer during a rally.

Warn with "Demystify Threats" Ceremonies

Many times what your travelers fear is more frightening in their imagination than in reality, so their fear will naturally dissipate once they move into action and find their foe is not so scary after all. Other times the threat is real enough to intimidate them into giving up before they even start to fight. When they're ready to give up, you should ceremonially unmask the enemy, demonstrate that the battle isn't as scary as it seems, and demystify the threat to keep travelers in the game.

By taking some teeth out of the monster, you can make people feel confident that the challenges are surmountable while exposing the enemy's weaknesses and flaws. Have your travelers imagine the difficulties ahead and the ways to combat them, which gives your troops the opportunity to envision the process in their minds. Help people feel like the battle is winnable by creating a safe environment where they can openly discuss the challenges they're up against and brainstorm possible ways to conquer them together.

Civil rights activists in the 1960s prepare for conflict by rehearsing how to stay nonviolent when being attacked.

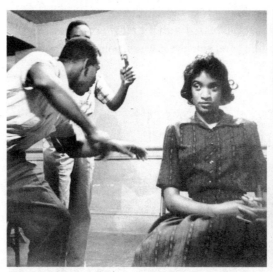 

During the civil rights movement of the 1960s, teams of activists staged peaceful demonstrations to draw the public's attention to inequality in the South. To prepare for the backlash they would encounter, protesters role-played interactions with the opposition beforehand. Some played activists staging a sit-in at a lunch counter, while others played the part of restaurant patrons and staff who shouted at, slapped, and spat on the peaceful protesters. Because they had mentally and emotionally walked in the shoes of their opponents, activists were able to take abuse and remain peaceful during the actual protests.

Apple ran the "Get a Mac" campaign, featuring a young, hip, laid-back, creative guy who introduces himself by saying, "Hello, I'm a Mac," while a stodgier man in a suit and tie who is overly concerned about work introduces himself as a PC. The two act out various vignettes that compare the weaknesses of the PC, especially ones running Microsoft Windows, to the strengths of the Mac OS. The ads were a lighthearted way to make PC users feel more comfortable purchasing a Mac even though they may have been unfamiliar with Apple products and even had a fear of changing.

FIGHT SYMBOLS

Fight symbols are images of what victory looks like. They could be weapons or spoils from vanquishing your enemy or tools you used during the battle itself. Motivating symbols help your travelers feel emboldened for battle, whereas warning symbols remind travelers of the danger in losing and how to ready themselves for battle.

Motivating Symbols

- **Visual:** The van Qualcomm took people around town in to test out their new cell phone technology has been placed in their museum to commemorate this defining moment; one of the van windows has been replaced with a screen that tells the story to visitors.

- **Auditory:** During the 1960s, the fledgling company Nike used the slogan "Crush Adidas" to inspire staff to defeat their competition.

- **Spatial:** J. C. Penney transformed the space in which they held an employee rally by hanging huge red banners around the building that read, "Fun," "Fight," and "Win."

- **Physical:** One public technology company hosts a ceremony whenever a sales team unseats a competitor's technology with its own. The salesperson who wins the deal parades around in a Viking hat as the team cheers, and a photo is taken with the president of sales to celebrate the achievement.

Warning Symbols

- **Visual:** Apple's "1984" commercial, directed by Ridley Scott, portrays a dystopian future of a world dominated by IBM. In it, a hammer-wielding heroine wears a T-shirt with an illustration of a Mac on it. Copies of the shirt were sent to the press before the commercial went live.

- **Auditory:** When Jennifer Aaker delivered her speech about the power of social media for good, she created a chilling effect by asking the audience to silently read the startling statistics on her slides about the lack of bone marrow for South Asians.

- **Spatial:** The Macintosh team flew a pirate flag above their building to exemplify their rebel spirit.

- **Physical:** Two African-American medal winners at the 1968 Summer Olympics raised their fists while on the medal stand as a gesture of pride and commitment to the Black Power movement. However, the Olympic Committee saw it as a symbol of aggression and banned the Olympians from further participation in the games.

SUMMARY

Instilling bravery communally helps people feel that they are stronger together than alone. Preparing travelers for the fight could be as simple as gathering the people to acknowledge that difficulties may lurk ahead—which they probably already foresee—and offering reasons to believe that a better future will come to pass. But no sooner do your travelers commit than they're hit with unexpected battles that knock even your most valiant trekkers onto their butts. Repeat moments of bravery over and over so travelers have the energy to combat the challenges ahead that hold you back.

Dr. Martin Luther King Jr. talks with children in a Chicago slum in 1966.

——

Civil Rights

The Fight stage can be brief and focused, or it can be long and expansive. In fact, the bigger your dream, the longer the battle may take to win. It may even take decades, as Dr. Martin Luther King Jr. and the civil rights movement discovered.

Dr. King Declares a Dream

Dr. Martin Luther King Jr. is arguably the most well-known civil rights leader in American history. His impact was far-reaching because he masterfully used persuasive communication techniques to inspire the nation and its people to imagine a different future for America, one in which all races would live together in harmony.

He was a gifted orator, to be sure, but he also understood how to mine the past for symbols, stories, and ceremonies and he brought them into the present to create moments that galvanized people.

His talent for creating transcendent moments was perhaps most evident during the March on Washington, D.C., in 1963, during the heat of the civil rights movement.

◀ Climb ceremony:
Renew Commitment

Dr. Martin Luther King Jr. delivers his "I have a dream"
speech from the Lincoln Memorial in 1963.

The goal of the march was to motivate President John F. Kennedy to introduce a bill that would grant full citizenship rights to African-Americans, from protecting their right to vote to desegregating schools and banning employment discrimination. The event drew more than two hundred thousand people, a sea of freedom-loving people that stretched for nearly a mile between the Lincoln Memorial and the Washington Monument.

On the one hundredth anniversary of the Emancipation Proclamation, Dr. King delivered his riveting "I have a dream" speech from the steps of the Lincoln Memorial, below a statue of the Great Emancipator himself. Veterans of the civil rights movement, including those who had endured beatings at sit-ins and on bus rides across the South, stood onstage to deliver testimony of their trials and issue a call for change.

When Dr. King began his remarks, he acknowledged the wins that the movement had achieved so far and expressed gratitude to those who had suffered along the way. But he also signaled that their journey was far from over, saying, *"Nineteen sixty-three is not an end, but a beginning."* He continued, *"There will be neither rest nor tranquility*

Climb symbol: Spatial ▶

Climb story: Endure the Struggle ▶

Climb speech: Progress ▶

(re)Dream ▶

in America until the Negro is granted his citizenship rights. The whirlwinds of revolt will continue to shake the foundations of our nation until the bright day of justice emerges."

Shortly afterward, President Kennedy drafted a civil rights bill that proposed sweeping reforms. Tragically, Kennedy was assassinated before his bill could be passed, but President Lyndon Johnson signed it into law in 1964. But this law wasn't enough for Dr. King. During his "I have a dream" speech, he had foreshadowed the direction he wanted to see the movement go next, saying: *"We cannot be satisfied as long as the Negro's basic mobility is from a smaller ghetto to a larger one."* With those words, he declared the next fight for civil rights: eliminating discrimination against African-Americans in all areas of their lives, including their homes.

Redrawing the Battle Lines

Even though segregation laws were rare in northern states, African-Americans still faced discrimination when they tried to apply for jobs or move into predominantly white areas. Those conditions prevented black families from getting ahead and fully enjoying "life, liberty, and the pursuit of happiness" as America's forefathers had envisioned. Instead, they were forced to live in crowded, dilapidated, and impoverished slums.

In the mid-1960s, the national mood was growing ever darker as televisions brought vivid images into people's homes of violence, from KKK attacks on African-Americans in the South to U.S. military bombs falling in Vietnam. As a result, tensions escalated. Fueled by anger and hurt, the Black Power movement began to tout a violent alternative to Dr. King's peaceful rhetoric. Their militant stance appealed to those who were tired of waiting for change, and some people resorted to rioting as a way to express their desperation. Dr. King recognized their tactics as a challenge to his peaceful methods, telling his team in the fall of 1965, *"In the North, we have heard much about the validity of violence. It has become a challenge to the nonviolent movement. . . . We must do a soul searching and profound analysis to properly chart our course."*

◀ Leap Ceremony:
Pledge Commitment

Fight symbol: Spatial ▶

Dr. King wanted to mount a campaign that would liberate people in the North while recommitting the movement to nonviolence. He and his team investigated several places to start a campaign. They considered metropolises such as Philadelphia, Cleveland, and Washington, D.C. But Dr. King ultimately chose Chicago—the second-largest city in the country at the time and a symbol of America's industrial strength. Also, a strong coalition of civil rights organizations already operated there that he could turn to for insight and support.

Fight symbol: Auditory ▶

Dream ceremony: ▶
Immerse Deeply

Leap symbol: Spatial ▶

After meeting with local activists to understand the mentality of Chicagoans and identify the best way to start, Dr. King and his team decided to launch their "War on Slums" campaign. It began in January 1966, when Dr. King and his wife, Coretta, moved into a tenement building in a poor area on the west side of Chicago, North Lawndale. By moving there, the Kings demonstrated their commitment to the community and got a taste of life in the slums. They furnished the apartment with used furniture from a local thrift shop because they wanted to live exactly as the locals did. What they didn't realize was that the conditions in their apartment still weren't as bad as the average resident's. As soon as the building's owner got wind that Dr. King was moving in, he swooped in to repair leaky pipes, broken heaters, and holes in the wall because he didn't want them to see what a hellhole it really was.

Dr. King and his wife, Coretta, sit in their rented apartment in a poor Chicago neighborhood.

Dr. King announces his War on Slums campaign in 1966.

That same month, Dr. King held a press conference to explain his plans for the Chicago movement. Behind him hung a banner emblazoned with a symbol—a giant circle made of the letters M-O-V-E, which symbolized their slogan "We're on the move to end slums." In his speech, Dr. King acknowledged that despair had spurred some to violence, an indirect reference to a riot that had occurred in Chicago the year before, but then he laid the blame on slums and the people in positions of power who profit from them. Quoting Victor Hugo, the author of *Les Misérables*, King said:

Fight speech: Underdog

Fight story: Come from Behind

> *"When men are in darkness, there will be crime; but those who have placed them in darkness are as much responsible for the crime as those who commit it. . . . Every condition exists simply because someone profits by its existence. This economic exploitation is crystallized in the slum."*

Laying out his objectives, King revealed that he wanted to force change at the federal level and raise consciousness nationwide about life in the slums, explaining:

> *"We would hope to get the kind of comprehensive legislation which would meet the problems of slum life across the nation . . . [and] create the kind of awareness in people that would make it impossible for them to be enslaved or abused."*

Soon after, Dr. King and local activist groups planned an event to gain more media attention and rally their supporters to commit time, energy, and money to the fight against this challenge of fair housing. Dr. King gave a keynote speech at the rally for the Chicago Freedom Movement, where more than sixty thousand people gathered at Soldier Field, a football stadium named for fallen American war heroes. Unlike the

Fight ceremony: Rally Spirits

Fight symbol: Spatial

inspiring, poetic tone of the speech he gave during the march on Washington, the tone of Dr. King's talk on this day was angry.

Fight speech: Battle ▶

Empathetic listening ▶

He mirrored the frustration of the poor people he had met in the city and empathized with their plight, announcing:

> *"We are here today because we are tired. We are tired of being seared in the flames of withering injustice. We are tired of paying more for less. We are tired of living in rat-infested slums."*

Yet Dr. King warned residents of the slums not to assume that someone else would solve the problem for them. *"We will be sadly mistaken if we think freedom is some lavish dish that the federal government and the white man will pass out on a silver platter. Freedom is never voluntarily granted by the oppressor. It must be demanded by the oppressed,"* he said. *"These forces will only respond when they realize that we have a powerful inner determination to be free."*

Fight symbol: Visual ▶
Fight story: ▶
Overcome the Enemy

At the same time, he counseled people to act peacefully, using vivid imagery of battles already fought. *"I have watched nonviolent power literally subpoena the conscience of a large segment of the nation to appear before the judgment seat of morality on the whole*

Dr. King inspires supporters during a rally at Soldier Field.

question of civil rights. . . . I am still convinced that nonviolence is a powerful and just weapon. It cuts without wounding. It is a sword that heals. Here in Chicago we must pick up the weapon of truth, the ammunition of courage . . . the breastplate of righteousness and the whole armor of God. And with this, we will have a nonviolent army that no violent force can halt."

Following in the footsteps of his namesake, Martin Luther, Dr. King posts a list of demands at Chicago City Hall.

Following the rally, King led people on a march to Chicago's City Hall. Once there, he pulled out a scroll, unrolled it, and taped it to the door, re-creating an act of protest performed by his namesake, Martin Luther, who posted his Ninety-Five Theses on the door of the Catholic church in Wittenberg in 1517. Dr. King's statements asked civic and business leaders to eliminate discriminatory practices, but he also called on the people of Chicago to boycott businesses that were unfair to African-Americans.

◄ Leap ceremony:
Pledge Commitment

The rally was covered by local Chicago media outlets, but Dr. King was disappointed to see they got little national coverage. To gain more attention, he turned to a tactic that had worked before—marching into hostile territory. He planned marches that would begin in predominantly African-American slums and end in suburbs occupied by mostly white residents. In contrast to the dirty tenements of the city, the well-

◄ Fight ceremony:
Rally Spirits

◄ Fight symbol: Spatial

Onlookers jeer at black activists marching in Chicago's white neighborhoods.

manicured lawns of the suburbs symbolized the American dream they couldn't obtain. By making the climb from the slums to the suburbs, marchers metaphorically reenacted the climb that they themselves hoped for but were denied by the powers that be.

The marches took place in a tense atmosphere because white residents resented being made an example of by Dr. King. As demonstrators walked peacefully down their streets, white onlookers shouted racial epithets. A march in the neighborhood of Marquette Park turned ugly when an onlooker threw a brick at Dr. King, hitting him in the back of the head with such force that he fell down on his knee, stunned. Afterward he told reporters who gathered around him, *"I have seen many demonstrations in the South, but I have never seen anything so hostile and so hateful as I've seen here today."*

Dr. King had hoped that the harsh rhetoric of his speeches combined with public marches would pressure the mayor and his cronies to bend the arms of the Chicago Real Estate Board and implore them to stop discriminating against African-Americans who tried to move out of the slums. But as the summer wore on, Dr.

Fight story: ▶
Come from Behind

King's team continued to demonstrate and city officials continued to resist. Then things came to a head when King decided to escalate the conflict by marching into the town of Cicero.

Fifteen years earlier, Cicero had been the site of a violent race riot. It had been a mostly Italian-American neighborhood until the owner of an apartment building offered to rent a flat to a black family. A mob of thousands of whites threw bricks and Molotov cocktails through the windows and raged outside the building for a full day and night as the black family cowered inside their new apartment.

◀ Fight symbol: Spatial

City officials feared the suburb would erupt again if Dr. King's people marched in. So the mayor ordered them to stand down. With his back against the wall, King deliberated for days with his team. During a heated summit meeting with city leaders, Dr. King and his team debated and pushed but finally came to an agreement— they would stop marching in return for changes in housing policies to reduce discrimination against African-Americans.

A small victory had been won, but it was far less than they had hoped to change in Chicago. Soon after, Dr. King and his wife moved out of their Chicago tenement and returned home to Atlanta. Publicly Dr. King had declared the War on Slums a victory, but privately he felt that he had failed. He was conflicted about the next direction to go with his organization. So he gathered his team for an off-site in Frogmore, South Carolina, in November 1966 to regroup. With the wounds of failure fresh and growing pressure from the Black Power movement, Dr. King needed to inspire his people and himself again.

Defining a New Goal

On the first day of the retreat, Dr. King gave a speech that, although perhaps less poetic than his speech in Washington three years earlier, strategically set the stage for the vision he documented in his final book, *Where Do We Go from Here: Chaos or Community?*

◀ Climb story:
Lose the Way

He knew his team was tired and some were wavering, so he used the moment to show how deeply he empathized with their feelings. No matter how passionate and committed they were, he understood they had plenty of reasons to lose faith. He emphasized:

Arrive speech: ▶
Surrender

> *"I know how many of you have suffered, and I know how many of you have sacrificed. . . . You are here because of your dedication to the Cause, and because of your real commitment to the principles and the ideals that have undergirded our struggle."*

Arrive story: ▶
Learn the Lesson

They had suffered setbacks and he felt compelled to acknowledge the failures. But he needed his travelers to recommit to the struggle because they had not yet won the war. He said, *"However difficult it is for us to admit, we must admit it: the changes that came about during this period were at best surface changes, they were not really substantive changes. While this period represented a frontal attack on the doctrine and practice of white supremacy, it did not defeat the monster of racism. . . ."*

Dr. King acknowledged that their movement was being attacked from inside, too, by activists who felt that nonviolent methods no longer worked:

> *"Now it is in this context that we must see the source of the cry of Black Power. [It] is really a cry of hurt. . . . It is the tragic conclusion that evil has so engrossed itself in the society that there is no answer within the society. . . . It is basically an unconscious belief in Black separatism and the feeling that the Black man can go it alone. Also it is an unconscious belief in the validity of violence to achieve certain ends. For this reason, I cannot accept the connotations of Black Power. . . ."*

(re)Dream ▶

Rather than leave his team feeling discouraged, Dr. King gave them a new mission, one that would unite all factions around a new vision—eradicating poverty. *"Why do you have 40 million people in our society who are poor? I have to ask that question. And it leaves me to ask the question of whether something is not wrong with the very structure of the society."* Changing the social system of America was a monumental task, one that would take more decades of struggle and sacrifice.

So he called on his team to renew their commitment and work together to achieve his great dream for humankind, saying:

> *"There have been too many hymns of hope, too many anthems of expectation, too many deaths, too many dark days of standing over graves of those who fought for integration for us to turn back now. We must still sing, Black and White together, 'We Shall Overcome.'"*

◄ Climb story:
Endure the Struggle

◄ Climb symbol: Auditory

In that speech, Dr. King laid out the purpose that became the focus of his life from then on. Essentially a human rights campaign, this new commitment was designed to uplift all the poor and downtrodden people around the world, from the Vietnamese who were in the midst of a terrible war to hungry children across the U.S. and beyond who deserved a better life.

Marking a Historic Moment

Though the last campaign that Dr. King completed seemed to end in failure, it actually resolved successfully. Two years after the Chicago War on Slums campaign, and just one week after Dr. King's assassination, President Johnson signed the Fair Housing Act into law, effectively implementing the federal antidiscrimination protection that King had demanded. At a ceremony to mark the passage of the law, President Johnson honored the memory of Dr. King and the promises that he'd fought to fulfill.

With a few choice words, President Johnson recalled one of the unforgettable refrains from Dr. King's speech on the National Mall, in Washington, five years before:

◄ Arrive symbol: Auditory

> *"I shall never forget that it was more than 100 years ago when Abraham Lincoln issued the Emancipation Proclamation—but it was a proclamation; it was not a fact. . . . This afternoon, as we gather here in this historic room in the White House, I think we can all take some heart that democracy's work is being done. In the Civil Rights Act of 1968 America does move forward and the bell of freedom rings out a little louder."*

◄ Arrive speech: Victory

Civil Rights Venture Scape Summary

In 1966, Dr. Martin Luther King Jr. led a civil rights venture in Chicago that built on tactics he had used successfully in previous campaigns. He stirred the anger of city leaders and suburban residents by confronting the conditions that allowed slums to flourish. But he ultimately won the battle for fair housing when the U.S. government passed a law banning housing discrimination.

01

Dr. Martin Luther King Jr. achieves many small victories in the fight for civil rights in the South. He and his team contemplate where to focus next in their fight against injustice. They decide to move into Chicago and mount an open housing campaign.

02

King and his wife, Coretta, move into a slum apartment in Chicago to symbolize their commitment to poor blacks in the city.

03

He holds a press conference to declare his strategy for Chicago. He stands before a sign that symbolizes their slogan *"We're on the move to end slums,"* saying, *"We would hope to create the kind of awareness in people that would make it impossible for [people] to be enslaved or abused and create for them the kind of democratic structures which will enable them to continually deal with the problems of slum life."*

04

King and other activist groups hold a rally at Soldier Field to motivate citizens to lend their support to the campaign.

05

King tells the crowd the power is in their hands: *"Freedom is never voluntarily granted by the oppressor. It must be demanded by the oppressed. . . . My friends, there is nothing more basic for us to learn than that 'the battle am in our hands.' We must not wait for President Johnson to free us."*

DREAM   LEAP

06

After the rally, King leads a march to Chicago City Hall to deliver their demands to city leaders.

07

He nails a list of twelve demands to the City Hall door, symbolically reenacting the act of protest that his namesake, Martin Luther, performed when he posted his Ninety-Five Theses on the door of the Catholic church in Wittenberg.

08

In addition to changes in city policies for housing, hiring, and other issues, the twelve demands include a request that citizens boycott businesses that violate the demands.

09

The city doesn't respond to King's demands, so he ups the ante by marching into white neighborhoods around Chicago.

10

King chooses a symbolic location for one of the last marches of the summer— the neighborhood of Cicero, where whites had attacked a building where a black family lived fifteen years before.

11

The mayor demands that King stand down from marching in Cicero; King calls a summit with city leaders to negotiate a resolution.

12

After days of tense meetings, King agrees to stop marching after the city agrees to small concessions on housing policies.

13

King leaves Chicago dejected over his lack of success in driving significant change. He calls an off-site with his team to regroup and figure out where their movement should go next.

14

After contemplation, King decides the next focus of their campaign should be overall human rights.

15

He encourages his team not to give up: *"We have come too far down the path now to turn back. . . . We must still sing, Black and White together, 'We Shall Overcome.'"*

16

King is assassinated in 1968, two years after his campaign in Chicago, yet he still succeeded because President Johnson signs the Fair Housing Act into law right after King's death. His legacy still lives on through nonviolent campaigns carried out by others to win rights for people around the world.

FIGHT   CLIMB   ARRIVE   ∞ (RE)DREAM

CHAPTER SEVEN

CLIMB

Climb

Moment of Endurance

The journey is bigger and longer than anticipated and enthusiasm is waning. In this fourth stage, your travelers start to lose sight of why they started this journey at all and need help strengthening their resolve to finish.

In this stage, you and your travelers have much to do because huge milestones still lie ahead. Weary from the recent battles, travelers will experience moments in the Climb stage that will feel like endless plodding along meandering paths and other times when it will feel like a treacherous trek over sheer cliffs and blind curves. Everyone's resolve gets tested. Even your staunchest and most eager travelers may rethink their commitment as they tackle an endless mountain of tasks, encounter problems, or run into disheartening setbacks. They'll have second thoughts and recalculate whether the risk is worth the reward. To top it off, you may grow impatient as your travelers grow weary.

Compound this doubt with the fact that around each corner of the climb new enemies may lurk and will force everyone to fight again. Even though the Fight and Climb stages look sequential, they're not. As you and your travelers advance, you fight, climb, fight, climb, and fight again. Sometimes, for every two steps forward, you take one step back. It's exhausting. When travelers encounter seemingly insurmountable vistas and discouraging crossroads, they once again must commit to stay the course in this test of endurance.

You can infuse your team with a spirit of endurance by reflecting on the progress they've accomplished so far and reiterating a compelling view of the rewards of reaching the summit. Remind them what marks you've hit along the way and use each setback to learn how to improve. By this point, your troops have pushed through the fight, have taken risks, and are beginning to be changed by the effort. The silver lining during this toughest, darkest part of the journey is that bonds between travelers will deepen as your team gets tested. Use this moment to refresh their spirits.

Understand What Your Travelers Are Feeling

In the Climb stage, exhaustion starts to set in. Travelers who were once energized for the journey may find their spirits flagging, unless you give them encouragement to keep their motivation high. Others may be ready to quit altogether, feeling as if they're so far from the final destination that their efforts no longer matter. Warn them of the risks of sticking to a doomed plan or stopping short of the final goal.

If They're **Committed,** You'll Hear Them Say . . .	Use **Motivating** Communication to Keep Them Going.
"I've been here before." **"You can lean on me."** **"Go, team!"**	Help your travelers see how far they've come and energize them to continue for the long haul. Give them challenges and rewards that fuel them with bursts of excitement so they'll have more energy to endure the rest of the journey. At moments of decision, push them to make new commitments. Appeal to their desire for community by emphasizing their essential role in the group's success.

If They're **Resistant,** You'll Hear Them Say . . .	Use **Warning** Communication to Get Them Unstuck.
"This is just too hard." **"We're doomed."** **"Why bother?"**	Don't allow complacency to creep in, because you still have a long journey ahead. Have you encountered unexpected setbacks or been blindsided by an unseen problem? Sound a warning call if your allies are straying from the path to success and reorient them with an honest picture of the problems. Admit how you may have played a role in arriving at the wrong place. Ask for help bringing those who are struggling back into the fold.

Endurance Communication Toolkit

To keep your travelers moving forward, reassure them that they have the strength to endure and that the journey is worth the effort. Use speeches, stories, ceremonies, and symbols to celebrate their accomplishments and reinvigorate their desire to see your venture succeed.

CLIMB SPEECHES

Motivate with "Progress" Speeches

Progress speeches are status reports with a soul—information about the state of your venture wrapped in a reason to believe. One of the founding fathers of America, Thomas Paine, acknowledged the difficulty of the struggle for independence when he spoke to fellow patriots who were growing weary after months of war. He showed that he understood their pain by saying, *"These are the times that try men's souls."* But he called on them to persevere because their continued effort would be rewarded, or as he said it, *"The summer soldier and the sunshine patriot will, in this crisis, shrink from the service of their country; but he that stands by it now, deserves the love and thanks of man and woman. . . . What we obtain too cheap, we esteem too lightly: it is dearness only that gives everything its value."*

At times, you, too, must revisit the dream and remind yourself why it's worth it to keep yourself and your travelers going. Recognize small wins and acknowledge what's completed but caution against slowing down, because only through persistent effort can travelers close the gap between what is and what could be.

///

UPS is on a mission to change how businesses think about logistics. When David Abney, now the company's CEO, spoke at the Alternative Clean Transportation Expo in 2013, he talked about the company's vision for environmentally sound transport of goods and the potential to transform millions of carbon-emitting trips into "green miles."

What Is: *"In just the last 5 years, we've committed to invest more than a quarter of a billion dollars to deploy more than 2,700 alternative fuel and alternative technology vehicles around the world. Since 2000, our vehicles have traveled more than 300 million miles on alternative fuels—the average distance from Earth to Mars and back."*

What Could Be: *"We're still early in our journey, but we're picking up the pace. . . . We expect to reach 500 million miles in 2015. That will get us to the average distance from Earth to Jupiter. And, based on what we know today, we will reach 1 billion green miles by the end of 2017! That would get us out to Saturn."*

New Bliss: *"Those are exciting destinations, but we can't do it alone. Together we can create a sustainable cycle of adoption, move alternative fuels into the mainstream, and improve the global environment for the 21st century."*

UPS has continued to invest in alternative-fuel vehicles, with more than fifty-five hundred in deployment as of mid-2015. As a result, the company reached its goal of 500 million miles a year ahead of schedule, in 2014.

IBM has long championed the idea of using technology to improve business performance, and under the guidance of CEO Sam Palmisano the company began evangelizing the concept of "Smarter Cities," which run on advanced technology infrastructure. At a meeting of urban planners in Brazil in 2011, Palmisano described how technology was fueling progress in cities around the world.

What Is: *"When you understand that the world has become pervasively instrumented and interconnected . . . it inevitably leads you to see our planet not as a collection of countries or industries . . . but as a system of systems. . . . At IBM, we've seen this future taking shape . . . in the work we do with clients in more than 2,000 Smarter Cities engagements."*

What Could Be: *"The systems being created by the new breed of Smarter Cities don't just achieve great efficiencies today. They also generate virtuous cycles that will last for a generation or more."*

New Bliss: *"The world's emerging global cities are the crucible in which a new model of leadership is being forged . . . a new generation of forward-thinkers who are making our world literally work better."*

Warn with "Crossroads" Speeches

Sometimes the best-laid plans fail and a course correction is needed. In those moments, your travelers face a critical choice either to keep executing the plan or to sound the alarm that it's time for a new plan. In act three of William Shakespeare's *Hamlet*, the prince of Denmark faces a tough situation and asks himself a life-or-death question. *"To be, or not to be?"* says Hamlet. *"That is the question—whether 'tis nobler in the mind to suffer the slings and arrows of outrageous fortune, or to take arms against a sea of troubles, and, by opposing, end them?"*

In the case of your venture, the life or death of your dream may be what's up for debate. You or your travelers may have become too attached to the course you're on and run the risk of failing altogether unless you reexamine the current state of affairs and redirect your efforts. Understand if and how the path is flawed and then explain how a different path can fulfill your vision.

///

During his testimony at a congressional hearing in 2010 about an auto recall, Toyota CEO Akio Toyoda (grandson of the company's founder) apologized to drivers and offered condolences to the relatives of a San Diego family killed in an accident caused

by vehicular malfunction. While showing remorse for the accident, Toyoda displayed resolve to get the company back on track. When speaking to Toyota employees one day later, he told them that the company was at a crossroads and needed to rethink its operations to ensure that they could continue to provide the highest-quality cars to customers.

Akio Toyoda expresses remorse after Toyota vehicles cause injuries.

What Is: *"Quite frankly, I fear the pace at which we have grown may have been too quick. . . .We were not able to stop, think, and make improvements as much as we were able to before, and our basic stance to listen to customers' voices to make better products has weakened somewhat. . . . I am deeply sorry for any accidents that Toyota drivers have experienced."*

What Could Be: *"I, more than anyone, wish for Toyota's cars to be safe, and for our customers to feel safe when they use our vehicles. . . . A step will be added in the process to ensure that management will make a responsible decision from the perspective of 'customer safety first.'"*

New Bliss: *"When the cars are damaged, it is as though I am as well. . . . You have my personal commitment that Toyota will work vigorously and unceasingly to restore the trust of our customers."*

Many corporations are as large as nations, so it's no wonder that government officials stop to listen when business leaders speak their minds on economic matters. During the depth of the recession in 2009, the CEO of the multinational company General Electric, Jeffrey Immelt, spoke to the Detroit Economic Club about choices facing the U.S.

What Is: *"We've seen a great vanishing of wealth. . . . As a nation, we've been consuming more than we earn, saved too little and taken on far too much debt. . . . We have already lost our leadership in many growth industries, and other new opportunities are at risk."*

What Could Be: *"Our country was built on great undertakings that brought out the best in government and business alike. . . . We should clear away any arrogance, false assumptions, or a sense that things will be 'OK' just because we are America. Rather, we should dedicate ourselves to be the most competitive country in the world."*

New Bliss: *"We should create an American Industrial Renewal. . . . From economic chaos we will create new opportunities for the people of . . . this country. We will once again be prosperous but, more importantly, we will be proud."*

CLIMB STORIES

Through Climb stories, you can illustrate tangibly what it looks like when people stick with the program or stray off course. Motivate or warn your travelers at key points along their climb with tales of the milestones achieved—or missed—in the present or the past. Renew their spirits with stories that illustrate the core values that drive them to persist when others quit.

Motivating with "Endure the Struggle" Stories

Everyone knows an endurance story because these are the tales that give us the will to go on. People who persevered through difficult circumstances—Ernest Shackleton's death-defying Antarctic expedition, Louis Zamperini's harrowing shipwreck and wartime captivity, Uta Pippig's gritty finish in the Boston Marathon—show us what triumph of the human spirit looks like. When your travelers need to believe that they have what it takes to keep going, tell them a story about persistence. When did you or someone else make progress toward a goal and muster the resolve to continue? What motivated you or them to keep going?

///

When Duarte, Inc., was two years into a transformation to unify our processes, we knew that people were tired of change and some were on the fence about staying. We needed them to stand together and support one another, so we told the "Bundle of Sticks" story from Aesop's Fables, about a father who wanted his sons to join together. As the fable recounts:

> "He told them to bring him a bundle of sticks. When they had done so, he placed the bundle into the hands of each of them and ordered them to break it in pieces. They tried with all their strength, and were not able to do it. He then unbundled the sticks and handed them to his sons one at a time, and they broke them easily. 'My sons,' he told them, 'if you are of one mind, and unite to assist each other, you

Duarte employees use "bundles of sticks" (actually colored pencils) to show that unity equals strength.

will be as this bundle, uninjured by all the attempts of your enemies; but if you are divided among yourselves, you will be broken as easily as these sticks.'"

What was Aesop's moral of the story? Strength in unity. We knew our travelers would endure if they banded together.

Famous fashion designer Coco Chanel endured much suffering. Her first personal tragedy happened when she was only twelve years old. Her ill mother had died and her dad abandoned her at an orphanage at the chapel of Aubazine, a Cistercian abbey. The nuns taught Chanel how to sew and during her seven years there, she found beauty in sparseness. The minimalism of the nuns' robes and orphans' smocks contrasted with the opulence of the religious garb and liturgical elements. This paradox left an indelible mark on Chanel and underpins all of her designs. The brand's famous interlocking C's were inspired by stained glass windows in the chapel that featured interlaced curves. Coco Chanel created symbols of other kinds as well, including the trademark little black dress, which was a revolutionary design in the 1920s. The color black was associated with mourning and she transformed it into chic evening wear. Chanel and her brand modeled an undying commitment to simplicity and the ability to endure.

Warn with "Lose the Way" Stories

If your climb starts to feel more like a downward spiral, tell a tale that lets your travelers know where you're headed if they don't stay on track. Use a story that illustrates how you are collectively wandering off course from the right path. How do you know you've lost direction? Or if it looks like people are at risk of giving up altogether, tell them what it will look like if they stop climbing on. Perhaps recall a time when you personally wavered and lost something dear as a result. When did you decide that the struggle was no longer worth it? What made you get back in the game?

The path from start-up to success is paved with failures, as any founder knows (but rarely admits). Adrian Tuck, CEO of the solar energy provider Tendril, feared his company could go under if he didn't make some radical shifts. Not only was he brave enough to make changes, he also openly shares his story with others.

> *"Up until 2012, we won more business than our competition combined. We raised over $100 million. . . . Before we knew it, black limos were parked outside our fancy offices, and bankers were talking to us about billion-dollar valuations. But in the rush toward world domination, too many of our resources were focused on grabbing new ground instead of serving our current customers. . . . We stopped winning new business. . . . Over a period of six months we backed our way out of two-thirds of our customer engagements and reluctantly let go of two-thirds of our amazing people. . . . Today, for the most part, we have happy customers, happy employees, and happy investors. We're profitable. And we won big deals with more to come. This is a testament to the most amazing group of colleagues, customers, and investors I have ever had the pleasure to work with. All our success is due to them."*

Innovative thinkers love the thrill of reinvention, but sometimes they lose focus on the little things that can make the difference between good and great. On a fateful mountain climbing trip, Rowan Trollope, of Cisco Systems, learned a hard lesson about cutting corners. He then used the story as an inspiring lesson to help his team pay attention to details as they developed a breakthrough product, because if they didn't the product might not succeed.

"I was about 11,000 feet up on Mount Laurel when I started hammering a piton into the rock. I heard a loud ping with each strike of the hammer and decided it was in good enough; then I hammered in the second one and tied some knots. . . . Something in the back of my head told me to stop so I retied the knot. The moment I put weight on my line, that first piton popped out and hit me smack in the middle of the helmet. Had I not retied the other knot, I would have died on that ledge. . . . Before my climb on Mount Laurel, I was prone to cutting corners wherever I could and it almost got me killed. . . . When I think of those pitons, one of them represents 'good enough' and one of them represents greatness. I like to keep both of them in mind so I always remember what kind of choice I'm making."

CLIMB CEREMONIES

In some ways ceremonies in the Climb stage mirror the Leap stage because your travelers must once again dedicate themselves to the dream, only now its luster has begun to wear off. Unite your travelers by gathering everyone together with ceremonies that renew focus on the purpose. Let them release feelings of frustration (or sadness) so they can once again look forward with hope.

Motivate with "Renew Commitment" Ceremonies

Travelers get motivated when reminded of the reasons they jumped in originally. As their energy wanes from the climb, being asked to recommit again helps them gain energy. Acknowledge that it would be easier to quit than continue but that their remarkable strength to endure is admirable. When a group recommits, people feel additional accountability to each other as they muster the strength together to finish the job. Often after travelers recommit they begin to exhibit surprising new qualities and skills that they've learned from the struggle of the journey so far.

///

Cesar Chavez speaks at a rally to campaign for fair wages.

The Spanish rallying cry "Sí se puede!" was introduced by labor leader Cesar Chavez, cofounder of the United Farm Workers (UFW). Translated, it means "Yes we can!" Chavez devoted his life to campaigning for fair wages for laborers. So in 1972 when the Arizona governor signed a bill into law outlawing strikes at harvest time, Chavez began a political fast in protest. The fast took a physical toll on him, and he became bedridden as time went on, but Chavez's resolve was steadfast. Latino leaders met with him to discuss what they saw as the bleak political outcome. They argued with him that his fasting efforts were futile. They kept repeating in Spanish, *"¡No, no se puede!"* (*"No, no it can't be done!"*). Chavez replied with *"Sí, sí se puede"* (*"Yes, yes we can"*). The co-leader of the movement, Dolores Huerta, immediately made the response the official slogan of the campaign as protesters recommitted and prevailed in forcing growers to negotiate fair labor practices with the UFW, winning many improvements for workers.

In 1997, the carpet tile company Interface gathered its leaders for an off-site to revisit progress on their sustainability goals and cast a vision for the next stage of their venture. After hearing inspiring presentations and participating in brainstorming sessions, the leaders were asked to show their commitment to helping the company make a bigger impact by writing statements on a "personal legacy wall" next to a Polaroid photo of themselves that had been taken earlier during the off-site. The commitments they made were then published in a company-wide newsletter for all to see.

Warn with "Heal Wounds" Ceremonies

After leaving the fog of war, travelers can experience confusion and chaos. Some things went great; others caused rifts between people or uncovered flaws. Travelers with open wounds will be resistant to moving forward at this point. But by addressing their suffering, you can ease them out of a difficult rut. If the battle was bigger than anticipated, travelers may need to align, heal, and bond with each other before beginning again. Ceremonies that acknowledge it was a painful season help bring closure to this stage.

When Philip M. Condit took over as CEO of Boeing in 1996, he worked to heal the strain that had formed between management and disgruntled employees due to the forced overtime required to keep up with orders while going through dramatic changes at the same time. In his first one hundred days, the company announced a $1 billion stock-grant program for employees, and opened a daycare center at the plant in Everett, Washington. Condit also increased spending on training and dispelled employee fears that improvements would result in more job losses. He reassured them that the recent changes would create new opportunities rather than lead to cuts. He worked to break down barriers among senior managers, holding a series of weeklong meetings with them, concluded by a trip to his house for dinner. After the meal, the group gathered outside around a giant fire pit and told stories about Boeing. They wrote down the stories, keeping the inspiring ones and tossing the negative ones into the flames to banish the memory of them.

At an industry conference of almost seven thousand technologists in 2004, Craig Barrett, Intel Corp.'s CEO, got down on his knees to beg the audience's forgiveness for Intel's unpopular strategic decision to cancel the Pentium

Craig Barrett kneels to ask forgiveness for Intel product missteps.

4 chip. This decision caused many customers to switch to a competitor's chip. *"Is it a missed commitment? Absolutely. Would we have preferred not to miss that commitment? Absolutely . . . forgive us,"* Barrett told the crowd. *"We ate crow."*

CLIMB SYMBOLS

Climb symbols inspire your travelers to keep going. Motivating symbols are artifacts from earlier times when your team struggled and endured to the finish. They serve as reminders that even though the trek is hard, your travelers are strong, capable, and qualified to keep going, whereas warning symbols are mementos from times you stood at a crossroads and went the wrong direction, or needed to heal from pain already endured.

Motivating Symbols

- **Visual:** When Rowan Trollope told his team the story about the mountain climbing incident that nearly cost him his life, he brought a replica of the piton because the original was still in the crack in the rock. It showed them how paying attention to details was critical.

- **Auditory:** The phrase "Sí se puede" emerged from a period of sacrificial fasting by Cesar Chavez. Barack Obama lifted the phrase from Chavez for his New Hampshire—and then presidential—campaign rallying cry, "Yes we can."

- **Spatial:** The hallway in the lobby of Foundation Medicine, a genomic cancer-testing and treatment-identification company, is covered with photos of people the employees know who have been affected by cancer. This serves as a daily reminder about the importance of their work.

- **Physical:** For Duarte, Inc.'s Shop Day, employees wore shop aprons to signify that we would be doing some hard work. A poster promoting the event featured an anvil to further signify the metaphorical heavy lifting we were asking travelers to do on that day.

Warning Symbols

- **Visual:** When Nokia's revenue was falling rapidly, CEO Stephen Elop used the metaphor of a burning oil platform, including graphic descriptions of what it would be like to work on an oil platform in the North Sea and wake up to an explosion that set the platform on fire. Intended to warn employees, the fatalistic metaphor was leaked to the press and spooked investors.

- **Auditory:** Harriet Tubman made the old spiritual song "Go Down Moses" a code for fugitive slaves to use to communicate when fleeing Maryland.

- **Spatial:** Starbucks held its event for store managers in New Orleans because that city was enduring its own uphill battle to recover from Hurricane Katrina. Starbucks demonstrated the company's commitment to recover and endure by sending employees to perform acts of service in the New Orleans area during the event.

- **Physical:** To sincerely acknowledge mistakes and losses, Toyota's CEO, Akio Toyoda, openly wept at his congressional hearing about a death that had resulted in an auto recall.

SUMMARY

In epic journeys, the hero reaches a moment when, having endured great hardship, he or she starts to question whether the sacrifice is worth the reward. Then he or she has to muster renewed resolve to finish the journey, just as your travelers will have to do. This is a critical juncture in your narrative. People can't endure for long stints without time to regroup and refresh. If they don't recommit, your dream won't be realized. Travelers need the energy and motivation to keep pressing forward and be warned of the harm of staying put or losing their way.

charity: water CEO Scott Harrison visits with children who received clean water.

charity: water

Sometimes a seemingly small shift can lead you to a great purpose that's so vast and so important it becomes your calling. Once your heart has been moved, nothing will stop you until the world is made right.

charity: water Brings Clean Water to Millions

Scott Harrison, CEO of the nonprofit charity: water, delivers speeches that are so moving, if you don't choke up at least once while listening to him, you should check your pulse to see if your heart is still beating. He and his organization brilliantly use speeches, stories, ceremonies, and symbols to move people to support the mission of bringing clean and safe drinking water to everyone in the world.

As a gifted storyteller, Harrison built a model for charity: water that put communication and transparency at the center. From day one, the nonprofit has separated the funds raised for organizational operations and water projects, so that every penny donated for water projects goes directly to efforts in the field. charity: water also shares stories of the work and hope created, helping donors emotionally connect with their impact. Combining storytelling and being transparent with how donations are used has led charity: water to be the largest nonprofit in the United States focused on water. Leading the reinvention of nonprofits, Harrison has created a new model for charities and communicates in a way that builds emotional connections with donors that can easily spread socially.

Harrison travels the world to tell the unlikely story of his personal transformation that became his calling to start charity: water. In a speech delivered in Boston in 2013, he told a series of vibrant stories that moved that crowd alone to donate tens of thousands on the spot. He set the stage by telling the audience about the path he took in <u>finding purpose</u> in life.

Arrive story: ▶
Learn the Lesson

"At eighteen years old, I, like so many bad clichés, rebelled. I moved to New York City, grew my hair down to my shoulders, and joined a band. Unfortunately, the band immediately broke up because we all hated each other. I learned that the guy who was booking our band was really the one making all the money—he would give us fifty bucks to split between us but he'd walk out with the lion's share. This job was called a nightclub promoter, and I realized that as a promoter you could drink alcohol for free and all you had to do was get beautiful people to come into the club. And if you got the right people in the club, you could charge them eighteen dollars for a vodka and soda, or charge guys five hundred dollars for a bottle of champagne that only cost you forty dollars. So the next ten years of my life disappeared; there are chunks of time that I don't remember too well. This is me at twenty-eight years old [shows a photo], and you can see that I think I'm on top of the world. So much so that I'm holding out my Rolex so the photographer notices what an expensive watch I'm wearing.

"It was pretty pathetic. I was getting paid two thousand dollars a month to drink a bottle of Bacardi. I was getting paid another two thousand a month by Budweiser just to be seen in public drinking Bud. So I thought I had arrived. I had a BMW. I had a grand piano at my apartment. I had a Labrador retriever. And my girlfriend was on billboards.

"As you can imagine, you pick up a lot of vices in a decade of working in nightlife . . . whether that's recreational drug use, gambling, pornography, or strip clubs. I had

them all at this point. But while I was on a New Year's Eve trip to Punta del Este, Uruguay, with all of the beautiful people, I realized I was the worst person I knew. I was in this beautiful place with servants and horses. We spent a thousand dollars on shrimp and fireworks, and Dom Pérignon magnums were everywhere. But I realized, 'Man, I am never going to find what I am looking for where I am looking for it.' I was spiritually bankrupt, I was emotionally bankrupt, and I was certainly morally bankrupt. While I was hungover during the day, I started reading theology books and the Bible again. I started looking for the faith I had as a kid that meant so much to me. But I remember hating some of the religious stuff that I grew up with. I came across this verse that said, 'True religion is to look after widows and orphans in their distress and to keep yourself from being polluted.' I thought, 'Man, I'm oh for two. I haven't done anything for the poor in ten years, and I literally pollute the world.' I mean, I got people wasted for a living. So I came back to New York and said to myself, 'I have to do something radically, radically different. I need to change everything about my life. . . .'"

He went on to tell about his transition from high-flying party boy to social-impact leader. He returned from his trip committed to overhauling his life. He applied for every nonprofit job he could and was rejected because his party promoter skills didn't exactly fit the bill. Finally, he convinced an organization called Mercy Ships to take him as a volunteer photographer on a trip to Africa, for which Harrison had to pay them five hundred dollars to be a volunteer. On this trip he realized that dirty water was the source of many problems on the continent.

"I learned that leeches were a huge problem throughout the developing world. Now, I'm pretty sure no one in this room has struggled with a leech in their drinking water recently. But if you got your water from an open spring like this [shows photo], you would. The big ones are pretty easy to filter out. But the little leeches get through the filtration and then grow up inside you, and their favorite spot is the back of the throat. There are two ways to get a leech out of the back of your child's throat. You either use a stick to scrape it out, or you give your kid a little bit of diesel fuel—just enough to kill the leech but hopefully not enough to injure your child.

An African boy fills a jerry can with filthy water.

> *"Many communities cannot afford to buy charcoal to boil their water. So probably half of the world's schools do not have clean water, or toilets. So how can kids get a good education if they have to wake up in the middle of the night to go collect river water and then bring it with them to school?"*

Dream story: ▶
Heed the Call

Having been moved deeply by the trip, Harrison came home and wanted to do something more about it.

> *"I'd seen all of these problems while I was in Africa: the lack of education, people dying of AIDS, and people dying of malaria. I just could not get this image of a child in a swamp out of my mind. I thought, 'I can't believe we live in a world where this happens,' and that's where the idea for charity: water was born."*

Building Trust with a New Model

When he returned home to tell his friends that he planned to start a charity, Harrison was surprised they didn't want to get involved. He learned that his friends distrusted charities because they seemed like big black holes. They would tell him, *"I give them my money, but I don't know where it goes. I don't know how much actually reaches people."* Each of his friends seemed to have horror stories of some charity CEO making millions by embezzling funds to make expensive purchases. Still determined, Harrison wanted his friends, who didn't even blink at spending five hundred dollars for a bottle of champagne, on board. To address their concerns, he imagined a unique new nonprofit model for charity: water.

Harrison's proposed financial model turned the "black hole" excuse on its head, promising donors that 100 percent of their money would go directly to digging wells that provide clean water. People responded with *"That's crazy. How will you pay your staff and cover the rent on your office? How will you cover your costs to fly to the well sites so you can know what's going on there?"* Harrison had no idea how to answer these questions, but he started by opening up two separate bank accounts with one hundred dollars each. One account would be used to send 100 percent of funds to dig wells in the field and the other account would cover all the overhead of running the nonprofit. In fact, the overhead fund would even pay back credit card fees people used to make donations online so Harrison could stand by his 100 percent promise. Harrison hoped to recruit board members, entrepreneurs, private companies, and foundations to pay for overhead costs and he publicly promised that the money for wells would never be touched to fund the business side of charity: water.

The second part of Harrison's model was to prove to donors that their money was being put to good use, employing technology to show them what their donations went toward. He bought GPS devices at Best Buy and put one on each well that charity: water dug, sending out the status of wells to donors through Google Maps and Google Earth.

◄ Leap ceremony:
Dismantle Blockages

Harrison recalls in his speech,

> *"So, charity: water started with a party. That's the only thing I knew how to do. I was a nightclub promoter. So I got someone to donate a club. I threw my thirty-first birthday party. I got seven hundred people to come out. I lured them with open bar, and I charged them twenty bucks at the door. And this time instead of pocketing the fifteen [sic] thousand dollars, we took it immediately to a refugee camp in Northern Uganda called Bobi, where 31,638 people were living. We built three wells, we fixed three wells, and then we sent the photos and the GPS and the story back to those seven hundred people. This was a big deal. Some people didn't even remember the party. . . . Seriously, people could not believe that a charity would bother to report to them on a twenty-dollar gift. And that something actually happened with the money that they could see, that they could connect with. And we said, 'Let's just keep doing this. Let's keep closing the loop until the problem is solved.'"*

Fight story: ▶
Overcome the Enemy

As Harrison traveled, he saw community groups trying to solve their local water crisis, but they weren't experienced in fund-raising, marketing, or raising awareness. Some local partners identified a hundred projects that needed to be completed each year, but they had funds only for eleven. So Harrison used this finding to inspire another charity: water model: Work through the locals, who knew their community's issues and how best to implement new projects, while charity: water would take on the storytelling piece to shine the light on them and their hard work. And try to get people to care.

Walking in Empathy

charity: water excels at putting donors in the shoes of those without clean water. Harrison's stories in the company's annual reports start with lines like *"I turn on the tap, and mud comes out. I'm following Dominic Mosa, a slender, soft-spoken man with a slight frame and an off-white lab coat. We're in the laundry of the health clinic he runs, watching brown water flow from two taps into a stone basin. 'This is your water?' I ask. 'You've got to be kidding. You must be.'"*

Harrison shares stories about the conditions of the Mogotio Health Centre, in Kenya. The hospital relies on a stream of mud from the river to use at the clinic—water that makes everyone sick. The clinic staff did its best to provide patients with good care and medicine, yet their success was compromised by disease-filled water.

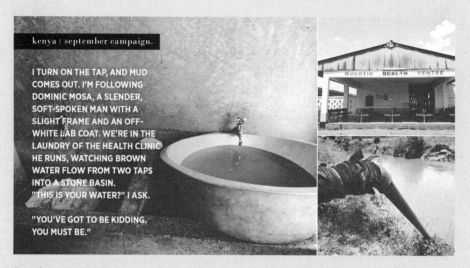

Page from charity: water's annual report about the Mogotio Health Centre

Because many health clinics in the Rongai district of Kenya didn't have access to clean water, patients had to bring their own five-gallon jerry cans full of water so they could receive treatment. What's a jerry can? It is a steel container originally intended to hold diesel fuel, but many people in developing countries use it to haul and store their drinking water. The standard five-gallon jerry can weighs about forty pounds when full. charity: water repurposed the jerry can to symbolize the water crisis. Millions of people, mostly women, spend hours each day with one strapped securely on their backs, held tightly to their hips, or balanced on top of their heads in an effort to provide clean water for their families.

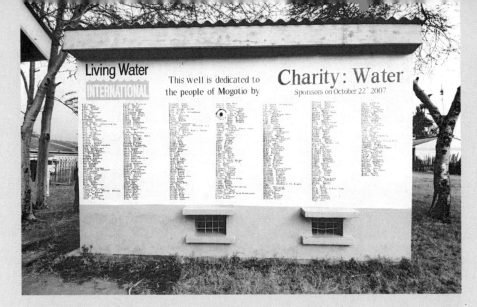

Wall honoring charity: water donors in a small African town

When charity: water came back from the Mogotio Health Centre, Harrison and his team told the story to everyone who would listen. charity: water was turning one year old and it was also Harrison's thirty-second birthday. He asked everyone he knew for a thirty-two-dollar donation as a birthday gift to drill a well there. In four weeks, donors committed $159,000 in funds to build water systems at three hospitals and one school in Kenya.

To honor his promise of providing transparency for the well projects, Harrison had the names of more than seven hundred donors inscribed on the pump house wall. Harrison recalled the ceremony, saying,

> *"Yes, we know it seems a bit much, and we still feel bad for the local artist who wrote 700+ names by hand, but we wanted to connect people. We wanted to show that it wasn't about how much they gave, but that they took the time to give, and their money really did something. We wanted to tie these 700+ people in America with some 5,000+ people halfway across the Earth whose lives were now changed. Whether they gave $1 or $1,000 they got their name on the Mogotio well."*

Leap ceremony: ▶
Pledge Commitment

Arrive ceremony: ▶
Honor Heroes

Attendees at the charity: water gala carry jerry cans full of water on a catwalk.

The charity: water team uses the powerful symbol of the jerry can to build hands-on awareness of the water struggle millions of people face every day. Sometimes first-world donors don't easily understand the plight of third-world sufferers who don't have clean water. Harrison's team travels with him to his domestic speaking gigs, and they host an annual gala where they set up a runway so attendees can pick up bright yellow jerry cans full of water and walk a hundred feet in the shoes of those who have to carry them for up to eight hours. The cans, originally a sign of oppression and suffering, have been turned into a symbol of hope to change the water crisis.

◄ Dream ceremony: Immerse Deeply

A Moral Dilemma

Harrison's promise to funnel 100 percent of contributions to the field and to communicate transparently helped donations pour in. People were so moved by his stories that the account to fund water projects was soon full of cash, which charity: water sent to fund projects as quickly as possible. The account to cover charity: water's overhead expenses, however, had run dry about eighteen months after the nonprofit was founded. Desperate, Harrison wrote e-mails to the founders of as many social media platforms as he could think of, asking for help. He had only five weeks of funding left. His friends told him to just move the money over from the water account to pay his overhead and then return it after he could replenish the overhead account.

He recalls, *"I remember being so frustrated because I had millions that I could never touch, and integrity was so important to me that I would never have even borrowed from the water account."* As a result of that mailing, social media entrepreneurs Michael and Xochi Birch, complete strangers to Harrison, took a two-hour meeting with him. After that meeting, Harrison was shocked to discover that the Birches had wired $1 million into his overhead account; they said, *"I believe in your vision, you just need more time."* Harrison used it to build a thriving operations side to the charity and realized he needed to create a more formal program to recruit large donors.

A boy celebrates when a freshly dug well begins to spout clean water.

Showing Love to The Well Members

Harrison created The Well as a program that recruited entrepreneurs and business professionals who understood the value of covering overhead costs for a growing organization. He began presenting charity: water to business leaders and several of them made multiyear commitments. Most of the money to support charity: water's staff and operations account comes from a small group of about a hundred people, who are excited about helping Harrison cover his costs. Before launching The Well, Harrison heard from many skeptics about their doubts regarding scaling an organization using his 100 percent model, but he has proved them wrong.

The success of The Well program is driven by how Harrison communicates. He hosts intimate dinners with The Well members so they can meet each other and build friendships, and he gives them behind-the-scenes updates about charity: water. He delivers informal, enlightening talks about the progress the organization is making and any special needs it has. He's open about what keeps him up at night, and The Well members get to hear new ideas he's experimenting with and help him vet them. The dinners are almost like mini–board meetings, where the members share their own stories, from which Harrison gains insight into how to drive his organization forward.

◀ Climb speech: Progress

To help connect The Well donors empathetically to what's happening in the field, Harrison takes some of them on immersive trips to meet the people benefiting from their donations.

Keeping the Torch Lit

Harrison's commitment to bring clean water to hundreds of millions is so ambitious, it's unclear whether he can solve this problem in his lifetime. It's hard to sustain the energy to pursue a daunting cause that takes years or decades to tackle. Torchbearers such as Harrison have learned how to renew and replenish their dreams with stories that remind them why they made a commitment in the first place. Even though Harrison's cause dramatically changes lives, there are moments, even for him, when he needs to reconnect to his purpose. Six years after founding the organization, he wanted to find a story that moved him to make a deeper commitment to those he was serving. He needed to rejuvenate himself for another long haul. So he took another trip, which he shared about in his Boston talk:

> *"Of all the stories I'd heard about people suffering from dirty water, there's one that struck me the most. Ethiopia is a country I'm deeply passionate about, and on a trip there last year I heard a story about a woman named Letikiros. We were staying in a six-dollar-a-night hotel room, and the hotel owner came up to us and said, 'You're the charity: water people. We know what you've been doing here. Let me tell you the story about this woman who lived in my village when I was young.'*

He said she used to walk eight hours a day to get water for her family; three hours out and five hours back. She used a clay pot that weighed ten to fifteen pounds when empty and then put another thirty pounds of water in it. One day, she came back to her village after the walk, she slipped and fell. The clay pot broke and all the water spilled out. She was so distraught about losing the water she worked all day to get that she took a rope and hung herself from a tree in the village. The hotel owner looked at me and said, 'The work you are doing is important.' This is not about a statistic of eight hundred million people. This is about people who have no hope, because of where they are born.

"The hotel owner's story seemed far-fetched and intended to shock, and I doubted whether I really believed it all. One day, I decided to go and see for myself. I wanted to see if anything had changed for the village in the fourteen years since the tragedy."

Harrison walked nine hours to reach the village. He walked the eight-hour path Letikiros had taken to get water and stood beneath the tree where she ended her life.

He discovered that Letikiros was beloved in the community. Her husband told Harrison, *"She was beautiful to me. We were in deep love."* Those who knew her well believed she must have been overcome with shame because she had spilled the family's water supply. Letikiros was buried beneath a pile of rocks behind the church. The pieces from the broken pot were strewn far from the village, where they'd never been seen again. Letikiros Hailu often talked about changing the lives of her people. She never got the chance in her lifetime, but perhaps she will in her legacy.

Dream ceremony: ▶
Immerse Deeply

The tree where Letikiros's body was found

The trip for Harrison was like a pilgrimage. This gut-wrenching story reminded him of what he was called to do. Having been moved by Letikiros's story, Harrison said, *"I returned home even more committed to help the people of*

Tigray, and even more passionate about the cause of clean water. I firmly believe, now more than ever, that water changes everything." Harrison will continue his tireless pursuit of emotionally connecting donors with the people their funds serve around the world.

Remarkable Growth

charity: water's key to success has been its promise to send 100 percent of donations to the field to fund clean-water projects and its transparency around this promise. A 2012 *New York Times* article stated that in four years, charity: water had *"grown by 400 percent while charitable giving in America has been going down, on an aggregate, by as much as 10 percent over the past three years."*

charity: water Growth

	2007	2008	2009	2010	2011	2012	2013	2014
Cumulative people served to date	235,400	531,194	1,048,309	1,742,331	2,360,000	3,223,000	4,222,867	5,228,494
Dollars sent to water programs	$932,367	$4,308,289	$5,439,218	$8,609,576	$17,646,927	$18,292,119	$26, 745,914	$30,568,181
Dollars spent on operations	$467,939	$909,418	$1,501,118	$2,814,203	$3,769,469	$5,195,519	$7,817,906	$8,883,020

Even great leaders struggle to keep going sometimes. Harrison has created a lot of momentum, yet it may be decades before everyone will be served with clean water. Finding a story to fuel charity: water again also compelled the hearts of donors to give. The story about Letikiros helped Harrison fall in love with what he is doing all over again, bringing the energy for another long haul.

charity: water Venture Scape Summary

When charity: water founder Scott Harrison felt called to bring clean water to the world, his friends were reluctant to support him. To them, charities didn't use their funds effectively. Harrison embarked on a venture to reinvent how charities raise funds, pledging to communicate transparently how charity: water's funds would be spent and promising donors that all their money would go to the cause of bringing clean water to those who have none.

01

Party planner Scott Harrison realizes his life has no purpose or meaning. He applies to several nonprofits and is rejected by all but one. That nonprofit, Mercy Ships, accepts him as a photographer in Africa. He has an epiphany there that many problems would be alleviated if people had clean water.

He returns to New York determined to make a difference.

02

He asks friends and family to donate to a charity instead of giving him birthday gifts.

03

His friends are skeptical because they believe giving to charity is like putting money in a black box and that no one is held accountable.

04

He resolves to create a model in which 100 percent of charity: water's proceeds will go toward digging wells and he'll provide proof of how donors' money is put to work.

05

Harrison hosts a party and his friends commit $159,000 to building wells.

06

When the wells are built, charity: water sends photos of the wells to donors, even to those who spent only twenty dollars. Word begins to spread and funds begin to pour in.

07

Harrison decides to have local partners dig wells and charity: water uses storytelling to raise funds to send to them.

DREAM   LEAP

08

People begin to challenge Harrison on the effectiveness of the 100 percent promise. As the account for water projects fills up, the account to cover operations runs dry.

09

Harrison sends notes to as many founders and entrepreneurs as he knows and tells them the charity: water story, asking them to help cover operations.

10

He receives a large donation for $1 million, which gives him enough resources for a year.

11

He creates a formal program called The Well, in which businesses and entrepreneurs make a multiyear financial commitment to cover charity: water's overhead.

12

Harrison travels to businesses, hosts dinners, and collaborates with The Well members to keep the innovative and entrepreneurial spirit of charity: water alive.

13

charity: water becomes the largest nonprofit in the United States focused on water. Even though they've reached more than five million people with clean water, they have plenty more to go.

14

Harrison rejuvenates his passion for water by visiting the family of a young woman who killed herself after carrying water all day. Her story ignites his passion to recommit to the long haul and bring clean water to a billion people.

∞

FIGHT   CLIMB   ARRIVE   (RE)DREAM

CHAPTER EIGHT

ARRIVE

—

Arrive

Moment of Reflection

You and your team have met a momentous milestone or crossed the finish line. In this fifth and last stage, it's time to declare wins, big or small. Recognize the hard work of your travelers and create opportunities for them to bask in their accomplishments.

You've arrived. You and your team have crossed the finish line. A significant milestone has been reached, capping perhaps one of the greatest journeys of your career (so far). Now it's time for you and your travelers to reflect on how you got here. Some leaders perceive partying as unproductive, and many deadline-driven organizations no sooner finish one big project than they are on to the next without acknowledging their previous achievement. But take this moment to pause and remember, to gather around the corporate campfire and tell tales about what just took place. Cast your big wins (and bloopers) in a warm glow of nostalgia that leaves your travelers feeling proud, happy, and grateful for the opportunity to be a part of this transformative experience.

Yet, to "arrive" doesn't necessarily mean you were victorious. Many times you simply need to call it quits and admit you've lost, yet still gather to recall what you've gained from the experience. Give a nod to the strong bonds forged in the foxhole during the toughest of times, and reiterate the common values and principles that held you together. Linger with the past long enough to pull insights into your folklore for the future. Torchbearers resurrect those memories and keep them alive in the collective consciousness.

If you succeeded, the committed ones will see it as a victory. But those who resisted will have to admit they were wrong. They may still dig in and say that the whole venture was stupid. On the flip side, if it actually does fail, the resisters may feel vindicated and happy about it.

If your venture was successful, congratulations—and a party—are in order for your travelers. If it wasn't, communicate the part you played in the demise, so your travelers can move on.

Understand What Your Travelers Are Feeling

Endings are bittersweet, and your travelers likely will feel mixed emotions now that your venture has reached its conclusion. You may find empathizing with the committed ones who share in your success easier than acknowledging the suffering of those who feel that the venture (or they) failed. You'll need to see both perspectives and speak to them with equal care to bring closure before beginning again.

If They Were **Committed**, You'll Hear Them Say . . .	Use **Motivating** Communication to Keep Them Going.
"Everyone gave their best." **"The sacrifices paid off."** **"We should be proud."**	As you look back on the journey and relive it with your travelers, draw out insights that will inspire and embolden them for future adventures. What triumphs did your travelers achieve? When did they struggle and when did they soar? When did the dream finally become real for them, and what helped them keep it alive during the long trek? Fuel fervor by appealing to their pride in achievement and celebrate how much wiser you are collectively. Acknowledge the sacrifices that made the win possible and honor those who helped you. Spread news of your victory and celebrate success with stories about your accomplishments and the impact they will have on the world.

If They Were **Resistant**, You'll Hear Them Say . . .	Use **Warning** Communication to Get Them Unstuck.
"That was a complete failure." **"It was a bad idea from the start."** **"I never wanted any of this."**	Not all stories have happy endings; sometimes your venture fails and you can't be overly simplistic or rosy. Losing at your own game probably left a bruise or two, so don't hide mistakes or the damage they caused. Be realistic about where you landed and why. What sacrifices were so courageously made? How were travelers tested, challenged, and changed even by failure? Own up to your own role in the debacle so people can move on. Acknowledge those who suffered in the struggle and lift them out of despair with evidence of learnings that equip them for your next journey together.

ARRIVE SPEECHES

In the Arrive stage, giving a speech is akin to plopping your hands into a square of wet cement on Hollywood Boulevard. You are effectively logging your venture's achievements, or lack thereof, in the historical record. Your words will leave a mark that lasts long beyond this moment, searing memories of the journey into your travelers' minds.

Motivate with "Victory" Speeches

Now is the time to look back and linger over the highlights of your journey. It's especially important to acknowledge the significance of the moment when arriving at your goal marks a historic achievement for you and your travelers. For instance, when Jawaharlal Nehru became the first prime minister of India after the country gained independence in 1947, he gave a speech to mark the occasion. He said:

> *"The appointed day has come—the day appointed by destiny—and India stands forth again, after long slumber and struggle, awake, vital, free and independent. The past clings on to us still in some measure and we have to do much before we redeem the pledges we have so often taken. Yet the turning point is past, and history begins anew for us, the history which we shall live and act and others will write about."*

Allow your travelers to savor their success by honoring what they have accomplished. Reflect on the journey and relive the trials and triumphs to show how far you've come. Acknowledge that the old reality could have led to ruin but you've transformed and emerged victorious to a new reality.

///

Turnarounds are never easy and certainly not fast, and the recovery of Ford Motor Company is no exception. When Alan Mulally took over as CEO in 2006, he outlined an ambitious plan for restructuring Ford to return it to a profitable status. The plan would take three years (and a loan) to achieve. After a series of sacrifices, from

Ford CEO Alan Mulally at New York International Auto Show

product discontinuations to staff layoffs, the company became profitable again. Mulally celebrated the win at the New York International Auto Show in 2010.

> **What Is:** *"It's going really well. . . . In the third quarter of last year all of the Ford operations around the world returned to profitability during the worst recession that we've ever had."*

> **What Could Be:** *"Ford will continue to be competitive with the best companies in the world. . . . We have the best product lineup that Ford has ever had."*

> **New Bliss:** *"We have a cost structure that allows us to make [our cars] and the profitability goes to the company so we can continue to invest in Ford . . . and not use our precious taxpayer money."*

On the fiftieth anniversary of the World Wildlife Fund (WWF), CEO Carter Roberts delivered a keynote address that surveyed the WWF's accomplishments and reiterated its commitment to securing the world's natural resources.

What Is: *"Half a century ago, our founders came together with the dream to build an unprecedented global network to save the world's great animals from extinction."*

What Could Be: *"At the end of the day, nature is not just achingly beautiful; it's also fundamental to meet our needs—it has value. And this kind of epiphany is spreading from the coasts of East Africa to the forests of Nepal to board rooms of the world's biggest companies."*

New Bliss: *"Look hard enough and you'll find this kind of determination in great abundance, in our staff, in our Board, in our volunteers, in our partners and in the faces of the extraordinary leaders with whom we work on the ground. I have faith that together we can and will save this remarkable planet and ourselves."*

Warn with "Surrender" Speeches

Despite all your efforts to realize the dream, you may have run up against such impossible odds that victory cannot be yours. When U.S. president Abraham Lincoln delivered his second inaugural address, the nation was in the midst of the bloody, four-year Civil War. He encouraged Americans to resolve their differences and surrender to the virtues of compromise, goodwill, and reconciliation so that the nation could move forward. He told them, *"With malice toward none, with charity for all . . . let us strive on to finish the work we are in, to bind up the nation's wounds to . . . achieve and cherish a just and lasting peace."*

When staring into the face of defeat, your travelers need to hear the truth so they can accept it and prepare to move on. Now is the time to throw in the towel and admit failure. Humbly apologize for what has happened, share the lessons you've learned, and assure them you've put systems in place so it won't happen again.

///

In 1985, Coca-Cola changed its popular soda formula, causing a public firestorm against the brand. Don Keough, president of the company at the time, gave a speech to admit failure and win back the support of consumers.

What Is: *"All of the time and money and skill poured into consumer research on the new Coca-Cola could not measure or reveal the depth and abiding emotional attachment to original Coca-Cola felt by so many people. They said that they wanted the original taste of Coca-Cola back and they wanted it soon."*

What Could Be: *"Yesterday afternoon, after Coca-Cola Classic was announced, we received [thousands of] calls. The overwhelming reaction of consumers is one of excitement. Most of them are emotional, honestly, many in tears, but their message is the same: We're glad to have our old friend back."*

New Bliss: *"Well what does this really mean? It only means what we say—that our boss is the consumer."*

In a speech promoting his book, *Where Does It Hurt?*, athenahealth CEO Jonathan Bush encouraged entrepreneurs to reform inefficiencies in the American health-care system. He told his audience how athenahealth eventually rose from the ashes of a failed venture after he experienced the bureaucratic inefficiencies in health care firsthand.

What Is: *"Back in the 1990s, I tried to reimagine the birth experience. . . . We took credentialed and skilled midwives to provide a safe, comfortable customer experience for mothers. We didn't just treat pregnancy as an illness to be eradicated quickly. Customers loved our service. . . . But we crashed and burned. We didn't have the data to prove to insurers how we generated savings. We were caught in the tangled knot of codes and regulations and outdated software. So insurers stopped offering Athena on their plans, even though we provided a service customers preferred over other options."*

What Could Be: *"In 1998, we made a pivot and became a back office company, athenahealth. Out of our troubles came a deep desire to make disrupting the*

system easier for others and we developed cloud-based software that became the
cornerstone of our new business."

New Bliss: *"Today athenahealth is a corporation worth more than four billion*
dollars, growing more than thirty percent a year. I'm not telling you this to sell you
my service—I want to give us all hope that making meaningful change in health
care is possible."

ARRIVE STORIES

To add vitality and vivid detail to the speeches that you give in this stage, include
stories within your speech to amplify its emotional power. Tales of travelers who
made great sacrifices all along your venture help everyone to relish the fact that
they've survived it or reflect upon and learn from their struggles.

Motivate with "Savor the Win" Stories

Ah, the sweet taste of success. Like the montage sequence in the movie *Up* that
replays happy moments from the life of a man and his beloved wife, your travelers,
too, want to relive the highlights of their lives. Take this opportunity to shine a light
on the times when they grasped victory, by retelling their feat in all its glory. Remind
them of what you have collectively accomplished by highlighting specific anecdotes
that illustrate the impact they had. How have you made your mark on the world,
and why are you all greater for having taken this journey together?

///

When talking about World Wildlife Fund accomplishments on their fifty-year
anniversary, CEO Carter Roberts highlighted the wins that his organization had
achieved, including bringing a beloved species back from the brink of extinction.
The animals that WWF has saved throughout its history have become iconic
symbols of environmental success.

"At the beginning of this past century white rhinos numbered less than 50 and black rhinos plummeted from 70,000 to just 2,000 in 1994. World Wildlife Fund mounted campaigns across two continents. With others we created parks, hired guards, and shut down poachers. Today we have 4,700 black rhinos and 15,000 white rhinos roaming the Earth. This was the first of many victories."

IBM's founder, Thomas Watson Sr., led the company through times of economic opportunity and times of scarcity, the worst of which occurred during the Great Depression. Many businesses had failed, but IBM survived in large part because of the determination of its sales team. During his address at the 1933 sales meeting, Watson used the story of his sales team's overcoming great odds to inspire them to keep striving.

"The officers of the One Hundred Percent Club have come into this business since 1929. . . . They found out that they had to get out and hustle. They had to do things right. They had to be on the job. The reason they were up there on the platform instead of some of the older men is that many of the older men came into the business in boom times, when it was just a question of going around and taking orders. . . . They learned to sail the boat in smooth water. . . . There never was a good sailor developed in fair weather. It is during storms when the seas are running high and the going is rough that you develop your sailors. And that is how you develop men. You have to test men just as you test metal. And, by Jove, men are getting the test today. . . . As long as you run on that basis, whether in good times or bad times, you are running on the right basis."

Warn with "Learn the Lesson" Stories

Learn the Lesson stories are some of the hardest to tell. Admitting you've failed puts imperfections on display. Telling a story about failure reminds travelers not to take that route again. Transparently own the role you played and what you learned from the failure. Travelers will follow a leader who admits that he or she has failed before they'll follow one who pretends to be perfect.

After an independent investigation revealed the mismanagement that caused ignition switch recalls and customer deaths, General Motors CEO Mary Barra addressed her employees in a televised speech. She told the whole story of the *"pattern of incompetence and neglect"* and individuals' failure *"to disclose critical pieces of information that could have fundamentally changed the lives of those impacted by a faulty ignition switch."* She didn't hold back in describing her company's failures in detail. But instead of telling her employees to push this failure story under the rug, she said that it should remain in their memories forever as a warning:

"I hate sharing this with you as much as you hate hearing it. But I want you to hear it. In fact, I never want you to forget it. This is not just another business crisis for GM. We aren't simply going to fix this and move on. We are going to fix the failures in our system—that I promise. In fact, many are already fixed. And we are going to do the right thing for the affected parties. But I never want to put this behind us. I want to keep this painful experience permanently in our collective memories. I don't want to forget what happened because I—and I know you—never want this to happen again."

Mary Barra, CEO of General Motors, delivers a speech to employees.

Jack Ma has launched eight successful businesses and in the process he's learned some hard lessons. He tells the story of how one of his companies, Alibaba, navigated a steep drop in its stock price and what that loss taught him about where to invest and whom to trust.

"[Businesses] believe that shareholders are number one. You only think about how to make your stock go up. But no shareholders can be trusted. . . . Before our IPO a lot of shareholders came to say, 'Jack, we are long-term shareholders, please give us more shares, we will keep them.' The day of our IPO our share price went from 13.50 in Hong Kong dollars up to 40 dollars in 24 hours, without us doing anything good. Then the financial crisis came and our share price went from 40 dollars to 3 dollars, without us doing anything bad. . . . Most shareholders are share traders; how can you trust them? So rely on your customers because they stay with you, grow up with you, and give you money, hope, and support. Secondly, rely on and serve your employees because . . . they make all your dreams realized."

ARRIVE CEREMONIES

Words are a potent way to acknowledge endings, but actions matter just as much. In this, the final stage of your venture, you need to ceremonially bring closure by gathering to party like there's no tomorrow or to part ways with the past.

Motivate with "Celebrate Wins" Ceremonies

When the Apollo 11 crew returned from their moon landing, astronauts were honored with several parades, state dinners, and awards, including President Nixon giving them the Presidential Medal of Freedom. Then they went on a forty-five-day international "Giant Leap" tour to twenty-five countries. Whatever your victory may be—winning a sale, displacing the competition, finishing an initiative, expanding into new territory, or meeting a financial goal—the win is grounds for celebration. Don't miss the opportunity to revel in success; suppressing celebration undermines morale just when it should be at a peak. Failing to celebrate will be widely perceived as callous lack of appreciation of a job well done. Victory should be sweet.

Throw a party (or at least ring a bell, doggone it). Fostering celebration reinforces camaraderie, recharges people, and offers a wonderful opportunity to highlight the reasons for success. You don't have to wait for final victory; you should also celebrate as teams reach milestones along the way. If celebrations burst out spontaneously, don't squash them. The only thing worse than squelching a spontaneous gathering of joy is not recognizing an accomplishment that needs to be celebrated.

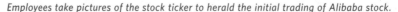

Employees in China celebrated Alibaba's U.S. public offering in front of a facade of the New York Stock Exchange. Employees took pictures in front of the fake backdrop and late in the evening, as the exchange was about to open in New York, green, white, and red fireworks broke out above the Alibaba campus. The 1980s pop song "Alibaba" blared on repeat as employees strolled through cutouts of the Empire State Building, yellow taxicabs, and a Wall Street sign. As the market opened, a website projected the trades on a large wall as revelers shouted and took pictures of the stock's successful results. Said one Alibaba alumnus, *"This is as exciting as having a new baby. It's a page in the history of China and the Internet."*

Employees take pictures of the stock ticker to herald the initial trading of Alibaba stock.

Steve Jobs wanted the signature of each member of the original Macintosh team engraved on the inside of the case of every Mac as a tribute to their work. Most customers would never see it, but the team took pride in knowing that their names appeared there. Andy Hertzfeld recalled, *"We held a special signing party where a large piece of drafting paper was placed on the table to capture our signatures. Steve gave a short speech about artists signing their work, and then cake and champagne were served."*

Warn with "Concede Defeat" Ceremonies

What do you do if your strategy is off base and you're not progressing as planned? Don't cover up mistakes; instead, expose them and explore your options for course correction. Sometimes you've just hit a stumbling block, but other times defeat is catastrophic and your whole plan must be scrapped. Admitting defeat is anathema to many leaders, but continuing to fight a losing battle can lead to failure, while retreating and mounting a new charge with a new plan might allow you to ultimately prevail. If you fail to concede defeat, you'll also likely face increasing desertions and lose trust. Your troops know when the fight is hopeless, and their frustration will build if they feel they're being thrown into the breach for a cause that's clearly lost. Conceding defeat is the first step in regrouping so you can start over. It gives the organization permission to hit the reset button. You can all collect your thoughts, assess the damage, formulate a new plan, and reload reserves for beginning again.

///

In 2004, Oracle acquired its rival PeopleSoft after eighteen months of a contentious hostile takeover battle. Oracle's plan was to discontinue use of the PeopleSoft software and move all the PeopleSoft clients over to Oracle's software, but the PeopleSoft board had fought valiantly to prevent this outcome. PeopleSoft resorted to threatening to use a "poison pill"—flooding the stock market with new PeopleSoft shares—if Oracle sought a 20 percent stake in the company. The move would have made PeopleSoft stock too expensive, even for cash-rich Oracle. When the two companies finally did strike a deal, both sides had to make concessions. Oracle paid more for the company and committed to continuing to offer and service PeopleSoft's software, and PeopleSoft didn't flood the market with new shares. For those at

Oracle, the takeover was a great victory. But PeopleSoft leaders felt very differently. Rather than officially announcing the deal to employees through the common method of an earnings call, executives chose to tell employees in person at a company meeting. They sobbed as they read their prepared messages. Employees wore black and turned a PeopleSoft sign into a makeshift shrine of flowers, candles, and company memorabilia.

The PeopleSoft sign becomes a makeshift memorial for employees mourning the company's takeover by Oracle.

In 1922, Ford's Model T began to see significant competition from the Lincoln, which had luxurious touches that made it one of the most prestigious and stylish cars on the market at a time when American consumers wanted to show off their prosperity. Consumers were willing to pay for flashier cars, but Henry Ford didn't want to change the classic model. By 1926, Ford had not made any significant changes to the Model T other than more color choices. Even though Henry's son, Edsel, had been urging his father to update the Model T, Henry refused. He believed

Henry and Edsel Ford drive the Model T off the assembly line.

he'd already created the perfect car that should last owners a lifetime. He had so completely misjudged consumer demand that sales dropped almost by half. Henry finally conceded that Edsel was right, and on May 26, 1927, he and Edsel ceremonially drove the fifteen millionth car off the assembly line together and closed the plant for six months to retool for manufacturing a new car. Edsel had designed a stylish replacement. And momentum built! In December 1927, ten million people stood in line for two days just to get a glimpse of the new Model A (all the Ford cars had been named alphabetically and Ford went back to the letter A to signify a new beginning). So the Ford ceremony was a concession ceremony for Henry and a victory for Edsel.

ARRIVE SYMBOLS

Arrive symbols reflect on the journey's wins and losses. Motivating symbols could be spoils picked up along the way or the receipt of the prize that motivated you to go for the win in the first place. Warning symbols reflect disappointment in having fought hard and still lost.

Motivating Symbols

- **Visual:** When Apple launched the new iMac, the name paid homage to the original Mac, which enclosed the monitor and processor in one case, just as the iMac does. The image on the screen said "Hello Again" in similar handwriting as in the original Mac "Hello" ads.

- **Auditory:** In the early days of Amazon, a bell would ring in the office every time someone made a purchase, and employees would gather around to see if they knew the customer. As the company grew, this bell had to be disabled because of the frequency with which it started to ring.

- **Spatial:** In Pixar's expansive two-story lobby (a.k.a. "the Atrium"), life-size versions of *Monsters, Inc.* characters greet employees and visitors at the door, and a display case shows Pixar's long line of Oscar, Golden Globe, and Annie Award statuettes. Also, prints on Pixar's walls show scenes from its films to celebrate its employees' accomplishments.

- **Physical:** An Ekin (Nike spelled backward) is an official company storyteller. Each Ekin undergoes an almost military-like nine-day training regime at Nike's headquarters. As a sign of completion, Ekins go to tattoo parlors to ink a Nike swoosh on their ankle or calf to symbolize the fact that they know Nike frontward and backward.

Warning Symbols

- **Visual:** After consumers protested when Coca-Cola changed its formula, aluminum cans of the classic Coke product became a symbol to everyone that customers can reverse a corporate decision.

- **Auditory:** During his apology speech, Coca-Cola president Don Keogh read letters from angry customers who said, *"Changing Coke is like God making the grass purple,"* *"Dear Chief Dodo, what ignoramus decided to change the formula of Coke?,"* and *"I don't think I'd be more upset if you burned the flag."* The letters added levity to the apologetic tone of the announcement.

- **Spatial:** When they heard that Oracle was going to acquire their company, PeopleSoft employees created a makeshift burial ground. They burned candles, placed photos, discarded branded memorabilia, and wrote letters that they laid next to the PeopleSoft sign.

- **Physical:** In Japan and other places, the crane is a symbol of joy and good fortune. But after atomic bombs fell in 1945, the crane took on new meaning. A girl named Sadako Sasaki committed to folding one thousand origami cranes as a statement of peace. Unfortunately, radiation from the bombs caused her to contract leukemia and she died before she could finish the task. Her classmates folded the remaining cranes in her honor, and today folding origami cranes is used as a symbolic act of remembrance.

SUMMARY

Endings are just as packed with feeling as beginnings, and this moment should amplify the emotions of your travelers. Provide an outlet for travelers to express all that's inside them—to cheer and clap, hug and cry, or sit in reverent silence while memories of the journey wash over them. The process of making a dream come true can feel transcendent, especially if your troops had to overcome great odds to realize your vision. As plans shifted right under their feet, they had to make sacrifices that felt harrowing at the time. By recounting the brave actions of your troops, you honor their achievements and celebrate the camaraderie and determination forged during the difficult days. Looking back also teaches important lessons to the travelers who may lead your next expedition. The next generation of adventurers will learn from your reflections on the defeats and triumphs and imagine how they might respond when faced with a similar venture.

Steve Nedvidek, Chick-fil-A's innovation and design specialist, persuades employees to practice innovation.

Chick-fil-A

Grabbing the number-one spot in your industry is no easy feat. Holding on to that spot requires a commitment to innovation, plus it rewards those who help get you there.

Recognize the Roots of Innovation

Truett Cathy, the founder of Chick-fil-A, established a rich history of innovation at his company decades ago. He turned his ideas into action: In 1946, he and his brother, Ben, opened their first restaurant. Then in the early 1960s, Truett developed a recipe for the chicken sandwich and came up with the name and logo for his new brand. He opened his first mall restaurant in 1967 and pioneered a unique licensing agreement for Chick-fil-A franchisees. In the mid-1980s, he chose to move Chick-fil-A out of the malls, as the "malling of America" was quickly tapering off. He anticipated trends and guided Chick-fil-A to become a successful regional chain in the U.S.

As Chick-fil-A scaled to accommodate growth and deliver a consistent customer experience, Truett built an operating model that rewarded consistency. Employees put their energy into optimizing efficiency and execution. The company began to hire employees who could get things done well. They hired responsibility-minded employees who were motivated to keep things moving along well and at scale. A mind-set of "don't mess it up" began to permeate as the staff made continual, incremental improvements to process.

With the steady, calculated growth of the chain, Chick-fil-A became a target for competitors entering the chicken sandwich market. One global hamburger chain started to experiment with a southern chicken sandwich with sweet tea on its menu and a local chain in Atlanta created a model that borrowed enough from Chick-fil-A to feel similar but different enough to be novel. Chick-fil-A went from the hunter to the hunted.

As the CEO torch was passed from Truett to his son Dan, executive leadership quickly realized that future growth would depend largely on how quickly the company could move away from just being a culture of continual improvement and transform into one valuing innovation. But innovation is messy and Chick-fil-A's deep-seated "don't mess it up" mind-set would require the business to adapt drastically.

Open Mind-sets to Innovation

Dream ceremony: ▶
Immerse Deeply

To research and be inspired by other innovators, a team of executives traveled around the country in 2008, visiting the innovation centers of Lucasfilm, Pixar, Google, Stanford d.school, and Hewlett-Packard. Upon their return, they held an innovation summit at Savannah College of Art and Design in Atlanta, where they built mock-ups of potential ideas for their own center. After negotiations and several rounds of budget revisions and architectural plans, Chick-fil-A opened a beautiful, large innovation center named Hatch.

Leap ceremony: ▶
Pledge Commitment

Leadership needed to convey to employees that it's okay to try new things at Hatch. Instead of a traditional ribbon-cutting ceremony, the VP of design and construction stood on a lift fifteen feet in the air and dropped three paint-filled eggshells onto the floor. The ceremonial act was a dramatic statement that Hatch was a different kind of work environment, where people could, and should, be breaking things, taking risks, and getting messy in the pursuit of innovation. The creative environment in

Paint-filled eggs splatter on the floor of Hatch, symbolizing that it's okay to get messy.

Hatch significantly differs from their corporate headquarters, where suits and ties have long been the norm. The splatters from Hatch's grand opening are preserved in a protective Plexiglas case to this day.

Next, CEO Dan Cathy gave a speech giving permission to employees to break with the past and now take risks and fail. After that, the vice president of menu strategy gave a speech, saying, *"I hope this symbolizes Chick-fil-A's approach to keeping the business relevant. We talk about reinventing continuously. Preserving the core but stimulating progress. This is the facility that's going to help us stimulate progress."* After him, the innovation and design specialist talked about the building as the place where employees will see and shape the future. He pulled a story from the past to reinforce that innovation is in Chick-fil-A's heritage as he recalled, *"Innovation has been going on since the founding of this business. Truett's innovation lab was his first restaurant. His customers helped drive him along the way. And so, this is your innovation center."*

◀ Leap speech:
Renunciation

◀ Leap speech: Pursuit

◀ Dream story:
Heed the Call

Right: Employees throw paint-filled eggs onto canvases.
Left: Paint-splattered canvases hang in the Hatch lobby.

Leap ceremony: Pledge Commitment ▶

Commit symbol: Visual ▶

After the speeches, more than 250 staff members threw paint-filled eggs onto canvases, which now hang in the reception lobby as art pieces. This mess-it-up ceremony empowered everyone to play a role in innovation. One executive said the launch *"was a one-of-a-kind, colorful touchstone moment."*

The Struggle to Change Minds

Leap ceremony: ▶
Pledge Commitment

Opening Hatch signaled the company's commitment to innovate, but leaders quickly realized that the real need was to help employees embrace an innovative mind-set. Employees didn't know why they needed to innovate, how to utilize the space, or how to prioritize projects. Hatch required a mind-set that was counterintuitive to the culture, which rewarded steadfastness and efficiency more than problem-solving or challenging the status quo.

To ensure the program's success, the executive committee asked a few executives to relinquish all of their responsibilities and stay narrowly focused on nurturing the employees into innovators. Steve Nedvidek, a senior manager of marketing, moved to Hatch as innovator in residence and was charged with coaching, teaching, and training innovation and design thinking to speed up the adoption.

The first thing Nedvidek did was ask fifty employees some questions. He asked whether Chick-fil-A had an innovative culture; the staff's answer came back with a near unanimous no. He also asked them how they defined innovation. He got fifty different answers, signaling that the company lacked a common language for innovation. The innovation team worked on a definition to share with everyone: "transforming new ideas into business value."

> *"It was pretty clear that just having a space to innovate was not going to be enough. Launching Hatch made a statement, but we needed momentum to get up the hill,"* Nedvidek says. *"It took us trial and error to determine the right levers to pull in order to shift a risk-averse mind-set. The executive committee, especially Dan Cathy, had our backs. Executive commitment took the fear of failure away."*

◄ **Fight ceremony:** Demystify Threats

Leaders Model Risk Taking

Nedvidek's innovation team started designing training programs, bringing in external innovators to speak, creating resources (tools, techniques, materials, and a website), setting up learning field trips, and streaming podcasts to infuse employees with innovative mind-sets.

To help employees get over their fear of failing, Nedvidek had executives tell their own stories of failure. Two senior VPs delivered a presentation admitting they had taken risks and failed. In a video speech distributed to employees, the senior vice president of finance said, *"Clearly to me, one of the big risks for Chick-fil-A is that we avoid risk, in order to try to hang on to what we have, we're fearful of small failures."* Yes, the finance guy said that. Another executive identified a key roadblock in the culture that may stop them from embracing innovation, saying, *"I think there's a general impression among many at Chick-fil-A that everything has to be perfect. But, if you expect everything to be perfect, you're going to be really frustrated and you're going to clamp down on the ability to give people room to experiment."* Then the executives shared the story of a risk they took in the 1990s when they opened a Chick-fil-A in South Africa. It was not successful. The senior vice president of operations added, *"We learned a lot about international business. . . . We had a chance for people individually to learn and*

◄ **Climb story:** Lose the Way

grow." The executives were willing to be transparent about one of their own failures and the value they got out of it. They modeled for employees that it is okay to take risks.

Creating Opportunities to Learn

As part of the transformation plan, Nedvidek delivered talks to different departments whose leaders wanted their teams infused with an innovative mind-set. In one talk to emerging leaders, he explained, *"We expect you to take risks, we expect you to fail. We expect you to keep your foot on the gas and move the business forward. And if you do, you will continue Truett's legacy of innovation."* Nedvidek explained to the emerging leaders that CEO Dan Cathy and the executive committee made their commitment clear: *"They built us Hatch. And they expect us to use it. Believe me. We have had many conversations with [Dan] about the space. Dan doesn't want to see team meetings over there. He doesn't want people over there just so that they can wear jeans. He wants to see people working on moving the business forward. This isn't just a wish. This is a mandate."* Nedvidek told them they stimulate progress and foster new ideas because they *"have to be responsible for not just maintaining the lead, but increasing the lead."*

Dream story: Heed the Call ▶

Just as employees tried to embrace innovation, an unexpected roadblock reared its head: time management. Many long-term employees felt the burden of getting their day-to-day work done, leaving no time for innovation. They resisted participating due to schedule constraints, saying too much was competing for their time. During training, Nedvidek countered their concern with a story: *"My wife taught me a lesson when we first got married over 26 years ago. I would have lots of excuses for not doing something. I didn't have time. I forgot. I was distracted. Whatever. One day, she looked at me and said, 'Steve, people do what is important to them.' And she had me. And at work, if my staff sees it's not important to me, it likely won't be important to them. Make it important."*

Fight motivating: ▶
Overcome the Enemy

Tireless in communications, Nedvidek spoke at several department meetings, empathetically explaining that innovation was *"not just Truett's job. This is something that we are all expected to use and employ."* Then he pointed out the leaders in the room whose teams had started adopting innovation and taking risks. He commended them for shifting their teams' mind-sets.

After the first year of Hatch, Chick-fil-A put even more support in place to fuel an innovation mind-set, building more classes, custom events, and workshops, and developing a robust every-other-week Lunch & Learn series bringing in experts on innovation. As mind-sets began to shift, employee participation gained traction. The executive team regularly communicated to the Hatch staff, encouraging them to continue to battle the old mind-sets every day until they saw results.

Ideas Begin Hatching

Eventually, Chick-fil-A saw change. Projects of all types began emerging from Hatch, such as customer simulations, restaurant prototypes, and exciting new products and experiences for the customer. The number of requests from people wanting to launch projects and solve tough business problems skyrocketed. New-project meetings were popping up several times a week. Rapid prototypes of concepts were being constructed at a regular clip, workshops and classroom offerings had a waiting list, Lunch & Learn sessions overflowed, and employees started using the design thinking models on their own without the help of the innovation team.

Because innovation at Chick-fil-A will be a continually renewing goal, there will not be an exact moment when employees will be able to say they're done innovating. So instead, Hatch has designed and hosts a touchstone event twice a year: a staff-wide Innovation and Design Day. The atmosphere is electric with food and music. External keynote speakers from places such as Pixar, Lego, and *Wired* magazine inspire the team. All-staff workshops such as "How to Make Ideas Stick" and "Techniques to Generate Better Ideas" are packed. Employees can walk through a symposium of projects that are mock-ups of how things might look in the future.

◀ Dream ceremony:
Immerse Deeply

The Launch Wall at Hatch showcases innovative projects that were born there.

The displays showcase real projects, help employees see progress, and foster cross-departmental innovation.

Arrive ceremony: ▶
Honor the Heroes

The innovation team designed a space within Hatch to recognize projects and the people who put them through the system. Nedvidek hosts a ceremony during Innovation and Design Day in which projects are mounted on a Launch Wall. Individuals receive a plaque and executives express their thanks. The wall now features many completed projects. Assets from the projects are on display and the people creating transformation feel honored. A core Chick-fil-A tenet rewards the behavior the company wants repeated.

Arrive speech: Victory ▶

Dan Cathy attends most of the Innovation and Design Day events. In a speech at one, he reflected about the event, *"To keep the business healthy and the brand healthy, we've got to spin up our thinking—Hatch is the future of our business. I think of this as* *a . . . <u>museum of the future</u>. Anytime the museum of the future is ten times the size of the museum of the past, that's a good sign."*

Driving Innovation Deeper

What's one of Nedvidek's next biggest challenges? Dan Cathy has asked him to create a reward system that honors employees who fail. Fail big-time. Some may never feel comfortable failing, but Hatch is drawing risk takers in like a magnet. They know that as long as it's messy, they are innovating.

Because of the momentum of Hatch, the Chick-fil-A innovation team is planning to move out of their current building into a much larger space. They have arrived only to start again.

CEO Dan Cathy attends Hatch events to show his support for innovation.

Chick-fil-A Venture Scape Summary

Moving the Chick-fil-A culture from a mind-set that valued steady execution to one that celebrated risk taking required significant investment and support. To launch its innovation venture, CEO Dan Cathy plucked an executive out of his day-to-day job to focus solely on changing mind-sets, engaging employees in problem solving, and celebrating risky projects.

01

Executive committee and CEO realize the company culture rewards steady growth and perfection more than risk taking and innovation.

02

A team of executives travel around the country to immerse themselves in how other creative companies foster innovation. They build mock-ups of ideas for their own innovation hub.

03

Budgets and architectural plans are approved for an innovation center called Hatch.

04

Hatch launches with much fanfare. Eggs full of paint sully the Hatch floor to demonstrate that innovation is messy.

05

Employees are released to take risks and innovate.

DREAM   LEAP

06

Executives quickly realize that the greatest challenge is mind-sets deeply seated in the corporate culture.

07

Two execs narrowly focus on cultural transformation.

08

Executive committee and CEO repeatedly help employees master their fear of taking risks.

09

VPs recall stories of when they took risks and failed, giving permission to others to fail and learn from it.

10

Nedvidek builds a multifaceted communication plan with training, guest speakers, and executive support.

11

Nedvidek delivers several speeches a month to departments and leadership teams.

12

Nedvidek honors the leaders who are facilitating innovation with their teams.

13

Innovation and Design Day is set up with packed workshops, symposiums to showcase prototyped ideas, and speeches from executives.

14

Completed projects, their artifacts, and a plaque with team member names are placed on a Launch Wall honoring projects completed at Hatch.

FIGHT   CLIMB   ARRIVE   ∞ (RE)DREAM

———

(re)Dream

Moment of Disruption

The Beat Goes On (and On)

Leaders are naturally restless. Just as your arrival seems imminent and your vision will become reality, a new dream begins to stir inside you. The very nature of the Venture Scape implies that you may see a new vision, or (re)dream, before your current one is realized. It's okay to percolate another dream before your travelers have accomplished the current one. In fact, (re)dreaming is healthy because an organization's longevity relies on being in a constant state of change and renewal.

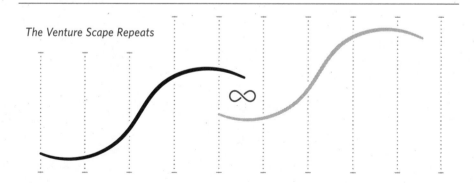

The Venture Scape Repeats

Ray Anderson reimagined Interface as a regenerative enterprise that gave back more than it took long before his company achieved its initial vision of becoming sustainable. Dr. Martin Luther King Jr. set his sights on the greater cause of human rights while struggles for basic civil rights raged on. Steve Jobs had envisioned Apple's Digital Hub strategy before developers were done migrating to Mac OS X.

Sometimes a new dream comes to you so suddenly that it startles you. When Anderson realized he was plundering the earth, the revelation felt like a sword in his chest—he couldn't ignore it. It's as if you were once blind and now you see. Other times dreams come from within. A new idea starts to form inside you and as you run it by others, they help you shape and refine it. Or a new dream may come out of necessity because the current venture is leading to your demise and you realize you will fail unless you change direction. Regardless of where that dream comes from, it holds the power to change the world if you have the tenacity to keep chasing it.

Every venture you undertake is part of a larger story. If you zoom out, way out, you'll see that each venture is just one small part of a larger tale with many ventures nested within it. When these ventures are strung together they create eras, long spans of time that mark the major thresholds an organization crosses throughout its lifetime.

These eras—which may be months, years, or decades in length—combine to create an epic tale, a continuous arc of transformation that keeps the organization and its ideas alive and healthy long into the future. Some public companies, such as GE,

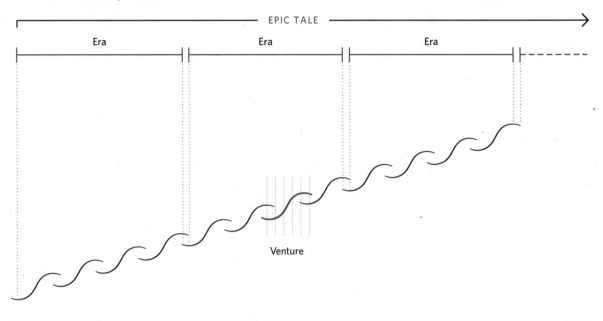

Ventures Become an Epic Tale

Each venture leads to the next, stringing together into an epic tale that moves your travelers from one era to the next.

IBM, and Ford, have crossed the hundred-year mark. Enduring companies like these have developed the ability to survive significant era shifts that surge them forward in wholly new directions.

Shifts in eras may be driven by the leader, such as when you create a new product category or enter new markets. Other times, new eras are ushered in by things out of your control, such as sudden shifts in customer sentiment, economic downturns, or internal decline. Sometimes your dream is a small, incremental shift and other times it is a direction-changing revelation.

Companies such as American Express have navigated several eras. Here are just a few of the major transitions that have occurred since it was founded:

American Express Eras

Freight Era	Money Order Era	Travel Era	International Era	Credit Card Era
1850–1881	1882–1918	1915–1919	1920–1958	1958–present
Founded by merging two express freight companies	Launched to compete with the U.S. Post Office and divested railroad freight	Company became synonymous with luxury global travel	Mergers led to global expansion	Launched premium credit card service

All's Well that Ends Well

Crossing into a new era can be incredibly disorienting for your travelers because of the magnitude of the change it brings. These dramatic, rather than incremental, changes make people feel like their world has turned upside down. Jumping from one venture to the next is hard, but moving to a new era is even more disruptive, and your travelers will have a tougher time breaking with their past when the future is massively different from what they know.

Because new eras create endings for beloved products, processes or programs, and even leaders, you may need to make it clear when an era is ending, so your travelers can move on. You can do this by symbolically decommissioning speeches, stories, ceremonies, and symbols that don't align with where you're going. But you must do it carefully. Travelers hang on to sacred ideas and shared moments more fiercely than anything else. So don't blow up the ones that don't seem to be relevant, because even though they are lying dormant they may have hidden power to unite or incite travelers.

Investment Banking Era	Divest Era	Holding Company Era	TBD
1980–1986	1987–1994	2008–2009	What's next?
Acquired several financial services companies	Brought focus by divesting Lehman Brothers and others	Converted to a holding company after the 2008 financial crisis	Will they disrupt the future as electronic payment changes the credit card landscape?

Case in point: At Duarte, Inc., we launched a short venture called Shrewd Dude in the fall of 2013. We'd had a great year, but it was a close call as to whether we'd be able to pay out our profit-sharing plan or not. We decided to curb spending, announcing the Shrewd Dude initiative to assure we'd make our margins and be able to pay employees their share of the profit. We made our numbers that year, but failed to communicate that the venture had ended. Months into the next year, a manager who had been approved to hire a key position on her team still hadn't because she was still operating in the Shrewd Dude mind-set. As a result, her team was strained for resources from a heavy workload. Even short and simple ventures need closure before starting a new venture.

Letting go may be tough for your travelers. Be explicit in marking an ending so they can begin again.

Look Back Before You Leap Forward

If you pull from familiar speeches, stories, ceremonies, and symbols, your communications will replace chaos, fear, and ambiguity with clarity, confidence, and hope. Show your travelers how the venture you're pursuing now connects back to the actions you've taken in the past to reassure them that this is the continuation of a plan that has brought success before. Doing so requires frequent, strategically planned communications plus intentional connections to the past to build a bridge that eases their crossing.

Hidden in every organization and culture are the communication tools you need to navigate these dramatic changes well. If you empathetically study the culture of your organization and your customers, you can build a toolkit of meaningful speeches, stories, ceremonies, and symbols from the past. Then consciously amplify the ones that hold potent meaning and align with your vision, and diminish the ones that may cause resistance in the future. Respecting the heritage and power of these elements of your folklore will set you up for success in the future.

> *"IBM has reinvented itself many times. But through it all, its DNA, its soul remained intact. . . . Its revolutionary idea was to define and run a company by a set of strongly held beliefs."*
> —Sam Palmisano, IBM chairman and CEO

A torchbearer must curate the past to communicate during the transition from venture to venture and era to era. Understanding how the future is connected to the past helps travelers make sense of the events happening around them and makes the new world feel somewhat familiar and less scary.

When IBM started a new era of services by introducing Smarter Planet in 2008, those who'd traveled with IBM over the years felt resonance with the concept right away because it was rooted in the company's past. When Sam Palmisano became CEO in 2003, he dug into IBM's archives in search of a vision. He spent hours poring over speeches given nearly ninety years earlier by the company's founder, Thomas

Watson Sr. Watson believed that engaged and intelligent workers could accomplish great things.

In IBM's archives Palmisano unearthed the story about how Watson conducted weekly morning meetings of sales managers. When the managers failed to come up with any good ideas about how to improve the business, Watson was so frustrated that he strode to the front of the room and said, *"The trouble with every one of us is that we don't think enough. We don't get paid for working with our feet. We get paid for working with our heads."* He then lectured them for ten minutes on the usefulness of thinking, writing "Think" on an easel, and that gave him the idea of making "Think" the company's slogan. He had it posted in bold letters on the conference room wall the following morning.

The slogan fit the mission of IBM perfectly: to create machines that help people think. The word *think* symbolized the core ethic that drove the company's success by encouraging everybody to be a thinker, from assembly line workers to engineers,

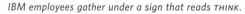

IBM employees gather under a sign that reads THINK.

from sales reps to mail clerks. This word was printed on notebooks and placards for desks, painted on walls, and engraved in stone walkways. You could see it just about anywhere you looked.

In that one word, *think,* Palmisano found the inspiration for the Smarter Cities program, which launched a new era of collaborative problem solving between IBM and government leaders. The Smarter Cities program evolved into the larger dream of Smarter Planet—a believable proposition because "Think" was so embedded in IBM's culture.

Similarly, orient your travelers to where you are in the history of your organization and how your ventures are in the service of an epic tale. Are you in the middle of a venture? Are you transitioning to a new era? Understanding the larger tale gives context so everyone knows whether you're starting something brand-new, supporting something that exists, or ending something whose time has come. In times of extreme upheaval, such as when your organization has had a near-death experience or when a longtime leader is transitioning out, you may need to look even farther back and into the historical narratives of your culture for insights and comfort.

> *"You can't connect the dots looking forward; you can only connect them looking backward."*
> —Steve Jobs

The Venture Transforms Your Travelers

With each new venture you pick up new skills that qualify you to tackle bigger problems and dream bigger dreams. Graham Weston simply wanted to renovate an old mall to create a new Rackspace campus, which turned into the dream of reinvigorating San Antonio with high-tech jobs. Steve Jobs, who had been ousted at Apple, returned as a stronger leader because of his experiences at NeXT and Pixar, and as a result he tackled one of the greatest reinventions of a business in history.

As you and your travelers trek along, you, too, experience transformative moments. These moments of inspiration (Dream), decision (Leap), bravery (Fight), endurance (Climb), and reflection (Arrive) test you and make you stronger. Remembering these moments gives you wisdom and skills to take on yet another venture together.

Apple CEO Steve Jobs onstage at Macworld, 1997

———

Apple

Launching a new era requires breaking with the past. When new leaders are charged with creating a new era, the first task may be to stabilize the organization before you have the space to create a new dream.

Apple Migrates from Mac Classic to Mac OS X

A computer's operating system (OS) is what controls its basic functions, such as the display on the screen and the types of tasks you can do. When personal computers first came out, the OS could only display lines of bright text on dark screen backgrounds. So, when Steve Jobs saw a demonstration at Xerox's Palo Alto Research Center of a computer mouse visually interacting with files on a desktop, he knew he'd seen the future of computing and launched Apple Computer Inc. When the Macintosh launched four years later, the revolutionary graphical user interface stunned the world and Apple gobbled up market share. The new OS features opened up a new world for software developers, who quickly jumped on board to write groundbreaking new applications to run on a Mac.

In the years between Jobs's ouster in 1986 and his return in 1996, Apple had lost some of its innovative energy and spent the decade trying to catch up with others by copying them instead of being different. Apple had three abortive attempts at modernizing its operating system to keep up with competitors such as Microsoft. Valuable developers suffered from each of Apple's failed attempts at OS updates, which cost them time and money. They became skeptical about continuing to develop on Apple's platform.

Apple stock value was falling and the company was losing money. Apple board member Gil Amelio stepped in as CEO to turn Apple around. One of the first things he did was concede defeat and kill the only remaining OS project because it was late and unstable.

Amelio looked outside of Apple for an existing OS to acquire and chose to purchase NeXT for $400 million. With that acquisition came Steve Jobs, who agreed to work with Apple as an adviser.

A Dream Is Declared

Only eighteen days after the acquisition of NeXT, Gil Amelio and Steve Jobs made their first public appearance together at a biannual event called Macworld Expo, in San Francisco. A lot was riding on this moment. Many developers were excited to see Jobs return, but still had questions and doubts about the company's strategy for the OS.

The two leaders' content and communication styles contrasted dramatically. Amelio chose to wing it instead of using the speech prepared by his speechwriter and ended up speaking for three hours instead of the hour the conference organizer had allotted him. Meanwhile, Jobs was like a caged cat backstage. By the time he was invited onstage, he delivered a tight, thirteen-and-a-half-minute talk in which he laid out his plan for Apple and the NeXT OS. Jobs was clear and confident, while Amelio rambled and appeared confused.

Dream speech: Vision ▶

Even though the audience was a blend of consumers and developers, Jobs understood the importance of luring developers to the NeXT OS, so he spoke with laser focus directly to them, as if they were the only ones in the room. Jobs used the word *developer* twenty-five times in his short speech; in contrast, Amelio said the word only a few times in the three hours he had the stage. Jobs knew if developers didn't begin writing software for the OS, Apple wouldn't succeed.

Jobs stated Apple's new vision:

> *"What we want to try to do is to provide relevant, compelling solutions that customers can only get from Apple. Because if we can't figure out how to do that, then I think there are a lot of other options for people to buy their computers from."*

This was a new direction for Apple because at this point, they were still copying the competition to catch up.

Jobs knew Apple would need the developers to make its platform second to none. He appealed to them by remarking on how developers put Apple on the map in the first place. He said, *"Apple can bring the marketing power to make the solution known, but it's the developers that bring the creative insight. . . . It's the developers that bring the market knowledge. It's the developers that bring that entrepreneurial energy."* He used a story from a decade earlier when PageMaker software combined with the LaserWriter printer to launch the entire desktop publishing marketplace.

◀ Dream story:
Ignore the Call

Xerox PARC, where Jobs first saw a computer mouse

Jobs then told a humbling story about his limited vision for the original Mac OS and how he failed to create as great an OS as he could have when the Mac originally launched, admitting, *"I'll tell you a story. When I went to Xerox PARC in 1979 and saw the original genesis of the graphical user interface there, they actually showed me three things. I was so blinded by the first that I didn't hang around to find out about the other two and it took me years to rediscover them."* Jobs confessed he didn't hang around long enough to see Xerox's modern OS or networking. He used the story to assure developers that the NeXT OS would build in all those features missing in the Mac OS.

Developers Resist the Dream

Once developers began to look under the hood of the NeXT OS, they were alarmed that it would force them to rebuild their software code from scratch. Large developers such as Microsoft and Adobe didn't want to jump in, and Jobs knew they needed to let off steam and get attached to the Apple brand again.

Since 1983, Apple has hosted an event catering only to developers, called the World Wide Developers Conference (WWDC). At WWDC 1997, five months after the NeXT acquisition, the developer community still expressed resistance to adopting the NeXT OS. To make matters worse, six months earlier, in Amelio's three-hour keynote, he had encouraged developers to continue developing applications using OS features that were killed by Jobs. This was not a happy crowd.

Empathetic listening ▶ To dissipate tension and help developers deal with the loss of features, Jobs chose not to deliver a splashy opening keynote. For this particular WWDC, he moved his own talk to the last spot on the last day of the event. He knew this moment needed to be a conversational Q&A format. He opened by stating,

Steve Jobs is animated during a Q&A at WWDC 1997.

"I wanted to come and just have a chat this morning. I know you've been getting lots of presentations all week, so I didn't want to do a big, fancy presentation, but what I want to do is to chat . . . and I want to talk about whatever you want to talk about. I have opinions on most things, so I figured if you just want to start asking some questions we'll go to some good places."

In a show of empathy, he allowed developers to drive the conversation.

Jobs remained calm and sincere as he was interrogated by angry developers who struggled to let go of the previous OS and commit to the new one. He was grilled about OS licensing (Jobs killed licensing), advertising (he refused to advertise), Newton (he'd killed it), and software (he'd killed several OS software features). They were all tough questions. Jobs stood behind his belief that the sacrifices, though hard on developers, were necessary to return Apple to health. Developers needed an outlet to mourn their loss and vent their frustrations.

Jobs apologized for the products that were sacrificed: *"I know some of you spent a lot of time working on stuff that we put a bullet in the head of. I apologize. I feel your pain, [laughter]*

◀ **Dream ceremony:**
Mourn the Loss

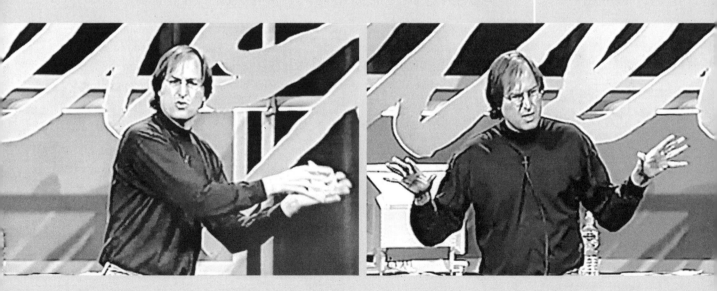

but Apple suffered for several years from lousy engineering management. [applause]"
He continued, *"The hardest thing is, when you think about focusing, you think, 'Well, focusing is saying yes.' No. Focusing is about saying no. Focusing is about saying no, and you've got to say, no, no, no. When you say no, you piss off people."*

Then an irate developer demeaned Jobs by saying, *"You don't know what you're talking about."* Jobs sat down to answer, paused for a long time, and then answered kindly, saying, *"One of the hardest things when you are trying to effect change is that people like this gentleman are right in some areas. . . . One of the things I've always found is that you've got to start with the customer experience and work backwards to the technology."* Jobs then reframed the argument by connecting the strategy back to what Apple customers (who are also the developers' customers) need: *"You can't start with the technology and try to figure out where you are going to try to sell it, and I've made this mistake probably more than anybody else in this room, and I've got the scar tissue to prove it, and I know that it's the case. As we have tried to come up with a strategy and a vision for Apple, it started with: What incredible benefits can we give to the customer? Where can we take the customer? . . . That's where Apple has got to get back to. . . ."* His commentary let developers know that he bore scars from <u>ignoring customers</u> in the past.

Leap story: Ignore the Reward ▶

Jobs listened to the developers' concerns at WWDC. He then tasked his team with beginning to modify the Mac operating system so developers' existing code could still be used and ported over to the new OS. Because it would take a year, he kept the project, code-named Carbon, a secret to avoid confusion in the developer community.

A Developer Makes the Leap

At Macworld 1997, a couple of months after Jobs became interim CEO, he closed his keynote with a major announcement he hoped would coax developers to continue to develop for the Macintosh. He announced that Microsoft was committing to develop on the Mac platform. Jobs knew a commitment from Microsoft could lure other developers to jump in.

Leap ceremony: ▶
Pledge Commitment

Bill Gates, CEO of Microsoft, joined via satellite, saying, *"Good morning. . . . It's very exciting to <u>renew our commitment</u> to the Macintosh."* Microsoft cemented its commitment by buying $150 million in nonvoting shares of Apple stock. At this time, Apple had cash reserves of $1.2 billion. The $150 million investment from Microsoft was more a ceremonial act of commitment than anything, communicating that Microsoft, Apple's largest developer, believed in Apple's future.

Apple Creates a Rallying Cry

That fall, Apple's "Think Different" campaign launched as a rallying cry to connect the hearts of customers, developers, and employees back to the brand. It reignited consumer affection for the Apple brand, which began to create demand for applications that developers were in the middle of building.

When Jobs prescreened the campaign with employees and developers on campus, he said: *"Apple's core value is that we believe that people with passion can change the world for the better. That's what we believe. . . . We've had the opportunity to work with people like that, with you, with software developers. . . . We believe that, in this world, people can change it together for the better. . . . So, we wanted to find a way to communicate this. A lot of things have changed. . . . But the values, the core values, those things shouldn't change. The things Apple believed in at its core are the same things that Apple really stands for today."* Jobs choked back tears as he continued, *"And, what we have is something that I'm very moved by. It honors those people who have changed the world. Some of them are living, some of them are not. But the ones who aren't, as you'll see, you know, that if they had ever used the computer, it would have been a Mac."* The ads featured black-and-white images of iconic creative people with the words "Think different" and the Apple logo. Connecting creative risk takers such as Albert Einstein, Alfred Hitchcock, and John Lennon to the Apple brand pulled on the symbols already deeply embedded in our cultural psyche and used visual shorthand to transfer that affection to Apple.

◀ **Fight symbol:** Visual

The prose, originally written as an advertisement, became Apple's manifesto:

> *"Here's to the crazy ones. The rebels. The troublemakers. The ones who see things differently. While some may see them as the crazy ones, we see genius. Because the people who are crazy enough to think they can change the world are the ones who do."*

Climb speech: Progress ▶

Jobs closed the presentation by thanking developers and employees for their commitment. *"I really deeply appreciate all of the commitment that's in this room, and the people not in this room, to turning this company around. This company is absolutely going to turn around. As a matter of fact, I think the question now is not 'Can we turn around Apple?' I think that's the booby prize. I think it's 'Can we make Apple really great again?'"*

Jobs Demystifies a Threat

Fight ceremony: ▶
Demystify Threats

At WWDC 1998, Jobs conceded that Apple hadn't taken NeXT's OS solution far enough for developers. So he and his team launched Carbon, the tool they'd secretly created that would port most of the developers' existing classic Mac OS 8 and Mac OS 9 code over to the Mac OS X developer beta release. Jobs announced that when Mac OS X formally released, Apple would be making the biggest leap in an OS since the Mac was first introduced in 1984.

To lessen developers' fear of migrating to Mac OS X, Jobs brought other developers onstage who, within only two weeks, had ported the bulk of their applications to the Mac OS X beta—a process that would have taken several months without Carbon. Jobs demonstrated that he had listened and responded empathetically to developers by having Apple build a tool to help them. In fact, the CEO of Macromedia (later acquired by Adobe) expressed gratitude from the stage, saying, *"Steve and Apple have learned that it's really not about being a visionary; it's about being a listenary—listening to what customers need and giving it to them."* This WWDC was a major turning point for developers, and immediately afterward many more began getting their software ready to run on Mac OS X when it officially launched to the public.

Jobs Asks Developers to Recommit

As the 1998 summer Macworld presentation rolled around, Apple appeared to be returning to good health. But the company still had its detractors in the press, and some skeptical developers struggled to believe Apple would stick with the Mac OS X strategy. Jobs delivered a speech to silence the skeptics straight on and show how far Apple had come. The structure of his talk was a play on Maslow's hierarchy of needs, which he titled the "Apple Hierarchy of Skepticism." He said, *"Let me explain this to you. When I came to Apple a year ago all I heard was that Apple was dying, Apple can't survive. It turns out that every time we convince people that we've accomplished something at one level they come up with something new. I used to think this was a bad thing—When are they ever going to believe that we're going to turn this thing around?—but actually now I think it's great. Because what it means is we've now convinced them that we've taken care of last month's question and they're on to the next one. I thought, Let's get ahead of the game; let's try to figure out what all the questions are going to be and map out where we are."*

◄ Climb speech: Progress

Jobs used the Apple Hierarchy of Skepticism as the road map for his presentation. He stated that three needs in the hierarchy had already been met: Survival, Stable Business, and Product Strategy. Now that Apple had solved its basic need of survival, the company began focusing on addressing the higher-level needs of the hierarchy so it could thrive: Applications and Growth. The bulk of his talk was about applications. Sixty percent of his entire talk, in fact, was targeted at developers again because their applications would drive growth.

Jobs mentioned how Apple was building strong partnerships with developers but acknowledged that had not always been the case. One of the first things he did was listen to his developers. He said, *"When I first got back to Apple, I called a lot of the big developers up and they were just hopping mad at Apple. Hopping mad for having lost some market share but even more hopping mad for not having paid any attention to them. We knew we had to turn this around and we started asking some of these developers to re-partner and recommit to Apple so that we could together turn this situation around. I think when Microsoft committed to the Mac it helped a lot of the other developers get over whatever historical baggage and hurdles that they had and recommit to the Mac and it's been fantastic."* He went on to say that in nine short weeks, 177 brand-new applications had been announced for the Mac—unprecedented growth for any platform.

◄ Empathetic listening

Developers' feelings about Apple had significantly changed and Jobs thanked them for enduring the climb so far. At WWDC 1999 he said, *"The key message I want to start off with is thank you guys. You guys have been awesome and you've hung in there and you've given us the time to turn this thing around . . . and we really, really deeply appreciate it. . . ."* Jobs clearly empathized with how tough the climb had been for them.

Through it all, Apple had remained focused on the single strategy of Mac OS X. Jobs was pleased to point that out but also acknowledged they'd endured a lot of struggle, stating, *"The changes from . . . our software strategy . . . they're zero. Zero changes. Hopefully, we're making up from not having the drama of a strategy per year with exciting and timely implementation that is surprising you on the upside. . . ."*

At Macworld in 2000, he announced to the audience, *"We've already gotten pretty much the top one hundred developers committed."* And he brought several of them onstage to show their software. Momentum for the platform was building again.

Time to Move On and (re)Dream

Dream speech: Vision ▶

By early 2001, Jobs had already started to (re)dream. Since Apple had become profitable again and traction was building in the developer community with Mac OS X, now he was ready to lead the industry into a new era.

Jobs launched his "Digital Hub" vision at Macworld. This strategy put Mac OS X at the center of a user's digital life by managing all content across all devices and the Internet. Jobs knew that for this new dream to become a reality, he needed to once again get developers' buy-in to build the necessary applications.

When he addressed developers that summer of 2001, Jobs created a symbolically comforting atmosphere as his keynote at WWDC. Abandoning his traditional keynote presentation, he hosted a fireside chat. As attendees filled the hall, a crackling campfire flickered on the screens. The symbolism of a campfire created an environment that felt safe and intimate, setting the tone for a frank conversation with developers. Still, he didn't hold back; he pressed them with language that bordered on threatening, such as *"This is a total commitment on Apple's part, and we ask the same of you," "The train has left the station,"* and *"We have a mountain to climb. The mountain is the number of OS X apps that will ship."* Jobs pushed the new operating system hard. Yet skeptical developers still struggled to believe Apple could

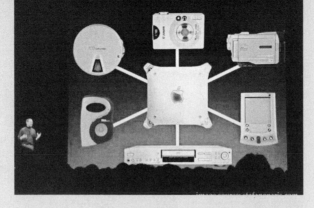

Steve Jobs dreamed of a Digital Hub with Mac OS X at the center.

ever truly focus on one strategy, given its rocky history. But Apple's strategy hadn't changed in more than a year, and Jobs felt compelled to restate his commitment to the Mac OS X. With dramatic flair, he made a public promise to stay focused on the new OS by pulling out oversize parchment paper and ceremonially delivering a sincere vow to Mac OS X—making it clear that Apple was betting its entire future on it.

Move On Through Mourning

By the time the developer conference rolled around in 2002, most developers had transitioned their applications to Mac OS X, yet some highly visible developers still had not. Jobs wanted all developers off Mac OS 9 and on to Mac OS X so everyone would be in a position to make the new Digital Hub strategy a reality.

To unseat the late adopters, Jobs kicked off WWDC 2002 with a mock funeral. A coffin was unveiled on the stage, and an image of a stained glass window was displayed on the screen behind it while mournful music played. The audience

◀ Dream ceremony: Mourn Endings

Jobs reads a manifesto declaring his vow to invest in Mac OS X.

Steve Jobs holds a mock funeral to show that the era of Mac OS 9 has come to an end.

gasped. Next Jobs solemnly placed an oversize product box labeled "Mac OS 9" into the coffin. Some in the audience applauded; others laughed awkwardly. Then he gave a eulogy:

> *"Mac OS 9 was a friend to us all. He worked tirelessly on our behalf, always hosting our applications, never refusing a command, always at our beck and call, except occasionally when he forgot who he was and needed to be restarted. Mac OS 9 came into this world in October of 1998 for a suggested retail price of ninety-nine dollars and was perhaps the best Internet OS of his generation."*

He used clever humor to give the occasion some levity, as eulogists often do to relieve tension at funerals:

> *"We are here today to mourn the passing of Mac OS 9. He's now in that great bit bucket in the sky, no doubt looking down upon us with that same smile he displayed every time he booted. Mac OS 9 is survived by his next generation, Mac OS X, and thousands of applications, most of them legitimate."*

At the end, he closed the lid, placed a red rose on top, and said:

> *"Please join me in a moment of silence as we remember our old friend—Mac OS 9."*

Bach's Toccata and Fugue in D Minor blasted through the speakers. The audience responded with muffled cries and sniffles in jest to honor the ceremony.

Leaving no ambiguity about his message, Jobs finished by saying:

> *"Mac OS 9 isn't dead for our customers yet, but it's dead for [developers]. . . . Today we say farewell to OS 9 for all future development, and we focus our energies on developing for Mac OS X."*

Through this ceremony, Apple decisively stated that developing for the Mac OS 9 was over. The faux funeral was a bold and creative way to tell the last straggling developers they had to move on.

From this moment forward, Jobs discontinued his persuasive effort to get developers to switch to Mac OS X. Apple had arrived and Jobs had already set his sights on a new vision.

Begin Again

Getting developers to migrate en masse from the classic Macintosh operating system to Mac OS X was a five-year trek. When Jobs reemerged to lead Apple, the developers had had no clear path for almost a decade and had a right to be skeptical. It took a while for them to trust Apple again. In spite of the obstacles, the developers went through the herculean effort of migrating. Jobs himself recognized that this was the fastest operating system adoption in history.

Torchbearers often begin a new dream before they've accomplished the current one. Even as Jobs was migrating developers from Mac OS 9 to Mac OS X, he had a new dream of Apple's Digital Hub. When you look back at the Macworld 2001 keynote, in which he introduced the Digital Hub, Jobs foreshadowed many of Apple's most disruptive products. The ideas he declared that day drove a new era of innovation at Apple for a decade. Convincing developers to let go of Mac OS 9 in its entirety made them ready to commit to building applications for the Digital Hub dream.

Apple Venture Scape Summary

When Steve Jobs returned to Apple, he knew the company's success relied on developers migrating to a new operating system, OS X. Yet the new OS required developers to make incredible sacrifices. Throughout the course of his venture Jobs communicated tirelessly to remove skepticism, and developers slowly began adopting OS X. As a new dream emerged, Jobs brought an end to the old OS era and ushered in the era of the Digital Hub.

01
After a decade of trying, Apple concedes it can't make a modern OS internally. Instead it looks to acquire a modern OS from an external source.

02
Apple buys NeXT's OS because its modern features will help create a long-term future for Apple. Jobs joins as an adviser with the purchase.

03
At Macworld 1997 Jobs announces Apple's dream for *"developers to provide relevant, compelling solutions that customers can only get from Apple."* He reminds developers that PageMaker was what made Apple successful the first time and how software will make them successful again. He also tells the story of how the NeXT OS has great features that he saw on his first trip to Xerox PARC years earlier, which he didn't build into the classic Mac OS.

04
Apple has to kill features in the classic OS that developers loved, which angers them.

05
Jobs hosts a Q&A at WWDC 1998 and tells developers that the features Apple killed will make the OS healthier.

06
To demonstrate that a big developer is on board, Jobs convinces Microsoft to invest in Apple. Microsoft then publically declares that it's committed to developing on the Macintosh platform. The investment is mostly symbolic, to demonstrate that others shouldn't be afraid to commit. Bill Gates verbalizes his approval, saying, *"We are excited to recommit to Apple."*

DREAM   LEAP

07

Apple launches the "Think different" campaign as a rallying cry, reminding everyone that Apple *"honors those who think different and move this world forward."* Developers' applications start to get interest from consumers again.

08

Developers push back on Apple's new OS because it requires them to rebuild their software from scratch.

09

Apple modifies its OS strategy with a tool that will leverage most of the developers' code with a smaller percent of rewrite. At WWDC, developers thunderously applaud Apple for meeting them partway on the trek. Apple demystifies the difficulty of developing on Mac OS X by having prominent developers onstage show what they produced in just two weeks.

10

Adobe, Macromedia, and other prominent developers start building in Mac OS X.

11

Jobs addresses skeptics and detractors head-on in a speech at Macworld, showing how much healthier Apple is and announcing that developer adoption is strong.

12

Jobs affirms to developers that Apple is sticking with one OS strategy and it won't make changes in its commitment to Mac OS X.

13

Jobs warns developers that if they don't jump in now, they could become obsolete, and he reads a manifesto of Apple's commitment to Mac OS X.

14

Jobs eulogizes Mac OS 9 at a mock funeral to communicate Apple is done persuading developers and their fate is in their own hands. He wants them to move on to the new dream of a "Digital Hub."

15

Apple announces a new dream of a Digital Hub strategy, in which OS X is the center of a user's digital life, managing content from across the Internet on all devices. Announced in a January 2001 Macworld keynote, the Digital Hub drives a new era of innovation at Apple for more than a decade.

∞

FIGHT   CLIMB   ARRIVE   (RE)DREAM

Confessions of a Torchbearer

by Nancy Duarte

When you choose to lead (or are chosen), your ability to see the way and illuminate it for others sets you apart. Torchbearers are dreamers, pioneers, and scouts who are energized to light the path for travelers. To boldly go into the future is one thing; to get others to go there with you is another entirely. Enter the power of communication. Effective and empathetic communication gives your team fuel to complete the journey—all while binding everyone to each other through moments they'll never forget.

Your determined, dogged desire to see your ideas become reality drives you to willingly take on the mantle of a torchbearer. But the torchbearer role is not an easy one. While studying the great leaders in this book, I was comforted to see them get frustrated, encounter hardships, and at times want to give up. Steve Jobs had to deal with backlash and skepticism. Howard Schultz described moments of sorrow and tears when he knew his decisions caused others pain.

I vividly remember the moment when Patti and I came across the speech Dr. King delivered at his staff retreat (page 169). It struck home for me because it vividly described the challenges of being a torchbearer. He and his staff were so tired; I could feel his desperation in trying to reinvigorate his weary travelers when he said:

> *"We on the executive staff often forget to express our gratitude. . . . I know how many of you have suffered, and I know how many of you have sacrificed. . . . So often when we are very close to a thing, we can't see how much we are doing. . . . [But] you are to be praised for your willingness to suffer so creatively."*

Then he visualized what their journey looked like. I gasped because Dr. King was describing a Venture Scape in his own words.

> *"Now first when you look at a revolution you must always realize that the line of progress is never a straight line. It has its curves and this again is a fact of history that there is never a straight line to the city of fulfillment or to what we think of as progress. It always has its dips and its curves, its meandering points. So it may move on a straight line for a period, then you get that dip, that curve, but the hopeful thing is that it keeps moving."*

King verbally painted a picture of the journey for his staff at a moment when they were mustering the will to continue. Leaders struggle to know what their travelers need, but the Venture Scape provides the tools you and your travelers need to picture the unknown and cope with it.

The Road Unraveled

Even though the visualization of the Venture Scape in this book shows the journey as a smooth curve, the process is nonlinear, messy, and unpredictable. A venture is much more complicated than a sloping S-curve can convey.

The five stages of the Venture Scape may take place sequentially. But more likely, you will traverse back and forth across stages—sometimes for years—inching forward through switchbacks and strategic adjustments.

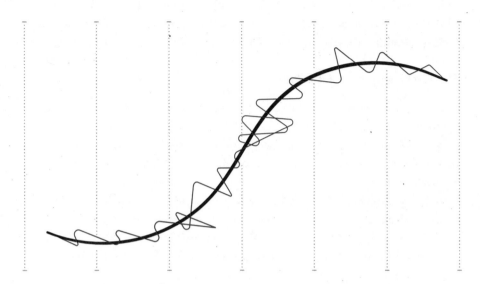

A typical venture is nonlinear and unpredictable.

Your venture may seem chaotic and discouraging at times when the reality of it is less predictable and looks like this: dream, leap, fight, climb, climb, fight, climb, fight, fight, recommit, climb, climb, fight, climb, arrive.

As travelers set out, some are zigging and others zagging, while competing priorities spring seemingly from everywhere. Travelers kick up a lot of dust as they bustle through the back-and-forth of your venture. As with military operations, chaos creates a level of ambiguity. Prussian military theorist Carl von Clausewitz wrote, *"War is the realm of uncertainty; three quarters of the factors on which action in war is based are wrapped in a fog of greater or lesser uncertainty."* Your communication toolkit will help minimize the uncertainty of the "fog of war."

Anytime ambiguity exists on your travelers' path, they will look to you for clarity. They need your help to forge the way for them. Your communication can blow away the fog, illuminate the unclear, and give them the confidence to move ahead again.

The Torchbearer's Toolkit in Practice

The most effective communication tools are those that emerge from an organization's or group's shared moments. At Duarte, Inc., every couple of years, I deliver a speech to employees in which I go through our values and tell the story of the experience that created each value. For example, one of our values is "The show must go on." That value emerged when our tiny company took on creating presentations for a huge event that was too big for our britches. An executive from Lotus (now IBM) showed up with a 35mm slide containing a complicated diagram that we had to redraw digitally. The image was of microscopic shapes combined in a webbed mess to convey monolithic code. We split the image into quadrants and my team worked until four a.m. to assemble a perfect digital representation of the slide. Forgetting to set the alarm, I was startled awake at seven a.m. by a call from the event producer, who stated that the executive was waiting for his slide so he could rehearse. Jumping from bed, I ran through the back side of the convention center, greeted the executive with a handshake and a smile, and handed him the diskette with the slide on it. He was pleased with how it looked, yet he didn't warm to me. When I dashed back to our greenroom to give my team high fives, they gasped. I was still in my red nightshirt, barefoot, and I had marks from the bedsheet across my face. That dogged commitment to serve each client well shaped our value that "The show must go on."

Over the years, our business continued to gain momentum. The show was going on and on and yet we never stopped to celebrate. As a deadline-oriented business, we were just too stressed to lift our heads above the fray and say thanks to each other. So, in 2002, one of our Duartians decided to institute a weekly ceremony to recognize staff members for a job well done during our company-wide meeting. She went to a local import shop and purchased a wooden giraffe as a small token of thanks. To this day, at staff meetings each week someone gives a small speech and then "passes the giraffe" to a staff member he or she wants to honor.

When the company hit a spot of meteoric growth in 2012, people were tired and stressed from the mounds of work. I sensed that we all needed to bond. I asked myself, "When giraffes gather together as a herd, what's it called?" To my delight, when I looked it up I found that a herd of giraffes is called a tower. What a great symbol of strength, community, and support. So I decided to make the giraffe the official company mascot and formally change the name from "pass the giraffe" to "Giraffirmations." Now the office is adorned with hundreds of giraffe statues in all sizes, T-shirts proudly displaying giraffes, rocks painted like giraffe fur, and hysterical photoshopped giraffe images sent around the office via e-mail. That symbol had been in use for more than a decade before we amplified it to an official symbol.

I delivered a speech to the company to announce the ratification of the symbol as a mascot. I told how a herd of giraffes is a tower and that in demanding seasons, we can pull strength from each other. After I told the stories that support each value, a beautiful booklet was distributed called "A Duartian's Guide to Giraffe Behavior." In it, the values were supported with stories and each page had giraffe facts, such as *"Each individual giraffe has a unique coat pattern. We're all unique and value each other's differences."*

The ceremony, story, speech, and symbol here weren't contrived. In fact, the leader didn't orchestrate them; the Giraffirmation ceremony was started and driven by our employees. I did decide to amplify the giraffe's status to infuse it with more meaning. The communication around the giraffe is codified in our culture and holds a lot of meaning for us.

Illuminating a venture is leading travelers through a story. Many times it's a tale of intrigue, full of suspense, challenges, friendships, and sometimes a pinch of horror. When your venture is done, mine the speeches, stories, ceremonies, and symbols, for they are treasures for which you paid a great price, and they can hold great meaning.

Plenty of other companies excel at mining their culture for speeches, stories, ceremonies, and symbols to have on hand during a venture. Story-driven companies such as Nike catalog their stories, make them searchable on an intranet, and train employees to tell them to Nike executives. Some stories turn into what Nike calls their maxims, which guide employees at all levels. Each maxim is founded in a story.

One maxim in particular, "Remember the Man," honors the founder of Nike, Bill Bowerman. By canonizing Bowerman's speeches and stories, Nike pulls on them for inspiration with phrases such as "There is no finish line" and "Everything you need is already inside." Even the "Just Do It" tagline came from Bowerman.

During Chick-fil-A's transformation toward innovation, at least fifteen different stories about how Truett Cathy innovated were embedded in the training systems and speeches, which were delivered over and over.

At Airbnb, the team wrote down hundreds of moments they had shared together. They hired an artist to visualize the moments and create lovely illustrations. Designer Timothy Goodman chose 115 of these moments and painted them on

At Airbnb, Timothy Goodman was commissioned to illustrate a wall of key moments in the company's history.

leftover plywood from the construction of the Airbnb building. The art piece covers sixty feet of linear wall space in Airbnb's office.

Ready, Set, Go… Again

After tasting victory, your travelers may have an even bigger appetite for adventure than you realize. The same people who quivered in fear at the start are today grizzled warriors with a thirst for challenge, ready for another chance to shape the future. By undertaking a bold and risky venture together, they learned that they were capable of more than they ever imagined. The nature of ventures is that they're transformative. Just as your travelers are different people than when they started the venture, you've been changed, too.

As you look back at your past ventures and listen anew to your travelers' tales, you will have the capacity for bigger ideas and broader dreams of where you could go next. This time around, even more may be asked of you than before and you may see that cloud of doubt. Perhaps the new dream that's emerging is larger than you ever imagined.

So when you discover a new ember, let there be light.

Duarte employees, or "Duartians," gather for a collective dreaming event.

—

Duarte, Inc.

When your travelers have jumped in and fought hard to see the dream come true, having wrangled plenty of roadblocks, they may feel too tired and disillusioned to complete the trek. Give them renewed energy and purpose by helping them bond with others and remind them why they are in the fray in the first place.

Change Is Hard for the Weary

When my book *Resonate* was published, our business spiked. We managed growth well but our structural systems started to show cracks and we realized our structure wouldn't be sustainable for growth beyond a hundred people or so. Research shows that if a service firm doesn't put the right systems in place, when it hits the hundred-person mark, the business fails. We were pressing up against that number quickly.

Duarte, Inc., was structured differently than other creative agencies. We had nine small teams running as mini-agencies operating under one roof. The creative staff answered to an account manager and each account manager ran that team how he or she saw fit. Other agencies are structured by function: account teams, project management teams, and creative teams. Our structure was not built for scale.

Two years later, Duarte, Inc.'s TED talk got a million views, which catapulted the company into a ripsnorting growth frenzy. The rapid spike in demand for our services almost crushed us because we didn't have unified processes or systems in place. We had already been worried we weren't well equipped for growth, and now with the additional surge in business, employees had to make incredible personal sacrifices to get work done.

Normally when we hold our company vision meeting, our focus is on moving into new markets or creating new services. But our vision this particular year was all about changing our internal systems—information, technical, operational, and structural. With everyone already stretched to their limits, fixing the underlying structure would be a huge task. The company would have to slow down growth and ask employees to squeeze change in on top of their real jobs. Where would we find the energy to do that?

Can a Growing Firm Bear Great Change?

So at Duarte, Inc.'s vision meeting in 2012, we introduced a new five-year vision to face this growth challenge to "Reimagine presentations to communicate vital stories and compel global action." To realize this dream, we needed to redesign our organizational structure to prepare for global readiness while preserving our ability to innovate quickly.

I kicked off the meeting by looking back at other times we had gone through reinvention. I showed a slide very similar to the sequence of Duarte's ventures on pages 2–3. My goal was to assure employees that we had the resilience and smarts to endure change because we had done it before:

> *"Getting where we got to today wasn't easy. We're reaping the benefit from a bunch of employees who believed we could get where we are now. Many of you who were here then made a lot of sacrifices of time, mental capital and drove the organization forward on sheer grit and passion."*

Arrive story: ▶
Savor the Win

Next, I had employees close their eyes while I played a recorded dramatization of a story excerpted from Jim Collins's book *Good to Great* about what it is like to have breakthrough momentum:

◀ Dream ceremony:
Immerse Deeply

> "*Picture in your mind a huge, heavy flywheel—a massive metal disk mounted horizontally on an axle, about thirty feet in diameter, two feet thick, and weighing about five thousand pounds. Now imagine that your task is to get the flywheel rotating on the axle as fast and long as possible.*

> "*Pushing with great effort, you get the flywheel to inch forward, moving almost imperceptibly at first. You keep pushing and, after two or three hours of persistent effort, you get the flywheel to complete one entire revolution.*

> "*You keep pushing, and the flywheel begins to move a bit faster, and with continued great effort, you move it around a second rotation.*

> "*Then, at some point—[whoosh] BREAKTHROUGH!*"

The metaphor worked because once the mass of a flywheel starts spinning, each revolution of the wheel takes less energy. For our company, this meant that once we had made the necessary changes, we'd gain momentum and would require less individual sacrifice on the part of employees, and unified processes would kick in to help bring efficiency. But we hadn't yet arrived at that stage; instead we were currently seeing two dangers emerge: The flywheel (our business) was starting to wobble, and we were trying to expand it while in motion. In physics, if an object wobbles or if you add mass, it loses energy. Losing energy slows down momentum.

In addition to our nonstandard structure, our lack of management systems made us wobble. I told a personal story about how my first few jobs didn't have formal management reviews and I vowed that if I had my own firm, my employees would know what's expected of them and how the organization values them. I was brokenhearted to learn of the gap between the care I dreamed the employees would receive and the care they were actually receiving. I apologized that I hadn't kept up with my own promise that I'd run my organization differently as we had grown.

◀ Arrive story:
Lose the Way

In an effort to foreshadow what big changes we would be making soon, I explained:

"I do not want to risk quality to gain mass. I do not want to sacrifice this culture to gain mass. But I also know that you're going to see some bold, sweeping changes that might make you question if we value our culture. You might feel like: WTF?"

Leap story: ▶
Seek the Reward

Then I said something that shows you just how ignorant I was about what we were about to get into:

"Yes, it will slow us down a bit—laws of physics dictate that. But I'm hoping it'll be like a small tap on the brakes and our flywheel will not be drained of energy. We want to be able to continue to spin as a highly functioning and wonderfully powered flywheel."

Leap ceremony: ▶
Pledge Commitment

Tapping on the brakes? We were about to see the carnage of a spinning flywheel untethered. After the vision presentation, executives reviewed a vision booklet with their direct reports and facilitated candid discussions about the role they would play in helping push the firm to achieve high-functioning teams and systems. As the management-led discussions began, deeply entrenched mind-sets reared up in force, challenging the proposed systems changes.

Leap story: ▶
Ignore the Reward

If we did restructure, almost everyone in the organization would have a new boss or be a new boss, which could provoke lots of upheaval. The pressure of heavy workloads and uncertainty as to whether people would like their new bosses caused some employees to leave Duarte, Inc.

Dream ceremony: ▶
Mourn Endings

Meanwhile, the uncomfortable process of change was fragmenting our culture. In a speech that June, I acknowledged the discomfort, bringing some closure to the pain of departing Duartians who didn't think the sacrifice was worth the reward. *"I know that the departures this year have been hard. Our turnover rate is low compared to the average business but because we're a family it is amplified and impacts us more deeply. It has made many of us question the strength of our community."* When you work hard to create a family atmosphere, people leaving hurts more deeply. The pressure to change was diminishing our family culture.

A Pivot, Not a Reorg

We underestimated the emotional toll this restructure would have. Even though no one was losing their jobs and we were moving toward a more common structure, people were freaked out just from the uncertainty of the change. Some thought we should move quickly, while others wanted us to take it slow and methodically. When the 2014 vision meeting rolled around, we were ready to announce the new structure. I explained:

> *"The word* reorg *can be intimidating and perceived as negative. Yet we're so excited about this, in fact, we've decided to avoid that word altogether. This new structure will set us up for so much success moving forward, we are calling this a pivot. For many of you, it's easy to see why this makes sense."*

The word *pivot* worked because we were literally rotating our organization chart by 90 degrees. As I announced the pivot, a series of slides animated the organization charts conceptually and walked through why we were changing the structure and how each shift benefited our clients, employees, and company. The journey so far had been much harder than we'd thought and now we were finally pulling the trigger on the new structure.

◀ **Leap ceremony:**
Dismantle Blockages

On top of the pivot, we had also begun implementing new systems, including a project management and accounting application that changed the way many people did their jobs. The new system, called Workamajig, took a lot of effort to implement. But our project managers rose to the challenge and did some heavy lifting to modify the tool to make it work for our needs. Over beer and chips, our president gave them each a star-shaped award engraved with their names and the title "Workamagician" in recognition of the magic they had brought to the project.

◀ **Arrive ceremony:**
Honor Heroes

Knowing that this system was creating some pain points for the company more broadly, I felt compelled to advise the teams that it would still be tough. I told them at the following staff meeting, *"This will be confusing before there's clarity. We will be less productive before we're more productive, which means it'll initially be harder before you see the benefits."*

◀ **Climb story:**
Endure the Struggle

Fight speech: Battle ▶
To acknowledge the employees who were <u>rising to the challenge</u> and taking on more responsibility, I said:

> *"There are going to be some gutsy, glorious people who will be tapped to become new leaders in this organization. Some haven't been managers before. Some people will take on positions of leadership but they don't have all the skills required. We need to make sure we give each other the room and the grace to make mistakes and be imperfect."*

Climb story: ▶
Endure the Struggle
As I ended the meeting, I relayed the Aesop's fable about the <u>bundle of sticks</u> to convey the importance of strength in unity, hoping to inspire the team to bind together to support our new managers and structure.

By the following May, we'd finished mapping out reporting structures, but strain caused disagreements about the best process for the new structure and fears arose about whether new managers would care about employees as much as their old managers had. Uncertainties dampened the mood. We needed to acknowledge again

Climb speech: Progress ▶
our empathy for <u>how tough it had been yet how far we had come</u>. I said:

> *"I worry about how much longer I can stand up here and say that it'll get better eventually. I wish more than anyone that this was easier. . . . I live for opening doors that help you realize your dreams. I know it hasn't felt much like that of late. Hopefully soon it will. I see a future. One where everyone communicates with open candor and continues to build one of the greatest companies on the planet."*

Toward the end of the year, people's fears started to calm, yet some areas still suffered from frayed nerves and confusion.

Uniting for the Final Push

After a ton of planning and meetings, the pivot was done, the dust settled, and many employees now had new bosses. The company began seeing positive results right away. New managers were learning new skills and the reorganization into functional teams was working out kinks of our processes. We still had more climbing to do. Roles were not defined well, tasks on projects became confusing, and we still had more heavy workloads ahead. We also started hearing worried comments from employees about how the change was impacting our culture. With even more change ahead, were we losing touch with the values and traditions that had helped us endure through the years?

Sensing the need to breathe new energy into the culture before we continued on our venture, a group of Duartians self-organized into a committee they called the "Culture Club" (apologies to Boy George!) and took up the task of designing a two-pronged process for listening to our employees and facilitating how to reenergize our culture.

To start, we held ninety-minute "discovery sessions," in which employees met in small groups to have candid conversations about what was working and what needed fixing in our culture. We gave the shop permission to be candid and caring. Our president told the team:

◀ Empathetic listening

> "Empathy without candor creates dysfunctional relationships. Candor without empathy creates distant relationships. Empathy with candor creates developing relationships."

Our facilitators created an atmosphere of candor to draw out stories of people's experiences at Duarte, Inc., which they graphically recorded on flip charts. When the sessions were done, the Culture Club combed through hundreds of flip charts and more than eighty pages of transcripts to distill the feedback into sixteen major themes.

Our facilitators synthesized listening sessions into visual notes.

We had asked for candor and we got it: Some of the employee insights were tough to swallow. Afterward, we asked employees to vote for the four themes they most cared about solving. It wasn't surprising that the eight topics that rose to the top of the employees' list had to do with the care and feeding of our people, such as a stronger recognition and reward program. These themes became the focus of what we called "Shop Day"—a full-day collaborative problem-solving event that coincided with our annual planning process.

Dream ceremony: ▶
Immerse Deeply

We absorbed the cost of closing down the shop for one full day to gather employees together in cross-functional teams to dig in to the challenges we faced. The goal was to create new ways of working together that would unleash the full potential of our people. The event's name carried double meaning as a time to focus on our business (which we often call a "shop") and as a time to make something beautiful, as in the "shop" classes we took in high school, with the poster promoting the event emblazoned with an anvil. As employees arrived for breakfast, they were handed a black shop apron so people knew immediately that this day was a different kind of workday.

Climb symbol: Physical ▶

The event began with informal remarks by our CEO, our president, and one of our key creative leaders, Doug Neff. Sitting on barstools upon a small stage, each leader spoke from his or her heart about the importance of the day and how it would shape

Shop aprons symbolize the heavy lifting that Duarte employees do on company initiatives.

A quick game of "Rock, Paper, Scissors" releases tension after hours of brainstorming.

the future of our shop. Doug explained that we would use our own creative process to create ideas, then filter those ideas, and end the day with each of the eight teams delivering two-minute pitches of their ideas to the entire company. He closed with a personal story that underscored how important it was for every employee to fully engage in the process to create a stronger Duarte culture:

◄ Climb story:
Endure the Struggle

> *"I remember the instant that I became a father. . . . This is a picture of my daughter, Meera [pointing to a photo of a beautiful tortoiseshell cat]. One morning seventeen years ago, my partner, Corey, was at the post office, where someone had abandoned a tiny kitten. Corey brought her home. When she looked up at me with those big green eyes, I realized that I was all she had in the world and it was up to me to protect her. And in that moment, I became a parent. You might not know it, but Nancy feels that way about Duarte, and she wants you to feel that way, too. So, today, I'm going to ask you to think like parents. Own your topics. Nurture your ideas. Be their champions and their defenders. And treat them as though you are all they have in the world."*

We knew that the intensive creative process from morning to afternoon would be draining for everyone. So the day was punctuated with moments to let off some steam and celebrate, including improvisation games, a massive roshambo match, and an artisanal coffee bar. We also created a piece of art together in the afternoon. We

Creating a collective art project bonds Duarte employees.

laid out paints, stencils, and small wooden disks (mimicking the circular Duarte, Inc., logo) at a long communal table and employees painted pieces of art that represented their personal mark on our company.

At the end of the day, we regathered for a closing ceremony in which employees hung their painted disks side by side on the wall to create a massive mural. High fives and hugs spread as we all stood back to admire each Duartian's unique expression and our collective act of creativity.

The next Monday morning at our all-hands meeting, we watched each team's pitches from Shop Day. With those presentations fresh in their minds, employees voted on

Climb ceremony: ▶
Heal Wounds

their top three initiatives using a live polling app. Everyone erupted into applause when three initiatives—resourcing, recognition, and remote work—won by a mile. These people-management systems were the most important systems we needed, and the ones that would have the greatest impact on employees.

Leaders from the winning teams stood at the front of the room and took a pledge to lead the final phase of our transformation. Each one was given a teething ring as a reminder to be good "parents" to their fragile new ideas.

◀ Climb ceremony:
Renew Commitment

The following Friday, the entire company went on a weekend getaway in Monterey, California. Employees shared a meal with coworkers and their guests in front of million-gallon fish tanks and danced the night away. This celebration felt like the right way to cap off an immersive week of change. People felt close to each other and knew everything would be all right.

◀ Arrive ceremony:
Honor the Heroes

Each Shop Day team is now off on their own venture taking risks, fighting internal forces, and making the long climb to see their ideas fully realized. Of all the events we host throughout the year, Shop Day was an outlet for compiling what needed to be done and generating energy to get those things done. We empowered the staff to collectively build something new and already we can tell the outcome is going to be deeper and more thoughtful than if executives had developed these programs ourselves.

This galvanizing day knit our team together and fueled fervent participation to solve some of our most urgent problems. Our company became energized and uplifted during the final season of change and our team is excited for a new future together. Employees took on new responsibilities, jumping into the venture and proving they have the grit to complete it. At the time of publication for this book, the story is still being written, but from the momentum of the first round of team presentations, the flywheel is moving again!

Duarte Venture Scape Summary

When Duarte, Inc., set its sights on global growth, CEO Nancy Duarte saw the need for a more scalable business foundation. Her venture to pivot the structure and overhaul systems resulted in improved operations . . . and exhausted employees. Designing moments of empathetic listening and collective effervescence gave Duartians a much-needed boost and infused the venture with new ideas to carry Duarte, Inc., into the future.

01

Duarte, Inc., grows so fast, we have fragmented processes and varying client experiences. While growing, we couldn't put in systems that would ready us for scale.

02

Nancy declares a new vision: to reimagine presentations and ready ourselves to service a global customer base, requiring us to have new systems. We liken the transformation to pushing a flywheel.

03

In the vision meeting, we honor the fact that we've successfully been through other seasons of reinvention and emphasize that we can master this change.

04

Executives meet with teams to review a vision booklet together to immerse them in the strategy. The booklet explains the commitment each role would have in making it happen.

DREAM   LEAP

05

A few Duartians buckle under the pressure and resign. The new systems are cumbersome and place a burden on the already-strained staff.

06

We determine that a reorganization will align employees and processes faster to deliver a unified client experience.

07

We honor those who have been putting systems in place (on top of their regular jobs) with awards.

08

We launch the pivot and tie it back to the benefits to employees and customers.

09

Employees begin to feel that the culture is drained of the family feel because of all the changes.

10

Employees self-organize Shop Day to reenergize the troops and get them recommitted for the journey ahead.

11

Eight teams present two-minute presentations at the end of Shop Day about how Duarte, Inc., can rejuvenate the culture while working hard on the systems.

12

Employees make a beautiful communal art piece to commemorate the day. Each disk represents employees' personal mark on Duarte, Inc.

13

Employees vote on which initiatives are the most critical to solve and teams are formed to address them.

14

The first two employee update presentations show promising momentum that we'll arrive at completion of our global scalability goal by the end of 2015.

15

In the meantime, our vision to reimagine presentations is launching a new dream for technology tools that will help our clients transform their communications and better connect with their audiences.

∞

FIGHT   CLIMB   ARRIVE   (re)DREAM

THE
JOURNEY BEGINS
AGAIN

The trek of a torchbearer goes on and on.
Just as you reach one peak, you spy another beyond.

Tough terrain and dark passages test your resolve,
yet still you push through in pursuit of your dream.

Finally the day arrives when you meet the future,
and discover that you and your travelers have changed.

Now that you're stronger and wiser, with greater capacity to lead,
the spark of a new dream begins to stir.

You pick up the torch to light the way,
so you and your travelers can venture forth once again.

ACKNOWLEDGMENTS

The authors are indebted to the work of many thoughtful scholars whose research in the fields of sociology, dramaturgy, communication theory, and leadership we devoured while writing this book and whose insights shaped our own leadership philosophies. These bright minds include Émile Durkheim, Edith Turner, Victor Turner, Arnold van Gennep, Catherine Bell, Howard Gardner, Robert Cialdini, Bill Moyer, Gene Sharp, Marshall Ganz, Walter Brueggemann, Jordan B. Peterson, John P. Kotter, Dan S. Cohen, John W. Gardner, Lawrence Miller, and Jim Collins.

We are also deeply grateful to the leaders we profiled in these pages. Their bravery, creativity, and empathy lit us up and inspired us to teach more torchbearers how to lead the way as brilliantly as they do. We're forever grateful to Graham Weston, Ray C. Anderson, Scott Harrison, Howard Schultz, Louis Gerstner Jr., Sam Palmisano, Steve Jobs, Dr. Martin Luther King Jr., and many others who light the path to the future.

Of course, we couldn't have written as thoughtfully about those leaders without help from the people who provided crucial information to flesh out the examples in this book. Among these are Lisa Cape Lilienthal, Steve Nedvidek, David Barnett, and Gina Woods. Still others made this book better in subtler ways by suggesting interview subjects, reviewing our early concepts, or dropping bits of wisdom that sent us spinning off in fruitful new directions. These gentle geniuses include Ron Ricci, Rowan Trollope, Sheryl Connelly, Jennifer Aaker, Joe Childs, Tricia Emerson, Ellen Snee, David Yu, Anthony Duarte, Linda Clarke, Eric Albertson, and Alex Varanese. We are eternally grateful to our furry muses, Darla and Archie, who fill our hearts with joy.

Shaping our words and concepts into clear prose and stunning visuals was a job in itself, which was performed by several people who walked alongside us throughout the creative process. We want to thank the entire Duarte, Inc., content team for their mad research skills and well-timed words of encouragement, including Doug Neff, Dave DeFranco, Greta Stahl, Amanda Dyer, Katie Gray, Paula Tesch, Jeff Davenport, Amanda Holt, and Stephanie Patterson. We are also incredibly grateful to our creative director Diandra Macias for her uncompromising dedication to excellent design and to the many talented designers who worked with her to craft beautiful illustrations, images, and layouts for this book, including Princeton Wong, Fabian Espinoza, Tyler Lynch, Denise Ho, Annette Filice, Jay Kapur, Veli Akman, Megan Paskin, Jonathan Valiente, Jacob Reid, Sareh Odom, Phoebe Sanchez, Kryshana Ananthan, Ira Pietojo, Erik Chappins, Ben Saluti, Joe Perez, Kelly McLachlan, Dave Nguyen, Johnny Rios, and Steve Wishman. We are especially indebted to our editors, Emily Loose and Stephanie Frerich, for careful readings and constructive criticism of our manuscript; intern Romy Saloner whose fact-finding skills gave us a jump start early on; photo researcher Marisa Lum for her resourcefulness and problem-solving abilities; our legal counsel Deepti Sethi for her savvy advice and steady presence; and marketing maven Ashley Faus for getting the book out there. We'd also like to thank Ramon from Faz restaurant, who fed and hydrated us as we wrote day after day in the Erica Room at the Sheraton hotel.

Creating this book was quite a long journey, which lasted nearly four years from the initial seed of an idea to the day it went to press. Just like any venture, it was exciting and exhausting in equal measure. Keeping our fingers moving, our bellies full, and our spirits strong the whole time took an army of helpers, too many to give proper credit to here. So to them we'll just say, "Gracias a la familia Duarte por su amor y ayuda. Larga vida y prosperidad!"

Nancy's muse, Darla   Patti's muse, Archie

REFERENCES

Foreword

1 **six years of operation:** "Business Establishment Age," U.S. Bureau of Labor Statistics, accessed May 26, 2015, http://www.bls.gov/bdm/entrepreneurship/entrepreneurship.htm; "Entrepreneurship and the U.S. Economy," U.S. Bureau of Labor Statistics, last modified May 7, 2014, http://www.bls.gov/bdm/entrepreneurship/bdm_chart3.htm.

Chapter One: Leaders Move Others Forward

10 **The shape of the curve plots the life cycle of a business:** Ichak Adizes, *Managing Corporate Lifecycles* (Paramus, NJ: Prentice Hall Press, 1999), 17–19.

10 **epic tale of growth and achievement:** Paul Nunes and Tim Breene, "Reinvent Your Business Before It's Too Late," *Harvard Business Review*, January–February 2011, https://hbr.org/2011/01/reinvent-your-business-before-its-too-late.

15 **returning home weary but wiser:** Tom Drake, "Six Elements of the Epic," University of Idaho, accessed May 26, 2015, http://www.webpages.uidaho.edu/engl257/General%20lit/six_elements _of_the_epic.htm.

18 **describe the feeling of such experiences:** Paul Carls, *Internet Encyclopedia of Philosophy*, s.v. "Émile Durkheim," http://www.iep.utm.edu/durkheim.

18 ***"transported into a special world":*** Émile Durkheim and Karen E. Fields, *The Elementary Forms of Religious Life*, trans. Joseph Ward Swain (New York: Free Press, 1965), 249–50.

20 ***"that have not yet come to pass":*** Fran Walsh, Peter Jackson, and Philippa Boyens, "The Lord of the Rings," IMSDB, accessed August 19, 2015, http://www.imsdb.com/scripts/Lord-of-the-Rings -Fellowship-of-the-Ring,-The.html.

20 ***"change the course of the future":*** Ibid.

21 ***"when all other lights go out":*** Ibid.

21 **his journey to destroy the ring:** "Galadriel," *TheOneRing.net* (blog), accessed May 5, 2015, http://www.theonering.net/torwp/the-hobbit/characters/galadriel.

Chapter Two: Listen Empathetically to Light the Path

24 **cope with the chaos of change:** Ronald H. Humphrey, "The Benefits of Emotional Intelligence and Empathy to Entrepreneurship," *Entrepreneurship Research Journal* 3, no. 3 (2013): 287–94, http://dx.doi.org/10.1515/erj-2013-0057.

24 **others are viewed as higher performers:** William A. Gentry, Todd J. Weber, and Golnaz Sadri, "Empathy in the Workplace: A Tool for Effective Leadership," Center for Creative Leadership, April 2007, http://insights.ccl.org/wp-content/uploads/2015/04/EmpathyInTheWorkplace.pdf.

25 **productivity, and creativity:** Cary Cherniss, "The Business Case for Emotional Intelligence," Consortium for Research on Emotional Intelligence in Organizations, 1999, http://www .eiconsortium.org/reports/business_case_for_ei.html.

25 **author of *Emotional Intelligence*:** Emma M. Seppälä, "The Unexpected Benefits of Compassion for Business," Psychology Today (blog), April 22, 2013, https://www.psychologytoday.com/blog/feeling-it/201304/the-unexpected-benefits-compassion-business.

25 **are more committed to the organization:** Adam M. Grant, "Motivating Creativity at Work: The Necessity of Others Is the Mother of Invention," *Psychological Science Agenda* 25, no. 7 (July 2011), Agenda, http://www.apa.org/science/about/psa/2011/07/motivating-creativity.aspx.

25 **share information freely with one another:** Mila Hakanen and Aki Soudunsaari, "Building Trust in High-Performing Teams," *Technology Innovation Management Review*, June 2012, http://timreview.ca/article/567.

25 **and changing their own views:** Richard Salem, "Empathic Listening," Beyond Intractability, July 2003, http://www.beyondintractability.org/essay/empathic-listening.

25 **"Hope rekindled. Energy returned":** Anne M. Mulcahy, "Social Responsibility: Building a Culture of Strong Ethics, Good Deeds and Smart Business" (lecture, Bentley College, Waltham, MA, April 12, 2005).

26 **Attitudes, and Lifestyles (VALS) study:** Sarah R. Stein, "The '1984' Macintosh Ad: Cinematic Icons and Constitutive Rhetoric in the Launch of a New Machine," *Quarterly Journal of Speech* 88, no. 2 (2002): 169–92, https://www2.bc.edu/~lissk/co378/1984.pdf.

26 **the time or inclination to learn programming:** "Macintosh Production Introduction Plan," Making the Macintosh: Technology and Culture in Silicon Valley, June 2, 2000, http://web.stanford.edu/dept/SUL/library/mac/primary/docs/pip83.html.

26 **and the companies that made them, such as IBM:** Kevin Blackwell, "Introduction to End-User Computing," in *Historical Changes in Computer Use* (Independence, KY: Course Technology, 2004), http://faculty.olympic.edu/kblackwell/docs/cmptr185/Online%20Book%20Preview/Chapter%201/0-619-21510-0_01_op.pdf.

26 **"NEVER TRUST A COMPUTER YOU CAN'T LIFT":** "Steve Jobs Demos Apple Macintosh, 1984.MP4," YouTube video, 4:48, from a presentation given in January 1984 by Steve Jobs, posted by "Volkan Kalpakçi," January 29, 2013, https://www.youtube.com/watch?v=pptb1Uzn7SQ.

26 **Big Brother figure from George Orwell's novel *1984*:** Apple, Apple Macintosh Computer, television, CBS, January 22, 1984.

26 **with simple yet powerful technology:** Chris Higgins, "How Apple's '1984' Ad Was Almost Canceled," *mental_floss*, 2012, http://mentalfloss.com/article/29867/how-apples-1984-ad-was-almost-canceled.

Case Study: IBM

31 **IBM was destined to be big:** "IBM Is Founded," IBM, accessed June 1, 2015, http://www-03.ibm.com/ibm/history/ibm100/us/en/icons/founded.

31 **who took the helm in 1914:** Ibid.

31 **carved into IBM's building in New York:** "The Creation of the World Trade Corporation," IBM, accessed June 1, 2015, http://www-03.ibm.com/ibm/history/ibm100/us/en/icons/ibmworldtrade.

31 **"year to year until the end of time":** "The Making of International Business Machines," IBM, accessed June 1, 2015, http://www-03.ibm.com/ibm/history/ibm100/us/en/icons/makingibm/impacts.

32 **storage systems, and application software:** "The Making of International Business Machines," IBM, accessed June 1, 2015, http://www-03.ibm.com/ibm/history/ibm100/us/en/.

32 **technology shifts in the 1980s and 1990s:** D. Quinn Mills, "The Decline and Rise of IBM," *MIT Sloan Management Review*, July 15, 1996, http://sloanreview.mit.edu/article/the-decline-and-rise-of-ibm.

32 **premium-priced mainframe business:** "Chronological History of IBM," IBM, accessed June 1, 2015, http://www-03.ibm.com/ibm/history/history/decade_1990.html.

32 **had racked up $8 billion in losses:** Ibid.

32 **with the company for thirty-three years:** Jack Schofield, "Obituary: John Akers, the IBM CEO Who Lost the PC Market," *ZDNet*, August 25, 2014, http://www.zdnet.com/article/obituary-john-akers-the-ibm-ceo-who-lost-the-pc-market.

32 **from outside IBM's ranks:** "Chronological History of IBM."

33 **his first official day of work:** Louis V. Gerstner Jr., *Who Says Elephants Can't Dance? Leading a Great Enterprise Through Dramatic Change* (New York: HarperBusiness, 2003), 12–5.

33 **to be done in his first ninety days:** Ibid., 21–5.

33 ***"with internal processes,"* he later wrote:** Ibid., 41–2.

33 **was bleeding so badly:** L. A. Lorek, "Shareholders Unleash Anger on IBM Board," *Orlando Sentinel*, April 27, 1993, http://articles.orlandosentinel.com/1993-04-27/business/9304270822_1_ibm-gerstner-blunk.

33 ***"plain old hard work":*** Ibid.

34 **company difficult to work with:** Gerstner, *Who Says Elephants Can't Dance?*, 46–7.

34 ***"is now a customer running IBM":*** Judith H. Dobrzynski, "Rethinking IBM," *BusinessWeek*, October 3, 1993, http://www.bloomberg.com/bw/stories/1993-10-03/rethinking-ibm.

34 **he understood their pain:** Gerstner, *Who Says Elephants Can't Dance?*, 47–8.

34 ***"to these things,"* Gerstner said:** Dobrzynski, "Rethinking IBM."

34 **called customers on his own:** Gerstner, *Who Says Elephants Can't Dance?*, 49–50.

35 **talking to twenty thousand workers directly:** Dobrzynski, "Rethinking IBM."

35 ***"draw conclusions,"* Gerstner said:** Ibid.

35 **a market-driven innovator:** Gerstner, *Who Says Elephants Can't Dance?*, 73–80.

Case Study: Market Basket

37 **customers boycotted your products:** Adam Vaccaro, "Market Basket Deal: Arthur T. Demoulas to Buy Out Grocery Chain," Boston.com, August 27, 2014, http://www.boston.com/business/news/2014/08/27/demoulas-sides-reach-deal/YHVqrKp65XS3DBzJd2PulI/story.html.

38 ***"secretly taped meetings, and more":*** Brad R. Tuttle, "Meet America's Most Beloved CEO—Too Bad He Just Got Fired," *Time*, July 23, 2014, http://time.com/money/3024511/market-basket-ceo-demoulas-protest.

38 **and attended employees' funerals:** Ibid.

38 **the loss of a father:** Callum Borchers, "Arthur T. Demoulas's Personal Touch Can Cut Both Ways,".

Boston Globe, August 22, 2014, http://www.bostonglobe.com/business/2014/08/21/arthur-demoulas
-profile-personal-touch-that-can-cut-two-ways/lqkmJ1i7A4AFKpLenN8vBM/story.html.

38 **and fired his cousin Arthur T.:** Jana Kasperkevic, "A Timeline of the Market Basket Supermarket
Family Feud," *Guardian*, August 14, 2014, http://www.theguardian.com/money/us-money
-blog/2014/aug/14/timeline-market-basket-supermarket-arthur-family-feud.

39 **missed work to attend protests:** John Collins, "More than 2,000, Market Basket Employees Put
Their Job on the Line for 'Artie T.'," *Lowell Sun*, July 18, 2014, http://www.lowellsun.com/
breakingnews/ci_26174386/more-than-2-000-market-basket-employees-put#ixzz3aEFbXVW0.

39 **"is to bring ATD back!":** "Tom Trainor's Speech at the Market Basket Rally," YouTube video, 14:08,
from speech given at Tewksbury, MA, on July 21, 2014, posted by "Bills GoPro," July 21, 2014,
https://www.youtube.com/watch?v=Aeq_q5nGcaA.

39 **throughout store aisles:** Jack Newsham, "Market Basket Managers Ordered to Take Down Protest
Signs," *Boston Globe*, August 14, 2014, http://www.bostonglobe.com/business/2014/08/14/market-
basket-managers-ordered-take-down-protest-signs/sNAquX1X0kwD96xtYjfEnO/story.html.

39 **employee-run blog, *We Are Market Basket*, was created:** *We Are Market Basket* (blog), accessed
June 1, 2015, http://wearemarketbasket.com.

39 **competitors on store windows:** Newsham, "Market Basket Managers Ordered to Take Down
Protest Signs."

39 **more than forty-five thousand signed it:** "Save Market Basket," Care2Petitions, accessed June 1,
2015, http://www.thepetitionsite.com/137/178/861/save-market-basket.

39 **"can't fire me, I quit!":** Stephanie Woods, "Dozens Protest in Support of Market Basket,"
WMUR.com, August 15, 2014, http://www.wmur.com/news/dozens-protest-in-support-of
-market-basket/27517164.

39 **"at Shaw's this week":** Ibid.

39 **garnered almost ninety thousand likes:** Save Market Basket's Facebook page, https://www
.facebook.com/pages/Save-Market-Basket/136649323208808.

40 **"most importantly, our customers":** "Friday, July 25. The Grand Finale," *We Are Market Basket*
(blog), July 23, 2014, http://wearemarketbasket.com/friday-july-25-the-grand-finale.

40 **members' shares for $1.5 billion:** Dan Primack, "Exclusive: Blackstone Group Is Market Basket's
Mystery Backer," *Fortune*, August 28, 2014, http://fortune.com/2014/08/28/exclusive-blackstone
-group-is-market-baskets-mystery-backer.

40 **"human soul. [extended applause and cheers]":** "Raw Video: Arthur T. Demoulas on Return to
Market Basket," WMUR.com video, 12:23, August 24, 2014, http://www.wmur.com/money/raw
-video-arthur-t-demoulas-on-return-to-market-basket/27770312.

41 **"within the communities we serve":** "We Are Market Basket," *We Are Market Basket* (blog),
September 11, 2014, http://wearemarketbasket.com/where-do-we-go-from-here.

41 **"to have him actually come back":** Dan Adams and Jack Newsham, "Happy Ending for Market
Basket Employees, Customers," *Boston Globe*, August 28, 2014, http://www.bostonglobe.com/
business/2014/08/28/happy-ending-for-market-basket-employees-customers/8DYrQ8orJYtv
HM1BdYSEyK/story.html.

Chapter Three: The Torchbearer's Toolkit

45 **"pits, pits, pits":** Fran Walsh, Peter Jackson, and Philippa Boyens, "The Lord of the Rings," Hitpages, accessed May 25, 2015, https://www.hitpages.com/doc/5077877825470464/15.

51 **another significant economic downturn:** World Economic Forum, *World Economic Forum Annual Meeting 2013: Resilient Dynamism* (Davos-Klosters, Switzerland: World Economic Forum, 2013), http://www3.weforum.org/docs/AM13/WEF_AM13_Report.pdf.

54 **increases attention levels and reduces boredom:** Bruce D. Perry, "How the Brain Learns Best," Scholastic, accessed May 26, 2015, http://teacher.scholastic.com/professional/bruceperry/brainlearns.htm.

55 **"to demarcate transitions" in life:** Bjørn Thomassen, "The Uses and Meanings of Liminality," *International Political Anthropology* 2, no. 1 (2009): 5–27.

56 **and strong interpersonal relations:** Richard Sosis and Candace Alcorta, "Signaling, Solidarity, and the Sacred: The Evolution of Religious Behavior," *Evolutionary Anthropology* 12, no. 6 (2003): 264–74, https://www.yumpu.com/en/document/view/10713105/signaling-solidarity-and-the-sacred-department-of-anthropology/3; Durkheim and Fields, *The Elementary Forms of Religious Life*.

57 **more likely to be remembered:** Sosis and Alcorta, "Signaling, Solidarity, and the Sacred."

57 **the smallest unit of ritual in cultures:** Victor Turner and Roger D. Abrahams, *The Ritual Process: Structure and Anti-Structure* (New Brunswick, NJ: Aldine Transaction, 1995), 19.

57 **our very beginnings as human beings:** Yngve Vogt, "World's Oldest Ritual Discovered. Worshipped the Python 70,000 Years Ago," trans. Alan Louis Belardinelli, *Apollon Research Magazine*, November 30, 2006, https://www.apollon.uio.no/english/articles/2006/python-english.html.

VENTURE Case Study: Starbucks

62 **"the center of everything we do":** "Howard Schultz Transformation Agenda Communication #1," Starbucks, January 6, 2008, https://news.starbucks.com/news/howard-schultz-transformation-agenda-communication-1.

62 **they spent time just seeing:** Howard Schultz and Joanne Gordon, *Onward: How Starbucks Fought for Its Life Without Losing Its Soul* (New York: Rodale, 2011), 72.

62 **"to reinvent an icon":** Aimee Groth, "Howard Schultz Turned to This Guy to Help Him Reinvent Starbucks," *Business Insider*, July 3, 2012, http://www.businessinsider.com/sypartners-keith-yamashita-helped-howard-schultz-reinvent-starbucks-2012-7.

62 **"stayed true to their music":** Schultz and Gordon, *Onward*, 74.

63 **a better job sharing coffee knowledge?:** Ibid., 109–10.

63 **approximately $6 million in profit:** Ibid., 6.

63 **"dedicating ourselves to honing our craft":** Melissa Allison, "Starbucks Retraining Goes Down Smoothly," *Seattle Times*, February 26, 2008, http://www.seattletimes.com/business/starbucks-retraining-goes-down-smoothly.

64 **"we'll make it right":** Erin Calabrese, "Pledge of Perfection," *New York Post*, February 28, 2008, http://nypost.com/2008/02/28/pledge-of-perfection.

64 **"could take many steps forward"**: Schultz and Gordon, *Onward*, 5.

64 **"who believed in me?"**: Ibid., 103.

64 **"as we grow"**: Ibid., 104.

64 **"one neighborhood at a time"**: "Our Mission," Starbucks, http://www.starbucks.com/about-us/company-information/mission-statement.

65 **"we need each other now"**: Schultz and Gordon, *Onward*, 112.

65 **the center of every business decision**: Ibid., 109–10.

65 **"to look at the company"**: Ibid., 111.

66 **display of their commitment**: Ibid., 112–5.

67 **"reclaiming its coffee authority"**: Ibid., 87.

67 **to be shuttered**: Michael J. de la Merced, "Starbucks Announces It Will Close 600 Stores," *New York Times*, July 2, 2008, http://www.nytimes.com/2008/07/02/business/02sbux.html.

67 **"best days are ahead of us"**: "By far, this is the most angst-ridden decision we have made in my more than 25 years with Starbucks," *Starbucks Gossip* (blog), July 1, 2008, http://starbucksgossip.typepad.com/_/2008/07/by-far-this-is.html.

67 **"for today and the future"**: Ibid.

68 **were in the audience that day**: Schultz and Gordon, *Onward*, 171.

68 **"and specifically yesterday"**: Ibid., 170.

68 **"I know people are mad"**: Ibid., 172.

69 **it was the right thing to do**: Ibid., 193.

69 **plant trees, and build playgrounds**: Coleman Warner, "10,000 Starbucks Employees Volunteer While in Town for Convention," *Times-Picayune*, October 28, 2008, http://www.nola.com/news/index.ssf/2008/10/city_gets_latte_helping_hand.html.

70 **"we are trying to balance"**: Schultz and Gordon, *Onward*, 201.

70 **"coffee that is not ours?"**: Ibid., 202.

71 **"as great as our past"**: Ibid.

71 **"of their store experiences"**: Ibid., 197–8.

72 **from soil to cup**: Ibid.

72 **were their own businesses**: Starbucks Corporation, Fiscal 2008 Annual Report (Seattle: Starbucks Corporation, 2009), http://phx.corporate-ir.net/External.File?item=UGFyZW50SUQ9MTExNzN8Q2hpbGRJRD0tMXxUeXBlPTM=&t=1.

72 **"in being your partner"**: Schultz and Gordon, *Onward*, 171.

73 **"actions we've taken to transform the business"**: SA Transcripts, "Starbucks F3Q09 Earnings Call," nasdaq.com, http://www.nasdaq.com/aspx/call-transcript.aspx?StoryID=150308&Title=starbucks-f3q09-qtr-end-6-28-09-earnings-call-transcript.

73 **"driving meaningful operational improvements"**: Ibid., 297.

73 ***"significantly improved store economics"***: SA Transcripts, "Starbucks F3Q09 (Qtr End 6/28/09) Earnings Call Transcript," *Seeking Alpha*, July 21, 2009, http://seekingalpha.com/article/150308 -starbucks-f3q09-qtr-end-6-28-09-earnings-call-transcript?page=2.

73 ***"customer satisfaction, up 9 points"***: Ibid.

73 ***"and do it so quickly"***: John H. Ostdick, "Rekindling the Heart & Soul of Starbucks," *Success*, March 6, 2011, http://www.success.com/article/rekindling-the-heart-soul-of-starbucks.

Chapter Four: DREAM

82 ***"Let a new age dawn!"***: Nelson Mandela, "Nobel Lecture," Nobelprize.org, 1993, http://www .nobelprize.org/nobel_prizes/peace/laureates/1993/mandela-lecture_en.html.

83 ***"example that we would set"***: "Pebble That Produced a Tsunami," YouTube video, 22:55, from an address given by Ray C. Anderson on August 18, 1995, posted by "Ray C. Anderson Foundation," July 10, 2013, https://www.youtube.com/watch?v=aj3CET3RMRM.

84 **about how business got done:** Gerstner, *Who Says Elephants Can't Dance?*, 68.

84 ***"our customers all around the world"***: "Louis V. Gerstner, Jr. Outlines IBM's Focus on Network Computing," IBM Archives, https://www-03.ibm.com/ibm/history/multimedia/comdex_trans.html.

85 ***"give me liberty or give me death!"***: Patrick Henry, "Liberty or Death" (speech, Second Virginia Convention, St. John's Church, Richmond, VA, March 23, 1775).

85 ***"our industry for tomorrow's needs"***: Graham Weston and Duarte, Inc., "Preparing for the Future of San Antonio" (speech, San Antonio, 2013).

86 ***"for the next world war to begin"***: "The Next World War Will Be Fought in Silicon Valley," YouTube video, 22:11, from a presentation given by Nawaf Bitar at the 2014 RSA Conference in San Francisco, posted by "RSA Conference," February 25, 2014, https://www.youtube.com/ watch?v=XKkwL0gTN4w.

87 ***"challenge today in San Antonio"***: Weston and Duarte, Inc., "Preparing for the Future of San Antonio."

88 ***"and they saved our apartment"***: "Joe Gebbia—The Airbnb Story," YouTube video, 22:56, from a presentation given at the 2011 PSFK Conference in New York, posted by "tiyo avianto," November 26, 2013, https://www.youtube.com/watch?v=NKxNhkzfTWg.

88 **quest to conserve water:** Megan Barnett, "PepsiCo's Indra Nooyi: Capitalism with a Purpose," *Fortune*, October 5, 2011, http://fortune.com/2011/10/05/pepsicos-indra-nooyi-capitalism-with -a-purpose/.

89 ***"as Peter finally grew cold"***: Gary Haugen, "The Hidden Reason for Poverty the World Needs to Address Now," TED video, 22:08, filmed in Vancouver, March 2015, http://www.ted.com/talks/ gary_haugen_the_hidden_reason_for_poverty_the_world_needs_to_address_now.

90 **its first day on sale:** Phil Patton, "The Car of the Year (and a Half)," AmericanHeritage.com, October 2006, http://web.archive.org/web/20080828154601/http://www.americanheritage.com/ articles/magazine/ah/2006/5/2006_5_52.shtml.

91 ***"you have never done before"***: Helen H. Wang, *The Chinese Dream: The Rise of the World's Largest Middle Class and What It Means to You* (CreateSpace Independent Publishing Platform, 2010), 170.

91 ***"goodbye with something special"***: "Nike Football Launches CTR 360 Limited Edition Boot," Nike, April 4, 2014, http://news.nike.com/news/nike-football-launches-ctr-360-limited-edition-boot.

91 **they opted for healthier choices:** Interview with Fortune 100 company executive, May 7, 2014.

92 **embedded in Interface's heritage:** Ray C. Anderson and Robin White, *Confessions of a Radical Industrialist: Profits, People, Purpose: Doing Business by Respecting the Earth* (New York: St. Martin's, 2009), 6.

92 **what it's like to be an icon:** Schultz and Gordon, *Onward*, 73–4.

92 **the company in his presentations:** "Joe Gebbia—The Airbnb Story."

92 **point of their role in the world:** Wang, *The Chinese Dream*, 170.

92 **your eye off the ball:** Alyson Shontell, "There's a Hidden Message on the Sign Outside Facebook's Campus—It Reminds Employees to Stay Motivated," *Business Insider*, December 7, 2014, http://www.businessinsider.com/why-suns-logo-is-on-the-back-of-facebooks-sign-2014-12.

92 **"to San Antonio or live in Austin?":** Weston and Duarte, Inc., "Preparing for the Future of San Antonio."

93 **to shed light on the problem:** Adele Peters, "This Is What a Salad Bar Would Look Like Without Bees (Hint: Not Much Salad)," *Fast Company*, April 22, 2015, http://www.fastcoexist.com/3045124/this-is-what-a-salad-bar-would-look-like-without-bees-hint-not-much-salad.

93 **being generous toward employees:** Jack Newsham and Stephanie Vallejo, "2014 Bostonians of the Year: Market Basket Employees," *Boston Globe*, December 21, 2014, http://www.bostonglobe.com/magazine/2014/12/21/why-market-basket-employees-are-our-bostonians-year/o3P4vXbnDO70tjVpfzoEBl/story.html#.

DREAM Case Study: Interface

95 **carpet tiles—that blew his mind:** Ray C. Anderson, *Mid-Course Correction: Toward a Sustainable Enterprise: The Interface Model* (Atlanta: Peregrinzilla Press, 1998), 28–36.

96 **and functional products exploded:** Ibid., 36–8.

96 **"be sure we were in compliance":** Ray C. Anderson, "The Journey from There to Here: The Eco-Odyssey of a CEO" (speech, U.S. Green Building Conference, Big Sky, MT, August 14, 1995), Interface Global, http://www.interfaceglobal.com/pdfs/ECO_ODYSSEYbooklet_Sept2011.aspx.

96 **moment of "pure serendipity":** Anderson, *Mid-Course Correction*, 39.

96 **the "plunderer of the Earth":** Ibid., 5.

96 **like a "spear in the chest":** Ibid., 40.

97 **show them what was at stake:** Ibid., 40–4.

97 **"I know you'll figure it out":** "Pebble That Produced a Tsunami."

97 **"and stunned them," Anderson said:** Anderson, *Mid-Course Correction*, 43.

97 **"the basic laws of thermodynamics":** Tamar Harel, "Interface: The Journey of a Lifetime," ed. Geanne van Arkel, Freek van der Pluijm, Berend Aanraad, James Ede, and Scott Perret, *Natural Step* (2013): 7, http://www.naturalstep.org/sites/all/files/case_study_interface.pdf.

98 **"lead this effort if not us?":** Ibid.

98 **just six years from that day:** Anderson and White, *Confessions of a Radical Industrialist*, 29–30.

98 **called it "Mount Sustainability":** Ibid., 5–6.

99 **"'know that I get it now'":** Christine Arena, *Cause for Success: 10 Companies That Put Profits Second and Came in First* (Novato, CA: New World Library, 2004), 8.

99 **dumped many shares of stock:** Mikhail Davis, "20 Years Later, Interface Looks Back on Ray Anderson's Legacy," *GreenBiz*, September 3, 2014, http://www.greenbiz.com/blog/2014/09/03/20-years-later-interface-looks-back-ray-andersons-legacy.

99 **"reach opposite conclusions":** Anderson, *Mid-Course Correction*, 43.

99 **"to help it. It's your call":** Ray C. Anderson, "The Business Logic of Sustainability," TED video, 15:54, filmed at Long Beach Performing Arts Center, Long Beach, CA, February 2009, http://www.ted.com/talks/ray_anderson_on_the_business_logic_of_sustainability/transcript.

100 **accomplishments in company newsletters:** Anderson and White, *Confessions of a Radical Industrialist*, 52–5.

100 **saved the company $49.7 million:** Interface Research Corporation, *Interface Sustainability Report 1997* (Atlanta: Interface Research Corporation, 1997), http://interfaceglobal.com/App_Themes/Interface/Pdfs/Interface_Sustainability_Report_1997.pdf.

100 **Wailea hotel, in Maui, Hawaii:** Anderson, *Mid-Course Correction*, 152–64.

100 **the impact each person could have:** Ibid.

101 **"people of Earth. Please be seated":** Ibid.

101 **Anderson addressed the room:** "RCAnderson Maui MTG PRGM-QuickTime H.264," Vimeo video, 27:26, from speech given in Maui by Ray C. Anderson in 1997, posted by "MagicWig Productions, Inc.," May 13, 2013, https://vimeo.com/66116341.

101 **"our work together is not finished":** Ibid.

102 **"for all of our partners in the climb":** Ibid.

102 **"What if everybody did it?":** Anderson, *Mid-Course Correction*, 165.

102 **signed a "personal legacy wall":** Ibid., 169–70.

103 **attended an emotional closing ceremony:** Ibid.

103 **"to each bright and shining day":** "John Denver Live in Hawaii—Blue Water World (10th April 1997, Subtitled)," YouTube video, 3:54, posted by "Jason Wang," August 21, 2009, https://www.youtube.com/watch?v=uBXfCcksrC4.

104 **to make Interface a better company:** Anderson, *Mid-Course Correction*, 172–3.

104 **no one had believed was possible:** Davis, "20 Years Later, Interface Looks Back."

105 **the wake of their founder's passing:** "Interface—5 Minutes with Dan—I Am Mission Zero," Vimeo video, 4:45, of Dan Hendrix, posted by "KPKinteractive," October 17, 2012, https://vimeo.com/51634252.

105 **unusable carpet into dog beds:** "I Am Mission Zero: The Story of Employee Engagement at Interface Australia," YouTube video, 18:05, of Dan Hendrix, posted by "Interface Australia," August 21, 2012, https://www.youtube.com/watch?v=spWuVxu16bM.

105 **"that very few companies enjoy":** Dan Hendrix, "All-Hands Meeting" (speech, Interface Corporation, 2014).

Chapter Five: LEAP

112 **that's far more valuable to you:** Oxford Dictionaries, s.v. "sacrifice," def. 1.2, accessed May 5, 2015, http://www.oxforddictionaries.com/us/definition/american_english/sacrifice.

114 ***"one which we intend to win":*** "1962-09-12 Rice University," video, 18:28, from John F. Kennedy's speech at Rice University, Houston, September 12, 1962, John F. Kennedy Presidential Library and Museum, http://www.jfklibrary.org/Asset-Viewer/MkATdOcdU06X5uNHbmqm1Q.aspx.

114 **to the Intel x86 platform:** Ina Fried, "Apple Throws the Switch, Aligns with Intel," *CNET*, June 7, 2005, www.cnet.com/news-apple-throws-the-switch-aligns-with-Intel.

115 ***"excited to keep pushing the frontiers":*** "Steve Jobs Announces Switch to Intel & Podcasting—WWDC (2005)," VoiceTube video, 1:00:38, from speech at 2005 Worldwide Developers Conference in San Francisco, December 3, 2014, posted by "Ashley Chen," https://www.voicetube.com/videos/19379.

116 ***"moved to make the violence stop":*** Haugen, "The Hidden Reason for Poverty the World Needs to Address Now."

117 ***"children of your Father in heaven":*** Matt. 5:7 (New International Version).

117 ***"to rise again to secure our future":*** *An Inconvenient Truth*, directed by Davis Guggenheim (Beverly Hills, CA: Participant Media, 2006).

118 **via traditional technology such as PCs:** Dan Berthiaume, "Forrester: Responsive Design Represents Future of Multi-Touchpoint Web Design," *CMSWire*, August 2, 2012, http://www.cmswire.com/cms/customer-experience/forrester-responsive-design-represents-future-of-multitouchpoint-web-design-016786.php.

118 ***"[mobile apps] into their strategy":*** "Keynote: Oren Michels (Mashery)—from London Web Summit," video, 18:31, Lanyrd.com, March 1, 2013, http://lanyrd.com/2013/london-web-summit/scdpgx/.

119 ***"be very pleasantly surprised":*** "Steve Jobs Announces Switch to Intel & Podcasting."

119 **small and medium-sized enterprises in 2009:** Aaron Chew, "APEC SME Summit: Small Is Beautiful, Says Alibaba's Jack Ma," *City News*, November 20, 2009, http://www.citynews.sg/2009/11/apec-sme-summit-small-is-beautiful-says-alibabas-jack-ma/.

120 ***"because we are still surviving":*** "Jack Ma on 'Small Is Beautiful' at 2009 Singapore APEC SME Summit—Part 1 of 4," YouTube video, 9:47, posted by "Alibaba.com," November 12, 2009, http://youtu.be/t-ARfP5rW1Q?.

121 ***"first hearings on global warming":*** *An Inconvenient Truth*.

121 **rising to dangerously high levels:** Roger Revelle, "Atmospheric CO2 at Mauna Loa Observatory," chart, https://meigakuglobalchallenges.wordpress.com/2012/04/26/an-inconvenient-truth-transcript-part-i/, accessed May 8, 2015.

121 ***"what are they waiting for?":*** "Keynote: Oren Michels."

122 **first successful semiconductor company:** Dean Takahashi, "Silicon Valley's Pioneers Gather for Screening of PBS's American Experience Documentary," *VentureBeat*, January 31, 2013, http://venturebeat.com/2013/01/31/silicon-valleys-pioneers-gather-for-screening-of-pbss-american-experience-documentary/.

123 **the founders of Silicon Valley:** Leslie Berlin, "Tracing Silicon Valley's Roots," SFGate, September 30, 2007, http://www.sfgate.com/business/article/Tracing-Silicon-Valley-s -roots-2520298.php.

123 **into one larger company:** Marjorie Cortez, "Southwest, Morris Air Will Say 'I Do,'" *DeseretNews*, February 15, 1994, http://www.deseretnews.com/article/336706/SOUTHWEST-MORRIS-AIR -WILL-SAY-I-DO.html?pg=all.

124 **want to control the market:** Christopher DeMorro, "The Tesla Patent Wall: Before and After," Gas2, June 23, 2014, http://gas2.org/2014/06/23/the-tesla-patent-wall-before-and-after/.

124 **one marked "executives only":** Bill Snyder, "Meg Whitman: Don't Fixate on What Is Wrong with a Company," Stanford Business, April 22, 2015, https://www.gsb.stanford.edu/insights/meg -whitman-dont-fixate-what-wrong-company.

124 *"that we wanted to build":* Meg Whitman, "Transparent Communication," *HP Next* (blog), April 17, 2013, http://www8.hp.com/hpnext/posts/transparent-communication#.VVuyp9NVikp.

125 **people can identify new employees:** Shelley Portet, "10 Weird and Wonderful Things You Didn't Know About Google," *ZDNet*, November 28, 2011, http://www.zdnet.com/article/10-weird-and -wonderful-things-you-didnt-know-about-google/.

125 **what is right for the greater good:** "Inaugural Address, 20 January 1961," video, 15:30, from John F. Kennedy's inaugural address, Washington, DC, January 20, 1961, John F. Kennedy Presidential Library and Museum, http://www.jfklibrary.org/Asset-Viewer/BqXIEM9F4024ntFl7SVAjA.aspx.

125 *"will and effort in the air":* Patrik Henry Bass, *Like a Mighty Stream: The March on Washington, August 28, 1963* (Philadelphia: Running, 2002), 142.

126 **to symbolize a kiss:** Terry Maxon, "With Hoopla, Southwest Airlines Closes Its Purchase of Rival AirTran Holdings," *Dallas Morning News*, May 2, 2011, http://www.dallasnews.com/business/ airline-industry/20110502-with-hoopla-southwest-airlines-closes-its-purchase-of-rival-airtran -holdings.ece.

126 **a terrible fate for the planet:** *An Inconvenient Truth*.

126 **proposals to the Commons:** Isabel Hardman, "Sledging Isn't Confined to the Cricket Pitch— Just Ask Ed Balls," *Telegraph*, December 12, 2013, http://www.telegraph.co.uk/news/ politics/10513679/Sledging-isnt-confined-to-the-cricket-pitch-just-ask-Ed-Balls.html.

126 **for electric cars to be adopted:** DeMorro, "The Tesla Patent Wall."

126 **petition for the soda's return:** Jay Moye, "Surge Returns: Back by Popular Demand, Brand Now Available Exclusively on Amazon.com," Coca-Cola, September 15, 2014, http://www.coca -colacompany.com/stories/surge-returns-back-by-popular-demand-brand-now-available -exclusively-on-amazoncom.

LEAP Case Study: Rackspace

129 **six of the past eight years:** Lanham Napier, "Why Rackspace Was Named One of Fortune's 100 Best Companies to Work For," *Rackspace Blog! & Newsroom* (blog), January 16, 2014, http://www .rackspace.com/blog/why-rackspace-was-named-one-of-fortunes-100-best-companies-to-work -for/.

130 **this is no ordinary company:** Garrett Heath, "Get an Inside Look at the Rackspace 'Castle' Via Google Street View," *Rackspace Blog! & Newsroom* (blog), February 26, 2013, http://www .rackspace.com/blog/get-an-inside-look-at-the-rackspace-castle-via-google-street-view/.

130 **eight hundred employees per year:** Kate Murphy, "Revitalizing a Dead Mall (Don't Expect Shoppers)," *New York Times*, October 30, 2012, http://www.nytimes.com/2012/10/31/realestate/commercial/rackspace-revitalizes-a-defunct-mall-into-an-unorthodox-tech-campus.html?pagewanted=all&_r=2%2C.

131 **just west of London:** Laura Lorek, "Rackspace Expands Its 'Castle' Headquarters," *Silicon Hills News*, December 9, 2011, http://www.siliconhillsnews.com/2011/12/09/rackspace-expands-further-in-its-castle-mall/.

132 **that was down on its luck:** David Barnett, in discussion with the authors, March 16, 2015.

132 ***"thought I was crazy":*** Murphy, "Revitalizing a Dead Mall."

133 **complex redevelopment incentive package:** Nan Eckman, "City of Windcrest Secures 111 Acres for Mixed-Use Project," *CoStar*, March 24, 2008, http://www.costar.com/News/Article/City-of-Windcrest-Secures-111-Acres-for-Mixed-Use-Project/99607.

133 **and how they would do so:** Barnett, in discussion with the authors.

133 ***"we'll be attacked!":*** Ibid.

133 **the area wasn't safe:** Cody Shawver, "Windsor Park Mall: San Antonio, TX," DeadMalls.com, December 3, 2005, http://www.deadmalls.com/malls/windsor_park_mall.html.

133 ***"never want to go back":*** Graham Weston, in discussion with the authors, February 26, 2015.

134 **young professionals wanted to live:** Ibid.

134 ***"'in the community instead?'":*** Ibid.

134 **community groups and volunteer work:** "Rack Gives Back," Rackspace, accessed June 28, 2015, http://www.rackspace.com/en-us/information/events/rackgivesback.

135 **could relax and play:** "Rackspace Foundation," Rackspace Foundation, accessed May 5, 2015, http://www.rackspacefoundation.com/.

136 ***"with people who are happy":*** Dan Goodgame, e-mail message to Patti Sanchez (author), May 28, 2015.

137 **use of recycled building materials:** Cameron Nouri, "Rackspace Achieves LEED Gold Certification for Corporate Headquarters," Rackspace, April 6, 2010, http://ir.rackspace.com/phoenix.zhtml?c=221673&p=irol-newsArticle&ID=1409693.

137 ***"and what we aspire to be":*** Weston, in discussion with the authors.

Chapter Six: FIGHT

146 ***"they'll never take our freedom!":*** *Braveheart*, directed by Mel Gibson (Los Angeles: Paramount Pictures, 1995).

147 **companies in Silicon Valley:** Alyson Shontell, "In 1999, Alibaba's CEO Told Employees 2 Things They Needed to Do to Be Successful: Beat Americans and Work Longer Hours," *Business Insider India*, September 22, 2014, http://www.businessinsider.in/In-1999-Alibabas-CEO-Told-Employees-2-Things-They-Needed-To-Do-To-Be-Successful-Beat-Americans-And-Work-Longer-Hours/articleshow/43163952.cms.

147 ***"because of our innovative spirit":*** "Jack Ma in 1999: Selling Alibaba from His Apartment," *Bloomberg* video, 2:11, from speech to Alibaba employees in 1999, accessed May 8, 2015, http://www.bloomberg.com/news/videos/b/1a567592-5ff0-4feb-9823-6db536289a96.

147 **Alibaba's success was unstoppable:** Helen H. Wang, "How eBay Failed in China," *Forbes*, September 12, 2010, http://www.forbes.com/sites/china/2010/09/12/how-ebay-failed-in-china/2/.

148 ***"beyond rescue into prevention"*:** "Fighting Human Trafficking with Technology: Announcing a New Initiative," YouTube video, 1:41:45, from a presentation given by Jacquelline Fuller in Washington, DC, posted by "Google Ideas," April 9, 2013, https://www.youtube.com/watch?v=1LQAYtpF5PM.

148 ***"to outlive the menace of tyranny"*:** Winston Churchill, "We Shall Fight on the Beaches" (speech, House of Commons, London, June 4,1940), Churchill Centre, http://www.winstonchurchill.org/resources/speeches/1940-the-finest-hour/we-shall-fight-on-the-beaches.

148 **to join the commonwealth as an ally:** Richard Toye, "'We Shall Fight on the Beaches': 3 Things You Never Knew About Churchill's Most Famous Speech," *History of Government* (blog), Gov.uk, December 2, 2013, https://history.blog.gov.uk/2013/12/02/we-shall-fight-on-the-beaches-three-things-you-never-knew-about-churchills-most-famous-speech/.

149 ***"spending money to pervert democracy"*:** Jay Yarow, "Watch Elon Musk Make an Emotional Speech About How Auto Dealers Are 'Perverting Democracy' to Destroy Tesla and Hurt Customers," *Business Insider*, March 12, 2014, http://www.businessinsider.com/elon-musk-on-teslas-auto-dealer-model-2014-3.

149 **a fight Musk clearly relishes:** Matthew Debord, "Is Elon Musk Finally Giving Up on Selling Teslas Direct to Consumers?" *Business Insider*, October 23, 2014, http://www.businessinsider.com/r-michigan-becomes-fifth-us-state-to-thwart-direct-tesla-car-sales-2014-10.

150 ***"because I sure can't do it alone"*:** Gerstner, *Who Says Elephants Can't Dance?*, 203–6.

150 **outnumbered, yet hold their own:** Fran Walsh, Peter Jackson, and Philippa Boyens, "The Lord of the Rings," IMDB, accessed May 25, 2015, http://www.imdb.com/title/tt0167260/plotsummary?ref_=tt_ql_6.

151 **particularly challenging to show:** "Qualcomm: Not Exactly an Overnight Success," *Bloomberg*, June 1, 1997, http://www.bloomberg.com/bw/stories/1997-06-01/qualcomm-not-exactly-an-overnight-success.

152 ***"probably would have been dead"*:** Ibid.

152 ***"the likes of Dr. King and Gandhi"*:** "The Next World War Will Be Fought in Silicon Valley."

152 **by his opponent Apollo Creed:** *Rocky*, directed by John G. Avildsen (Beverly Hills, CA: United Artists, 1976).

153 ***"to find matches within a year"*:** "Jennifer Aaker: Case Study: Increasing the Bone Marrow Registry," YouTube video, 9:30, from a presentation given by Jennifer Aaker on November 17, 2010, posted by "ecorner," November 29, 2010, https://www.youtube.com/watch?v=N1Mjjk32t00.

154 ***"processes aren't cutting it anymore"*:** Rowan Trollope and Duarte, Inc., "Creating a Renaissance of Innovation," Internal Meeting, Cisco, San Francisco, June 2014.

154 **as they showed off their skills:** *Encyclopaedia Britannica*, s.v. "war dance," accessed May 21, 2015, http://www.britannica.com/EBchecked/topic/635632/war-dance.

155 **a small band of rebels again:** Andy Hertzfeld, "Pirate Flag," Folklore.org, August 1983, http://www.folklore.org/StoryView.py?project=Macintosh&story=Pirate_Flag.txt.

155 **fuel everyone's competitive spirit:** Maria Halkias, "Morale at J. C. Penney Is Mending," *Dallas Morning News*, November 2, 2013, http://www.dallasnews.com/business/retail/20131102 -morale-at-j.c.-penney-is-mending.ece.

157 **peaceful during the actual protests:** Bruce Hartford, "Notes from a Nonviolent Training Session (1963)," Civil Rights Movement Veterans, 2004, http://www.crmvet.org/info/nv1.htm.

157 **even had a fear of changing:** Tim Nudd, "Apple's 'Get a Mac,' the Complete Campaign," *Adweek*, April 13, 2011, http://www.adweek.com/adfreak/apples-get-mac-complete-campaign-130552.

158 **that tells the story to visitors:** "The Qualcomm Museum," Qualcomm, https://www.qualcomm .com/company/facilities/museum.

158 **"Crush Adidas":** Craig Chappelow, "5 Rules for Making Your Vision Stick," *Fast Company*, September 5, 2012, http://www.fastcompany.com/3000998/5-rules-making-your-vision-stick.

158 **read, "Fun," "Fight," and "Win":** Halkias, "Morale at J. C. Penney Is Mending."

158 **sales to celebrate the achievement:** Interview with a Fortune 500 company VP of communication, June 20, 2014.

158 **before the commercial went live:** Apple, Apple Macintosh Computer, television, CBS, January 22, 1984.

159 **lack of bone marrow for South Asians:** "Jennifer Aaker: Case Study."

159 **exemplify their rebel spirit:** Hertzfeld, "Pirate Flag."

159 **from further participation in the games:** Ben Cosgrove, "The Black Power Salute That Rocked the 1968 Olympics," *Time*, September 27, 2014, http://time.com/3880999/black-power-salute -tommie-smith-and-john-carlos-at-the-1968-olympics/.

FIGHT Case Study: Civil Rights

162 **Lincoln Memorial and the Washington Monument:** "March on Washington for Jobs and Freedom," Martin Luther King, Jr. Research and Education Institute, accessed May 13, 2015, http://mlk-kpp01.stanford.edu/index.php/encyclopedia/encyclopedia/enc_march_on_washington_for_jobs_and_freedom/.

162 **the Great Emancipator himself:** Ibid.

162 **issue a call for change:** Ibid.

163 ***"bright day of justice emerges":*** Martin Luther King Jr., "I Have a Dream" (speech, March on Washington for Jobs and Freedom, Lincoln Memorial, Washington, DC, August 28, 1963), American Rhetoric, http://www.americanrhetoric.com/speeches/mlkihaveadream.htm.

163 **signed it into law in 1964:** "Civil Rights Act," History.com, http://www.history.com/topics/black -history/civil-rights-act.

163 **their lives, including their homes:** King, "I Have a Dream."

163 **crowded, dilapidated, and impoverished slums:** "The Political History of Public Housing in Chicago," Roosevelt University, http://www.roosevelt.edu/CAS/CentersAndInstitutes/NewDeal/HistoryFair/PublicHousing/PoliticalHistory.aspx.

163 ***"properly chart our course":*** J. Tracy Power, "The Chicago Freedom Movement," in *I Will Not Be Silent and I Will Be Heard: Martin Luther King, Jr., the Southern Christian Leadership Conference, and Penn Center* (Columbia, SC: South Carolina Dept. of Archives & History, Public Programs

Division, 1993), 8, http://lits.columbiasc.edu/edenslibrary/Digital%20Library/Power
_1%20Will%20Not%20Be%20Silent....pdf.

164 **for insight and support:** David J. Garrow, *Bearing the Cross: Martin Luther King, Jr., and the Southern
Christian Leadership Conference* (New York: William Morrow Paperbacks, 2004), 430–44.

164 **their "War on Slums" campaign:** "Transcript: Two Societies (1965–1968)," *Eyes on the Prize*, PBS,
January 22, 1990, http://www.pbs.org/wgbh/amex/eyesontheprize/about/pt_202.html.

164 **live exactly as the locals did:** Maria R. Traska, Joseph D. Kubal, and Keith Yearman, "Route 66
History: Lawndale's Dr. M. L. King Legacy Apartments," *The Curious Traveler's Guide to Route 66 in
Metro Chicago* (blog), January 19, 2015, http://curioustraveler66.com/2015/01/19/route-66
-history-lawndales-dr-m-l-king-legacy-apartments/.

164 **to see what a hellhole it really was:** "Dr. King Carries Fight to Northern Slums," *Ebony*, April
1966, Google Books, https://books.google.com/books?id=kUBLURuzOxEC&lpg=PA94&ots
=-JLHPFDFwR&dq=mlk%20war%20on%20slums&pg=PA157#v=onepage&q=mlk%20war%20
on%20slums&f=false.

165 **his plans for the Chicago movement:** "Chicago Campaign (1966)," Martin Luther King, Jr.
Research and Education Institute, accessed May 13, 2015, http://mlk-kpp01.stanford.edu/index
.php/encyclopedia/encyclopedia/enc_chicago_campaign/.

165 **"on the move to end slums":** "Dr. Martin Luther King and the Chicago Freedom Movement,"
Oxford African American Studies Center, http://www.oxfordaasc.com/public/features/
archive/0110/photo_essay.jsp?page=1.

165 **"for them to be enslaved or abused":** Martin Luther King Jr., "The Chicago Plan" (speech, press
conference, Chicago, January 7, 1966), King Center, http://www.thekingcenter.org/archive/
document/chicago-plan#.

165 **named for fallen American war heroes:** Tab Bamford, "10 Things You Didn't Know About the
History of Soldier Field," *Chicago Like a Local* (blog), February 13, 2013, http://www.choosechicago
.com/blog/post/2013/02/10-Things-You-Didn-t-Know-About-the-History-of-Soldier-Field/560/.

167 **"no violent force can halt":** Martin Luther King Jr., "Address to the Chicago Freedom Movement
Rally" (speech, Chicago Freedom Movement Rally, Soldier Field, Chicago, July 19, 1966), King
Center, http://www.thekingcenter.org/archive/document/speech-chicago-freedom-movement
-rally.

167 **on a march to Chicago's City Hall:** "Transcript: Two Societies (1965–1968)."

167 **the Catholic church in Wittenberg in 1517:** Ridgely Hunt and Daniel McCaughna, "The
Movement Goes North," *Chicago Tribune*, April 7, 1968, http://archives.chicagotribune.
com/1968/04/07/page/35/article/the-movement-goes-north#text.

167 **that were unfair to African-Americans:** Martin Luther King Jr., "Demands Placed on the Door of
Chicago City Hall by Martin Luther King, Jr.—July 10, 1966," Poverty & Race Research Action
Council, http://www.prrac.org/projects/Chicago96/King.pdf.

167 **marching into hostile territory:** King, "The Chicago Plan."

168 **American dream they couldn't obtain:** "Transcript: Two Societies (1965–1968)."

168 **"hateful as I've seen here today":** Frank James, "Martin Luther King Jr. in Chicago," *Chicago
Tribune*, http://www.chicagotribune.com/news/nationworld/politics/chi-chicagodays
-martinlutherking-story-story.html.

169 **into the town of Cicero:** Garrow, *Bearing the Cross*, 500–4.

169 **cowered inside their new apartment:** "Cicero Race Riots Happen," African American Registry, http://www.aaregistry.org/historic_events/view/cicero-race-riots-happen.

169 **discrimination against African-Americans:** "Transcript: Two Societies (1965–1968)."

169 **in November 1966 to regroup:** David J. Garrow, "Where Martin Luther King, Jr., Was Going: Where Do We Go from Here and the Traumas of the Post-Selma Movement," *Georgia Historical Quarterly* LXXV, no. 4 (1991): 722–26, http://www.davidgarrow.com/File/DJG%201991%20 GHQMLK.pdf.

170 *"that have undergirded our struggle":* "Transcript: Two Societies (1965–1968)."

170 *"defeat the monster of racism":* Ibid.

170 *"the connotations of Black Power":* Ibid.

170 *"the very structure of the society":* Ibid.

171 *"together, 'We Shall Overcome'":* Martin Luther King Jr., "Dr. King's Speech" (speech, Southern Christian Leadership Conference, Frogmore, SC, November 14, 1966), King Center, http://www .thekingcenter.org/archive/document/mlk-speech-sclc-staff-retreat.

171 **beyond who deserved a better life:** Gary May, "A Revolution of Values: Martin Luther King Jr. and the Poor People's Campaign," Moyers & Company, January 18, 2015, http://billmoyers.com/2015/ 01/18/revolution-values/.

171 **protection that King had demanded:** "Fair Housing Act of 1968," History, http://www.history .com/topics/black-history/fair-housing-act.

171 *"freedom rings out a little louder":* Lyndon B. Johnson, "Remarks on Signing the Civil Rights Act" (speech, Washington, DC, April 11, 1968), Miller Center, http://millercenter.org/president/ speeches/speech-4036.

Chapter Seven: CLIMB

180 *"that gives everything its value":* Thomas Paine, "The Crisis," USHistory.org, http://www. ushistory.org/paine/crisis/c-01.htm.

181 *"global environment for the 21st century":* David Abney, "The UPS Journey: Lessons from 300 Million Green Miles" (speech, Alternative Clean Transportation Expo, Washington, DC, June 26, 2013), https://pressroom.ups.com/pressroom/ContentDetailsViewer.page?ConceptType=Speeche s&id=1426415415188-199.

181 **a year ahead of schedule, in 2014:** UPS, e-mail message to Patti Sanchez (author), June 15, 2015.

181 **on advanced technology infrastructure:** Samuel J. Palmisano, "Shining Cities on a Smarter Planet," *HuffPost New York: The Blog*, June 22, 2009, http://www.huffingtonpost.com/sam -palmisano/shining-cities-on-a-smart_b_206702.html.

182 *"our world literally work better":* Samuel J. Palmisano, "Smarter Cities: Crucibles of Global Progress" (speech, SmarterCities Forum, Rio De Janeiro, November 9, 2011), http://www.ibm .com/smarterplanet/us/en/smarter_cities/article/rio_keynote.html.

182 **a life-or-death question:** "No Fear Shakespeare: Hamlet," SparkNotes, http://nfs.sparknotes.com/ hamlet/page_138.html.

182 **highest-quality cars to customers:** Jeffrey McMurray, "Toyoda Tours Plant, Says Company at 'Crossroads,'" *Seattle Times*, February 25, 2010, http://old.seattletimes.com/html/businesstechnology/2011185865_apustoyotarecallkentucky.html.

183 *"restore the trust of our customers":* "Toyota President Akio Toyoda's Statement to Congress," *Guardian*, February 24, 2010, http://www.theguardian.com/business/2010/feb/24/akio-toyoda -statement-to-congress.

183 *"importantly, we will be proud":* Michael Mandel, "Immelt Speech: U.S. Companies Begin to Realize Their Mistake," *Bloomberg Business* (blog), June 27, 2009, http://www.businessweek.com/the_thread/economicsunbound/archives/2009/06/immelt_speech_u.html.

185 *"'broken as easily as these sticks'":* Aesop's Fables, "The Bundle of Sticks," University of Massachusetts Amherst, accessed May 9, 2015, http://www.umass.edu/aesop/content.php?n=4&i=1.

185 **Aubazine, a Cistercian abbey:** Jean-Louis Froment, *Culture Chanel* (New York: Abrams, 2012).

185 **that featured interlaced curves:** Gabriella Davi-Khorasanee, "Flash Back Friday: The Legend of the Chanel Logo's Double C," *La Chanelphile* (blog), June 29, 2012, http://www.lachanelphile.com/2012/06/29/flash-back-friday-the-legend-of-the-chanel-double-c/.

186 *"All our success is due to them":* "Experience [Greater Than] Tech: Tendril CEO Adrian Tuck," Vimeo video, 14:32, from presentation in October 2013, https://vimeo.com/103770827.

187 *"kind of choice I'm making":* Rowan Trollope and Duarte, Inc., "Creating a Renaissance of Innovation" (speech given at internal meeting, San Francisco, June 2014).

188 **Chavez began a political fast in protest:** "History of ¡Si Se Puede!" United Farm Workers, http://www.ufw.org/_board.php?mode=view&b_code=cc_his_research&b_no=5970.

188 **many improvements for workers:** Ibid.

188 **company-wide newsletter for all to see:** Anderson, *Mid-Course Correction*, 165.

189 **rather than lead to cuts:** Andy Reinhardt, Seanna Browder, and Pete Engardio, "Booming Boeing," *BusinessWeek*, September 30, 1996, http://www.businessweek.com/1996/40/b34951.htm.

189 **to banish the memory of them:** Ibid.

190 **switch to a competitor's chip:** "The End of Moore's Law?" *Economist*, October 21, 2004, http://www.economist.com/node/3321802.

190 **told the crowd. *"We ate crow":*** Jason Kelly and Ian King, "Intel Chief Begs Forgiveness, Says Company Became 'Too Relaxed,'" *Bloomberg*, October 25, 2004, http://www.bloomberg.com/apps/news?pid=newsarchive&sid=aJ00txpKSIRI.

190 **was still in the crack in the rock:** Trollope and Duarte, Inc., "Creating a Renaissance of Innovation."

190 **rallying cry, "Yes we can":** "History of ¡Si Se Puede!"

190 **the importance of their work:** "Foundation Medicine hallway lobby," photograph, Foundationmedicine.com, accessed May 12, 2015, http://www.foundationmedicine.com/wp -content/uploads/2014/05/our-impact.jpg.

191 **the press and spooked investors:** Eric Savitz, "CEO's 'Burning Platform' Memo Highlights Nokia's Woes," *Forbes*, February 9, 2011, http://www.forbes.com/sites/ericsavitz/2011/02/09/ceos -burning-platform-memo-highlights-nokias-woes/.

191 **to communicate when fleeing Maryland:** "Songs of the Underground Railroad," Harriet Tubman Historical Society, accessed June 2, 2015, http://www.harriet-tubman.org/songs-of-the-underground-railroad/.

191 **New Orleans area during the event:** Schultz and Gordon, *Onward*, 194.

191 **had resulted in an auto recall:** Norihiko Shirouzu, Sue Feng, and Gao Sen, "Tracks of His Tears: Why Akio Toyoda Choked Up," *ChinaRealTime* (blog), *Wall Street Journal*, March 3, 2010, http://blogs.wsj.com/chinarealtime/2010/03/03/tracks-of-his-tears-why-akio-toyoda-choked-up/.

CLIMB Case Study: charity: water

193 **water to everyone in the world:** Nick Bilton, "One on One: Scott Harrison, Charity Water," *Bits* (blog), *New York Times*, January 2, 2012, http://bits.blogs.nytimes.com/2012/01/02/one-on-one-scott-harrison-charity-water/?_r=1.

194 **United States focused on water:** Max Chafkin, "A Save-the-World Field Trip for Millionaire Tech Moguls," *New York Times*, August 8, 2013, http://www.nytimes.com/2013/08/11/magazine/a-save-the-world-field-trip-for-millionaire-tech-moguls.html?pagewanted=all.

194 **that can easily spread socially:** Steven N. Pyser, "Millennials and the Reshaping of Charity and Online Giving," *Nonprofit Quarterly*, October 20, 2014, https://nonprofitquarterly.org/philanthropy/25017-millennials-and-the-reshaping-of-charity-and-online-giving.html.

195 ***"'change everything about my life'":*** Scott Harrison, "Founder, Scott Harrison, Explains charity: water's Role in Solving the Water Crisis, at the 2013 Inbound Conference," video, 1:04:12, Charitywater.org, 2006, http://www.charitywater.org/about/scotts_story.php.

196 ***"bring it with them to school?":*** Ibid.

196 ***"charity: water was born":*** Ibid.

197 ***"much actually reaches people":*** Ibid.

197 **his 100 percent promise:** Ibid.

197 **Google Maps and Google Earth:** charity: water, *charity: water Annual Report 2008* (New York: charity: water, 2009), http://www.charitywater.org/about/cw_08_annual_report.pdf.

198 ***"'until the problem is solved'":*** Harrison, "Founder, Scott Harrison, Explains charity: water's Role in Solving the Water Crisis."

198 **try to get people to care:** charity: water, *charity: water Annual Report 2008*.

198 ***"'be kidding. You must be'":*** Ibid.

199 **clean water for their families:** "The Story Behind the Jerry Can," charity: water Blog, December 9, 2011, http://www.charitywater.org/blog/jerry-can/.

200 **and one school in Kenya:** charity: water, *charity: water Annual Report 2007*, https://www.charitywater.org/about/cw_07_annual_report.pdf.

200 ***"their name on the Mogotio well":*** Ibid., 19.

201 **hope to change the water crisis:** charity: water, *charity: water Annual Report 2009* (New York: charity: water, 2010), http://www.charitywater.org/about/cw_09_annual_report.pdf.

201 **after the nonprofit was founded:** Josh Zelman, "(Founder Stories) Charity: Water's Harrison, 'We Were Going to Run Out of Money in Five Weeks,'" *TechCrunch*, December 20, 2011, http://

techcrunch.com/2011/12/20/founder-stories-charity-waters-harrison-we-were-going-to-run
-out-of-money-in-five-weeks/.

201 **he could think of, asking for help:** David Baker, "Charity Startup: Scott Harrison's Mission to
Solve Africa's Water Problem," *Wired UK*, January 4, 2013, http://www.wired.co.uk/magazine/
archive/2012/12/features/charitystartup.

202 ***"you just need more time":*** Zelman, "(Founder Stories) Charity: Water's Harrison."

202 **made multiyear commitments:** Mark W. Guay, "Reinventing the Non-Profit: An Interview w/Scott
Harrison from Charity : water," *HuffPost Impact*, November 26, 2014, http://www
.huffingtonpost.com/mark-w-guay/an-interview-w-scott-harr_b_6225218.html.

202 **helping Harrison cover his costs:** Zelman, "(Founder Stories) Charity: Water's Harrison."

203 **benefiting from their donations:** Chafkin, "A Save-the-World Field Trip for Millionaire Tech
Moguls."

204 ***"fourteen years since the tragedy":*** Harrison, "Founder, Scott Harrison, Explains charity: water's
Role in Solving the Water Crisis."

204 ***"We were in deep love":*** Scott Harrison, "The Last Walk for Water," *Medium* (blog), February 19,
2014, https://medium.com/charity-water/the-last-walk-for-water-979160375b4a.

204 **they'd never been seen again:** Ibid.

204 **but perhaps she will in her legacy:** Ibid.

205 ***"that water changes everything":*** Ibid.

205 **transparency around this promise:** Dan Schawbel, "Scott Harrison: How He Started Charity:
Water and What He Learned in the Process," *Forbes*, July 22, 2013, http://www.forbes.com/sites/
danschawbel/2013/07/22/scott-harrison-how-he-started-charity-water-and-what-he-learned-in
-the-process/.

205 ***"10 percent over the past three years":*** Bilton, "One on One: Scott Harrison, Charity Water."

205 **charity: water Growth:** "Financials," Charitywater.org, http://www.charitywater.org/about/
financials.php.

Chapter Eight: ARRIVE

214 ***"and others will write about":*** Jawaharlal Nehru, "Tryst with Destiny" (speech, Constituent
Assembly, New Delhi, India, August 14, 1947), *Norton Anthology of English Literature*, http://www
.wwnorton.com/college/english/nael/20century/topic_1/jawnehru.htm.

214 **(and a loan) to achieve:** David Booth, "Ford's Mulally Was Right on the Money," *National Post*,
http://www.nationalpost.com/story.html?id=905799eb-c2ea-410e-9ae0-7cc3ae20663b&k=51858.

215 ***"our precious taxpayer money":*** Alan Mulally, "Remarks on Ford," C-SPAN video, 36:06, from a
speech at the Washington Auto Show, Washington, DC, January 26, 2010, http://www.c-span.org/
video/?291662-1/alan-mulally-remarks-ford.

216 ***"save this remarkable planet and ourselves":*** Carter Roberts, "Epiphany," in *Annual Report 2011:
World Wildlife Fund's 50th Anniversary Year, WWF* (Washington, DC: WWF, 2011), 2–6, http://
assets.worldwildlife.org/financial_reports/1/reports/original/Annual_Report_2011
.pdf?134266769.

216   *"a just and lasting peace":* Abraham Lincoln, "Second Inaugural Address" (speech, Capitol Building, Washington, DC, March 4, 1865), Bartleby.com, http://www.bartleby.com/124/pres32 .html.

217   **public firestorm against the brand:** Elaine Woo, "Donald Keough Dies at 88; Helped Coke Stay Dominant During 'Soda Wars,'" *Los Angeles Times*, February 24, 2015, http://www.latimes.com/ local/obituaries/la-me-donald-keough-20150225-story.html.

217   *"our boss is the consumer":* "Don Keough Speech Classic Coke," YouTube video, 5:52, from a press conference given by Don Keough in New York, April 23, 1985, posted by "Coca-Cola Conversations," April 22, 2010, https://www.youtube.com/watch?v=t_djFC9Uhuw.

217   **the American health-care system:** Jonathan Bush, "Where Does It Hurt? An Entrepreneur's Guide to Fixing Health Care," athenahealth, accessed May 12, 2015, http://www.athenahealth.com/ jonathan-bush/where-does-it-hurt.php.

218   *"change in health care is possible":* "2014 Partners HealthCare Connected Health Symposium: Jonathan Bush, athenahealth," YouTube video, 22:28, from a keynote presentation, October 24, 2014, posted by "Partners HealthCare Connected Health," December 9, 2014, https://youtu.be/ eN9W1fdIDSk.

218   **from the brink of extinction:** Roberts, "Epiphany."

219   *"the first of many victories":* Ibid.

219   **during the Great Depression:** Kevin Maney, *The Maverick and His Machine: Thomas Watson, Sr. and the Making of IBM* (Wiley: Hoboken, NJ: 2003).

219   *"running on the right basis":* Peter E. Greulich, *The World's Greatest Salesman: An IBM Caretaker's Perspective: Looking Back* (Austin, TX: MBI Concepts Corporation, 2011), 271–3.

220   **in a televised speech:** "Text, Video of GM CEO Mary Barra on Switch Report," *USA Today*, June 5, 2014, http://www.usatoday.com/story/money/cars/2014/06/05/gm-ceo-mary-barra-speech -switch-recall-report/10012715/.

221   *"make all your dreams realized":* "Jack Ma on 'Small Is Beautiful.'"

221   **"Giant Leap" tour to twenty-five countries:** Suzanne Deffree, "Apollo 11 Celebration Begins, August 13, 1969," *EDN Network*, August 13, 2014, http://www.edn.com/electronics-blogs/nasa --revealing-the-unknown-to-benefit-all-humankind/4392240/Apollo-11-celebration-begins --August-13--1969.

222   **the stock's successful results:** Te-ping Chen, "Alibaba's IPO Sparks Hometown Celebrations," *Wall Street Journal*, September 19, 2014, http://www.wsj.com/articles/alibabas-ipo-sparks -hometown-celebrations-1411142808.

222   *"history of China and the Internet":* Ibid.

223   *"cake and champagne were served":* Andy Hertzfeld, "Signing Party," Folklore, February 1982, http://www.folklore.org/StoryView.py?project=Macintosh&story=Signing_Party. txt&topic=Apple%2BSpirit.

224   **read their prepared messages:** Adrienne Sanders, "Toppling PeopleSoft's Defense," *San Francisco Business Times*, February 27, 2005, http://www.bizjournals.com/sanfrancisco/stories/2005/02/ 28/focus1.html?page=all.

224   **candles, and company memorabilia:** Michael Liedtke, "Oracle to Cut 5, Jobs," LJWorld.com, January 15, 2005, http://www2.ljworld.com/news/2005/jan/15/oracle_to_cut/.

225 **car off the assembly line together:** Robert Casey, "Model T: 1908–1927," American Society of Mechanical Engineers, accessed May 12, 2015, https://www.asme.org/about-asme/who-we-are/engineering-history/landmarks/233-model-t.

225 **signify a new beginning:** "Last Day of Model T Production at Ford," History, accessed May 12, 2015, http://www.history.com/this-day-in-history/last-day-of-model-t-production-at-ford.

226 **the original Mac "Hello" ads:** Walter Isaacson, *Steve Jobs* (New York: Simon & Schuster, 2011), 354–5.

226 **someone made a purchase:** Drew Olanoff, "Bellbot Will Make Happy Sounds Every Time You Get a New User," *TNW News*, January 28, 2012, http://thenextweb.com/apps/2012/01/28/bellbot-will-make-happy-sounds-every-time-you-get-a-new-user/.

226 **employees and visitors at the door:** Adam B. Vary, "Inside Steve Jobs' Mind-Blowing Pixar Campus," *BuzzFeed*, June 25, 2013, http://www.buzzfeed.com/adambvary/inside-steve-jobs-mindblowing-pixar-campus#.yhMGZ1ZOl.

226 **know Nike frontward and backward:** Eric Ransdell, "The Nike Story? Just Tell It!," *Fast Company*, January 2000.

226 **can reverse a corporate decision:** Pamela G. Hollie, "Fans of 'Old' Coke Wouldn't Give Up," *New York Times*, July 12, 1985, http://www.nytimes.com/1985/07/12/business/fans-of-old-coke-wouldn-t-give-up.html.

226 **levity to the apologetic tone of the announcement:** "Don Keough Speech Classic Coke."

227 **laid next to the PeopleSoft sign:** "PeopleSoft employee Karla Hendrix places balloons next to a sign outside of the company's headquarters in Pleasanton, Calif.," photograph, LJWorld.com, accessed May 12, 2015, http://www2.ljworld.com/photos/2005/jan/15/54118/.

227 **cranes as a statement of peace:** "Legend of the Crane," Out of the Darkness Community Walks, accessed June 9, 2015, http://www.sos-walk.org/sos/crane.htm.

ARRIVE Case Study: Chick-fil-A

229 **Recognize the Roots of Innovation:** Steve Nedvidek, senior manager of marketing, Chick-fil-A, interview with the authors, May 28, 2015.

231 ***"your innovation center":*** "Hatch Launch" video, Chick-fil-A intranet.

232 ***"colorful touchstone moment":*** Steve Nedvidek, e-mail message summarizing Hatch to Nancy Duarte (author), November, 15, 2014.

233 ***"commitment took the fear of failure away":*** Steve Nedvidek, senior manager of marketing, Chick-fil-A, interview with the authors, May 28, 2015.

233 ***"fearful of small failures":*** "Innovation" video, transcript, Chick-fil-A intranet.

233 ***"give people room to experiment":*** Ibid.

233–34 ***"individually to learn and grow":*** Ibid.

234 ***"continue Truett's legacy of innovation":*** Steve Nedvidek, speech, May 20, 2014, training transcript, Chick-fil-A intranet.

234 ***"This is a mandate":*** Ibid.

234 ***"but increasing the lead":*** Ibid.

235 **"expected to use and employ":** Ibid.

237 **"past, that's a good sign":** "Innovation Day" video, May 2015, Chick-fil-A intranet.

Chapter Nine: (re)DREAM

244 **American Express Eras:** "American Express: Our Story," American Express, https://secure.cmax .americanexpress.com/Internet/GlobalCareers/Staffing/Shared/Files/our_story_3.pdf.

246 **Sam Palmisano, IBM chairman and CEO:** "Our Values," IBM, http://www-03.ibm.com/ employment/our_values.html.

247 **conference room wall the following morning:** Steve Lohr, "Even a Giant Can Learn to Run," *New York Times*, December 31, 2011, http://www.nytimes.com/2012/01/01/business/how-samuel -palmisano-of-ibm-stayed-a-step-ahead-unboxed.html?pagewanted=all&_r=2.

248 **"connect them looking backward":** "'You've Got to Find What You Love,' Jobs Says," *Stanford News*, June 14, 2005, http://news.stanford.edu/news/2005/june15/jobs-061505.html.

(re)DREAM Case Study: Apple

251 **computing and launched Apple Computer Inc.:** "Steve Jobs 1st Keynote Reappearance at Apple— Macworld SF (1997)," YouTube video, 44:25, from Macworld in San Francisco, January 7, 1997, posted by "EverySteveJobsVideo," December 21, 2013, https://www.youtube.com/ watch?v=4QrX047-v-s.

252 **instead of being different:** Peter Burrows, "Apple's Copland: New! Improved! Not Here Yet!" *BusinessWeek*, December 18, 1995, http://www.businessweek.com/1995/51/b345595.htm.

252 **competitors such as Microsoft:** "Apple Updates Operating System," *BBC News*, March 23, 2001, http://news.bbc.co.uk/2/hi/americas/1238769.stm.

252 **cost them time and money:** John Markoff, "Apple Expects It Will Lose $700 Million," *New York Times*, March 28, 1996, http://www.nytimes.com/1996/03/28/business/apple-expects-it-will-lose -700-million.html.

252 **for $400 million:** "Press Release: Apple Computer, Inc. Agrees to Acquire NeXT Software Inc.," Internet Archive, December 20, 1996, http://web.archive.org/web/20020208190346/http:/ product.info.apple.com/pr/press.releases/1997/q1/961220.pr.rel.next.html.

252 **organizer had allotted him:** "Worst. Apple. Keynote. Ever." YouTube video, 14:18, from presentation given at MacWorld Expo in San Francisco, January 1997, posted by "mickeleh," April 7, 2013, https://www.youtube.com/watch?v=PsBVyUDs-84.

252 **Apple and the NeXT OS:** "Steve Jobs 1st Keynote Reappearance at Apple."

253 **hours he had the stage:** Ibid.

253 **"buy their computers from":** Ibid.

253 **"that entrepreneurial energy":** Ibid.

253 **"years to rediscover them":** Ibid.

254 **features that were killed by Jobs:** Ibid.

255 **"go to some good places":** "Apple's WWDC 1997," YouTube video, 1:11:09, from Apple Worldwide Developers Conference in San Jose, posted by "superapple4ever," June 5, 2011, https://www .youtube.com/watch?v=GnO7D5UaDig.

256 **"to get back to"**: Ibid.

256 **"commitment to the Macintosh"**: "MacWorld Boston 1997—Full Version," YouTube video, 38:31, posted by "The Apple History Channel," March 6, 2006, https://www.youtube.com/watch?v=PEHNrqPkef1.

257 **of commitment than anything:** Matt Richtel, "Microsoft and Apple Startle Industry with Alliance," *New York Times*, August 6, 1997, http://partners.nytimes.com/library/cyber/week/080697apple.html.

257 **"would have been a Mac"**: "Apple Confidential—Steve Jobs on 'Think Different'—Internal Meeting Sept. 23, 1997," YouTube video, 16:01, posted by "MacBoock," November 5, 2013, https://youtube/9GMQhOm-Dqo.

257 **"are the ones who do"**: Rob Siltanen, "The Real Story Behind Apple's 'Think Different' Campaign," *Forbes*, December 14, 2011, http://www.forbes.com/sites/onmarketing/2011/12/14/the-real-story-behind-apples-think-different-campaign/.

258 **"'Apple really great again?'"**: "Apple Confidential—Steve Jobs on 'Think Different.'"

258 **developer beta release:** Benj Edwards, "Looking Back at OS X's Origins," *Macworld*, September 13, 2010, http://www.macworld.com/article/1154036/osxorigins.html.

258 **"and giving it to them"**: "Steve Jobs Reveals OS X Strategy—WWDC (1998)," YouTube video, 1:29:11, from Apple Worldwide Developers Conference, posted by "EverySteveJobsVideo," December 21, 2012, https://www.youtube.com/watch?t=4652&v=E5dWDg6f9eo.

259 **"and map out where we are"**: "Steve Jobs Previews OS 8.5—Macworld NY (1998)," YouTube video, 1:28:07, posted by "EverySteveJobsVideo," September 22, 2014, https://www.youtube.com/watch?v=HwZzkf-IReM.

259 **applications would drive growth:** Ibid.

259 **growth for any platform:** Ibid.

260 **"really deeply appreciate it"**: Ibid.

260 **to show their software:** Ibid.

260 **he hosted a fireside chat:** "Apple 2001 WWDC Keynote," Internet Archive, accessed May 26, 2015, https://web.archive.org/web/20010812030313/http://www.apple.com/hotnews/articles/2001/05/wwdc/keynote.html.

260 **that bordered on threatening:** Derrick Story, "Apple Not Resting on Its Mac OS X Laurels," *O'Reilly* (blog), accessed May 26, 2015, http://archive.oreilly.com/pub/post/apple_not_resting_on_its_mac_o.html.

261 **"OS X apps that will ship"**: Michael Gowan, "Apple Ships All Macs with OS X, LCD Monitor," CNN.com, May 23, 2001, http://www.cnn.com/2001/TECH/ptech/05/23/apple.osx.monitor.idg/index.html.

261 **new operating system hard:** Mathew Honan, "Jobs on OS X: 'The Train Has Left the Station,'" *Macworld*, May 1, 2001, http://www.macworld.com/article/1002154/21wwdc1.html.

261 **given its rocky history:** Neil Ticktin, "Viewpoint: Mac OS X . . . Are We There Yet?" *MacTech* 16, no. 10 (2000), http://www.mactech.com/articles/mactech/Vol.16/16.10/Oct00Viewpoint/index.html.

262 **others laughed awkwardly:** "Steve Jobs Announces the Death of OS 9—WWDC excerpt (2002)," YouTube video, 3:19, from Apple Worldwide Developers Conference in San Francisco, May 6, 2002, posted by "EverySteveJobsVideo," December 21, 2012, https://www.youtube.com/watch?v=2Ya2nY12y3Q.

263 ***"developing for Mac OS X":*** Ibid.

263 **system adoption in history:** "Steve Jobs Keynote Macworld NY 2001," YouTube video, 2:11:00, posted by "Evgeny Z," November 9, 2011, https://www.youtube.com/watch?v=Roda_vL-QEQ.

CONCLUSION: Confessions of a Torchbearer

268 ***"that it keeps moving":*** King, "Dr. King's Speech."

269 ***"greater or lesser uncertainty":*** "The Nature of Command and Control," MCDP 6, October 1996, http://www.au.af.mil/au/awc/awcgate/mcdp6/ch1.htm.

271 **what Nike calls their maxims:** Barbara Farfan, "Nike Company Mission Statement—About Inspiration, Innovation & World Athletes," About.com, http://retailindustry.about.com/od/retailbestpractices/ig/Company-Mission-Statements/Nike-Company-Mission-Statement.htm.

273 **linear wall space in Airbnb's office:** Dorothy Tan, "At Airbnb HQ, A Wall Filled with Hand-Illustrations of Employee Experiences," *DesignTAXI*, January 21, 2014, http://designtaxi.com/news/363254/At-Airbnb-HQ-A-Wall-Filled-With-Hand-Illustrations-Of-Employee-Experiences/.

Conclusion Case Study: Duarte, Inc.

275 **hundred-person mark, the business fails:** W.-X. Zhou, D. Sornette, R. A. Hill, and R. I. M. Dunbar, "Discrete Hierarchical Organization of Social Group Sizes," *Proceedings of the Royal Society B: Biological Sciences* 272, no. 1561 (2005): 439–44, http://rspb.royalsocietypublishing.org/content/272/1561/439.article-info.

280 **about the bundle of sticks:** Aesop's Fables, "The Bundle of Sticks."

PHOTO CREDITS

INDEX

contact@duarte.com   650.964.6745   www.duarte.com

See.
Change.

Amid the swells of change someone must stand alone—scanning the horizon, spotting the future, and pointing the way there. We'll help you craft inspiring communications that compel others to answer the call.